THE
GREAT CLASSICS

THE
GREAT CLASSICS

Automobile Engineering in the Golden Age

GALLERY BOOKS
An Imprint of W. H. Smith Publishers Inc.
112 Madison Avenue
New York City 10016

CONTENTS

FOREWORD

The history of this book is not sensational, although it is hardly conventional, and is, indeed, almost sentimental. It began in May 1971, when I was wandering round Scotland, retracing the footsteps of the composer Felix Mendelssohn. The 20-year-old composer had travelled with a friend to Scotland in 1829, a journey which left lasting traces in his compositions: an excursion by boat to the Hebridean island of Staffa was the inspiration for his overture 'Fingal's Cave' and the 'Scottish' 'Symphony in A minor. I kept strictly to the stages of the route taken by the young composer, which is how I happened to be on the island of Mull during the Scottish Six-Day Rally of the Veteran Car Club of Great Britain. Since the Scottish roads did not allow me to make a detour, the journalist in me made a virtue out of necessity: I spent the time photographing. On this day, 15 May 1971, I became infected by the classic car bacillus.

From the very start I was fascinated by the names of the cars, which resounded in my ears like the names of distant stars: Gobron-Brillié, Calcott, Darracq, Donnet-Zédel, De Dion-Bouton, Swift, Züst, Panhard-Levassor, Belsize, Argyll, to name but a few. Then I met their owners, who regaled me with glorious, ludicrous automobile stories. Suddenly a new journalistic dimension opened up before my eyes: to describe and relate the fascinating history of the automobile through the fate of the marques, designers, companies, drivers, extravagant owners, all against the background of history. During long walks on the high moorland of Mull the idea came to me that one day I should develop the topic for a book based on this chance meeting.

In the years that followed I was to be found, armed with cameras, note-pad and recording equipment, at veteran club meetings, racing events and rallies, in many different countries. Owners of classic cars would roll their often strange four-wheeled precious objects out of sheds and garages so that I could photograph them, and furthermore give me much valuable additional information. My library of slides grew to some 12,000 individual items, and printed material covered several metres of shelf space. During my research I discovered a whole technical subculture, in which amateurs preserve, with passionate devotion, valuable artefacts from the history of the development of the automobile for posterity. The veteran and vintage clubs have taken over the functions of modern automobile museums, which pass on their objects and technical and historical know-how to the succeeding generations.

'Only a lunatic would write a book like this!' – I will readily agree with this opinion expressed by an experienced publisher, for when I was in England, racing to catch the next continental ferry on a Sunday evening after some important veteran event, I would often ask myself: 'What's it all for?'. It cannot be explained simply as infatuation – infatuation with the infernal noise of the supercharged Bugatti, or with the hoarse barking of the E.R.A., or even with the breathtaking sight of the 24-litre Lion-Napier aircraft engine of 1924, which had been mounted in a Bentley chassis and had there reached the point of madness....

No, it is something more, for the whole climate of the classic-car brotherhood reflects the great pioneering years of automobile technology at the end of the 19th century. And automobile history is not only a question of the technology of yesteryear, but also of aesthetics. A genius such as Ettore Bugatti, for example, could develop automobile manufacture into an art form, and models such as the Bugatti 35 satisfy all the requirements of functionalism.

When I took my first classic-car photographs fifteen years ago, I was an absolute beginner in matters of automobile technology and history. Problem number one was the difficulty in equating British 'RAC horsepower' figures with international standards. The British h.p. figures stand for the control or operating horsepower, as opposed to the b.h.p. or brake horsepower. They are calculated from the formula: square of the cylinder bore in inches, multiplied by the number of cylinders, divided by 2.5. This 'RAC rating' occurs throughout the whole English-language classic-car literature and complicates research no end, and so I have attempted to calculate b.h.p. figures in the captions to the photographs. I find it astonishing that so many British owners seemed to have absolutely no interest in this figure. For them, the 'pedigree' of a car is much more important: when and from whom was it bought, how long it had been standing undiscovered in some dusty coach-house, where it had been placed in which races, how often it had been restored, by whom and when.

The British regard classic cars above all as part of their heritage, the legacy of a once illustrious empire which is worth preserving. An almost inexhaustible source of information for me was the 170 or more clubs, of which 160 alone are involved in individual marques, including a club as elite as 'Les Amis de Panhard et Levassor', or one as bizarre as the 'Volkswagen Split-Window Club', in which the club activities exclusively revolve around early 'beetles' with a divided rear window. Among the top clubs are undoubtedly the Rolls-Royce Enthusiasts Club, the Bentley Drivers Club, to say nothing of the Bugatti Owners Club. The last-named club even has its own racing track, Prescott Hill Climb in Gloucestershire, which winds uphill and downhill among apple trees and oaks. The finishing post is surrounded by a sea of broom bushes. The prescribed ritual at Prescott Hill involves the drivers spending the nights before the training days and race days in the damp meadows immediately next to the racing track. There gentlemen who would normally only be seen dismounting at the Ritz or Waldorf-Astoria are to be found on hands and knees in one-man pup-tents. An early summer morning under the fruit trees at Prescott would have inspired a painter such as Turner. Dew glistens on the tarpaulins and covers under which Bugattis, Alfa Romeos and Ferraris shelter. Morning mist envelops the idyllic scene in a grey veil, and an early riser offers to go in his Maserati to the next village to get some fresh rolls. He can but hope that his motor will respond, for the dampness of Prescott Hill, which penetrates into all the cables, is proverbial. On Prescott the snob appeal is in small details: next to 'Ettore's Field' are those very rustic lavatories, from which flows Bugatti-blue water when they are flushed....

If however the Vintage Sports Car Club of Great Britain invites one to Silverstone, one is not conscious of any romance. Rather, one very quickly becomes aware of the hectic pace at this former military airfield – which is also the impression at the Oulton Park track. British devotees on the other hand enthuse about the incomparable racing atmosphere that prevails at the Nürburgring, where the Automobile Club of Germany holds veteran races every August.

My visits to the many rallies and racing events in the British Isles raised a whole range of organisational problems, since they always had to be combined with completely different professional activities. Thus, the time-tables of the channel ferries ultimately dictated the rhythm of my life, and a typical weekend would be somewhat as follows. Three hours' drive on Saturday morning from Hamburg to Arnhem. A Bugatti meeting at a closed-off military airfield. No sightseers allowed, and therefore peace and quiet for taking photographs. A rare Bugatti 44 in front of the lens. In the afternoon continue on to Rotterdam to catch the overnight ferry to Hull. Arrive early morning. Then on the M62 and M6 motorways to the Oulton Park race track between Chester and Manchester. In the evening from there back to Leicester. The next morning, a visit to the automobile museum in Donington Park, and in the evening return via Hull to Rotterdam. Taking photographs was one side of the coin; the other was filing and writing captions for the slides, which as a rule meant much prior detailed, painstaking research. The fact that I could count on the tight information network of the various clubs, whose members did research work on my behalf in England, was indispensable for this Sisyphean task. Innumerable letters were written, and in many telephone conversations I enquired about technical details, in the course of which it is highly likely that on occasions I got on the nerves of both my English and German friends with my persistent desire for information.

I have already emphasised that the history of the automobile is far from being a science in the conventional sense of the term. It seems to me that in many books on 'old cars' the description of the technicalities is treated independently, without looking at the subject within the context of its historical framework. The present book aims to compensate for this deficiency. The car has completely altered human mobility and thereby also resulted in a new, more intensive life style, which is reflected in the activities of a photographer and author like myself. How else to explain the fact that an invitation to visit a small village in East Friesland to see, let us say, a Maybach-Zeppelin 12-cylinder – incidentally the official car of the former Nazi Foreign Minister von Ribbentrop – can make me excited? What's more, I'll go there despite the fact that I have 'flu, and I'll photograph the car between two breaks in the clouds, which then appears on the slide like a black and sombre chariot of the gods rising up from Hades.

He who would follow such trails must live in patience. Before the jacket photograph of this book was taken, again in pouring rain, I had already been allowed to see the individual parts of the completely stripped down Opel Grand Prix 1914 carefully arranged in rows and covered by tarpaulins. Its owner, Noel Mavrogordato, said on that occasion: 'I'll call you when I've rebuilt the car again. Then you'll get your photo!' And so it happened, two years later.

I will never forget how I took a photograph of the legendary Rolls-Royce Silver Ghost AX 201 in London on 7 April 1974. For the British, the AX 201 is purely and simply the Silver Ghost, for it was the first demonstration model of this most famous Rolls-Royce marque. You cannot simply photograph such a car by pressing the shutter release. First of all there was lunch with executives in their club. Then we drove across London in a Silver Shadow to the climatically controlled chamber, where the precious object on four wheels, insured for nearly half a million pounds, spent its retirement. Carefully sheltered from the normal workshop activity, the silver-plated coachwork of the Rolls-Royce Silver Ghost AX 201 shone in the pale afternoon sun of the London spring.

I did not intend in this book to write a complete history of the automobile. Many important marques, many interesting names and events have consciously been omitted. It was intended to be the completely personal book of a 'madman', who wishes to thank such renowned experts as Hans-Otto Neubauer, Peter Hull (Vintage Sports Car Club), D.B. Tubbs, Cyril Posthumus and Karl A. Klewer for their contributions and helpful advice. In this acknowledgment I should also like to include many informants whose names I cannot mention here, numbering as they do far more than one hundred.

In my research I strove for the greatest possible accuracy. Nevertheless a certain latitude should be allowed, for the afore-mentioned reasons. Each chapter has been read and checked by competent experts; for example, the chapter on Ferdinand Porsche was checked by his son, Dr 'Ferry' Porsche. The colour photographs are in snapshot style: none of the subjects was 'staged' or involved in long photographic sessions. In order to complete the overall visual impression, I have included a few colour photographs from other photographers. I hunted for the black-and-white photographs in European and American archives: they are a touching reminder of those largely unknown colleagues who were already taking fascinating pictures many decades ago.

I should be happy if the reader were to adopt the working motto of the book also as his own: 'These are picture and stories that smell of petrol – from the great, crazy period of the automobile, when to build and drive cars was still a gloriously exciting adventure for individualists'.

INGO SEIFF

GERMAN PIONEERING SPIRIT AND FRENCH 'ESPRIT'

In 1893 French automobile maker René Panhard presented his son Hippolyte with a new 4-horsepower Panhard & Levassor car for his 20th birthday. Panhard *père* had several good reasons for making his lavish gesture; he knew that his son hoped to become an expert in driving such machines, and this would undoubtedly be an opportunity to introduce him to the mechanics of the motor carriage, a knowledge vital to all who chose to venture on to the road with this novel mode of transport. On a 770 km test run from Paris to Marseilles Hippolyte got on extremely well with his birthday present, achieving an average journey speed of 12 mph – and extending his test-drive as far as Nice. After such a successful (even if not totally trouble-free) marathon young Hippolyte decided to make the return journey by the Alpine route. His confidence was misplaced, however; he had not counted on the 'mountain spirits'. The highly original wire-brush clutch was not up to the stress, and Hippolyte, together with the car, returned to Paris by rail. Panhard senior was satisfied nevertheless. This pioneering trip could be counted a resounding triumph for the car designed by his partner Emile Levassor – and he had discovered its weak spot.

GERMAN DISCOVERY AND
A FRENCH REVOLUTION

Paris 1889. Nearly thirty million visitors marvelled at the engineering masterpiece of the World Fair, the 300-metre-high steel tower built by Frenchman Gustave Eiffel on the Champ-de-mars – a skeletal colossus they called the 'Eighth Wonder of the World'. Other exhibits – especially the combustion engines of the Germans Karl Benz and Gottlieb Daimler, which endured a wallflower-like existence in the 'Machines et Moteurs' hall – had a very poor time of it, partly because relations between France and Germany were still somewhat strained after the war of 1870-1871. The 'hereditary enmity' was cultivated on both sides of the Rhine, accompanied by much bluster and sabre-rattling. France was still obsessed with the desire to exact revenge for the defeat, and for the loss of Alsace-Lorraine, and to this end the Third Republic devoted a great deal of effort to modernising the army and training its soldiers. The anti-German lobby in France had retreated temporarily behind the grandiose overseas policy of the French, but even two years before the opening of the World Fair, French Minister of War General Boulanger spoke of the immediate threat of a new Franco-German conflict.

It was therefore not surprising that there was no official German representative at this mighty spectacle on the Seine. Karl Benz left the promotion of his products to his French agent Emile Roger, while Gottlieb Daimler entrusted his to the charm and negotiating skills of his agent, Madame Louise Sarazin, called by some chroniclers the 'Maid of Orleans' of the French automobile industry. She was the widow of Edouard Sarazin, who had for many years represented the interests of the German firm Otto & Langen in Paris.

Madame Sarazin, Daimler's Paris representative

In 1886 the far-sighted Edouard Sarazin had already acquired the Daimler concession for Belgium and France. He and his old friend René Panhard often spoke of the technology and the future of 'self-propelled' vehicles, and of the fact that steam had reached its limits as a propulsive medium. They also discussed the possibilities of utilizing the brilliant pioneering work of Nikolaus Otto, Benz and Daimler 'for the glory of France'. Panhard formulated a plan: in 1886 he and his partner Emile Levassor bought up the woodworking machinery firm of Périn & Pauwels, in which they had an interest. Their sole aim was the acquisition of the machinery and production workshops. Then Sarazin's permission to build the Daimler engine

under licence was obtained. Thus the foundation stone of the French automobile industry was laid – somewhat ironically with an invention from the land of the 'hereditary enemy'!

There was no co-operation with Karl Benz however, even though Roger had bought one of the first Benz cars and left it with Panhard & Levassor, to 'get accustomed to it'. Despite some test drives with Karl Benz in 1888, Panhard and Levassor just could not take to his product.

Sarazin's death in 1887 appeared at first to halt the ascendancy of the Daimler engine in France, but the natural fears of René Panhard and Emile Levassor proved to be groundless. Madam Sarazin was a worthy successor to her commercially-minded husband. Even in his last hours, on Christmas Eve 1887, he implored his wife: 'Hold on to Daimler, if only for the sake of the children! Continue working with him and with Panhard and Levassor. Only you know how to get the best out of Daimler's patents'. Louise Sarazin fulfilled the wishes of her husband. She went to see Daimler in Cannstatt and begged him to appoint her the new general representative in France. The honest Swabian was captivated. That such a resolute and capable woman wanted to promote his work on the French market, he considered an exciting adventure to which he gladly agreed.

Louise Sarazin did nothing by halves: on her return journey her luggage included, in addition to a contract for the licence rights for Belgium and France, a new Daimler engine, which she took through customs with the connivance of a government minister. This valuable item from Cannstat was stripped down by Panhard and Levassor and examined to the last detail. The Daimler engine became the prototype for the later Panhard engine, intended as a drive unit for horseless carriages, boats and rail cars, and as a stationary power unit.

Madame Sarazin did the honours for Daimler at the Paris World Fair. Both the Benz and Daimler engines stood unobtrusively in a side hall, unnoticed by the vast majority of visitors, between various stationary steam and gas engines. Only when a Daimler engine drove a dynamo for demonstration purposes, which in turn illuminated some 30 electric bulbs, was public attention captured. Daimler's machine, it seemed, had the makings of becoming a fun-fair attraction.

It was not the invention of this combustion engine *per se* that was the revelation in the opinion of the visitors, but its applications. Many questions were raised: what can one start up, or move, with this engine, so much lighter and convenient than the power machinery of the past? What technical virgin territory can be opened up? Will horses become redundant? Has the death knell sounded for steam power? Answers to these questions were to be found in another exhibition hall, where two tiny *voitures à pétrole* were hidden between beautifully decorated horse-driven carriages. One of them was Benz's latest three-wheel carriage, the other Daimler's second automobile, the spidery *Stahlrad* or 'Steelwheeler', a four-wheel carriage with a two-cylinder V-engine that delivered 1.6 h.p.

Paul Daimler, Gottlieb's son, took the occasional interested customer on trial runs along the banks of the Seine; one was René Panhard. Gottlieb Daimler trusted his automobile so little, however, that he kept two boats for demonstration purposes in a specially prepared berth on the Seine in order to prove the capability and performance of his new *moteur*. Together with his friend and collaborator Wilhelm Maybach, he would run his petrol-driven boats *Violette* and *Passe-Partout* on the Seine as far as St Cloud and Suresnes. Levassor and the astute Louise Sarazin became regular passengers. At the time French journalist Pierre Giffard noted what little interest Paul Daimler's trial drives and Levassor's and Madame Sarazin's test runs in the engine-driven boats, created: 'No-one thought that the germ of today's technical revolution was to be found in this forgotten corner of the World Fair' he wrote.

Had Daimler's efforts at the Paris World Fair paid off? Public interest was slight, and he had certainly not achieved any great commercial success with his petrol-driven engine. True, a number of visitors had taken notice of his invention, but there were just three persons in all France who were willing to stake their future on his combustion engine, and prepared to lead the 'Grande Nation' into the age of the automobile: Louise Sarazin, René Panhard and Emile Levassor. Daimler confirmed in writing to Madame Sarazin that he assigned to her 'the exploitation of his French and Belgian patents and gas and petroleum engines', and moneys which would be 'payable when you have earned a profit on them, but at the latest within three years'. Daimler laid down the following two conditions: 'All improvements and refinements made by both sides and all products must bear my name, and you will not compete with me in other countries.'

Emile Levassor married Louise Sarazin on May 17 1890, an alliance of affection and commercial interest made just as Panhard & Levassor were starting on their car-making venture. They had in fact produced an experimental model a couple of months earlier.

However, a fourth name now appeared in the records of the infant industry; Armand Peugeot, a pioneer in that small band of French engineers, destined to become one of the most highly respected in the automotive field.

In 1890 the Peugeot family could already look back on a long tradition as manufacturers. Their firm had its origins in the 15th century. A marriage certificate from the village of Vaudencourt in 1435 names Hans Peugeot, craftsman and maker of pitch. A few generations later a certain Jean-Pierre of this lineage (1768-1852) was on the way to becoming an 'industrialist'. Some members of the Peugeot clan went into textiles, others into metallurgy. Jean-Pierre together with his brother Jean-Fréderic founded a steel foundry at Montbéliard on 26 September 1810. (The present-day automobile enterprise proudly refers to this date, with the statement 'founded in 1810', but in reality the founding company for automobile manufacture was created only in 1896 with the Peugeot limited liability automobile company.)

Peugeot and Panhard et Levassor

When Armand Peugeot decided to build an automobile driven by a petrol engine, the company, Les Fils de Peugeot Frères, had already had long experience of manufacturing agricultural machinery, tools, strip and bandsaws, heavy-gauge sheet metal articles and metal springs. They had even profited from the fashion for crinolines adopted in 1850, at the time of the Second Empire, producing steel frames or cages for the voluminous flared skirts and lace-up corsets. Peugeot had invented a successful clipping or shearing instrument for horses, and had supplied hair-cutting machines to the army during the 1870-1871 war. When the 'high-wheel' bicycle came into fashion Peugeot soon became one of the largest manufacturers of it in France, adapting the thin steel crinoline stays as cycle spokes.

Peugeot's experiments with a steam-driven three-wheeled carriage had proved unsatisfactory; he realised that the age of steam drive was a thing of the past, after the emergence of the Benz and Daimler engines; the low efficiency and large dead-weight prevented any further significant expansion of steam drive. Peugeot had a serious discussion with his friend Levassor, who had been a good customer of the Peugeot company for some years. In 1890 he obtained permission to build a Panhard-Daimler petrol engine in a Peugeot chassis.

The first Peugeot car was developed by the engineer Rigoulot, and represented a modified version of the Daimler Steelwheeler vehicle, predictably influenced by cycle construction. The most notable structural feature of the French car was the novel double-pivoting front axle, named after its initiator Ackermann. The German-born Rudolph Ackermann (1764-1834), a London book-dealer and publisher, had been very interested in carriages and coaches and between 1818 and 1820 had developed a technical device for adjusting to the two different radii described by a pair of front wheels steered through a road curve: the whole axle no longer turned in the curve but the wheels themselves swivelled. This invention had been almost completely forgotten in the ensuing 70 years – even Benz had not heard of the development when he decided to build a four-wheel vehicle, and had to work it out all over again.

Peugeot, being a bicycle manufacturer, had a great deal of experience in processing and machining steel tubing, and welding it cleanly at critical points. As Gottlieb Daimler had done with his Steelwheeler, Peugeot utilised the steel tube chassis as a cooling water system connected between the engine and the radiator. The V-type two-cylinder Daimler engine was mounted over the rear axle. The wheels, which were smaller than those of the Steelwheeler, ran on ball bearings instead of simple bush bearings, as was still customary with Daimler vehicles.

Panhard and Levassor were now trailing slightly behind the Peugeots as the improvement and refinement work on the Daimler engine occupied their time. Their experimental automobile introduced in 1890 still leant heavily on the construction principles of the carriage, with a wooden chassis and the very old-fashioned centre-pivot steering. The Panhard and Levassor car was larger and more robust than the Peugeot, but this was compensated for by a somewhat more powerful 2 h.p. engine, mounted over the rear axle. The Panhard and Levassor vehicle also differed from the Peugeot in the transmission. Levassor was no lover of belt drive and was sceptical of Daimler's giant sliding pulley arrangement. He mounted the engine centrally in a transverse position and opted for a chain drive arrangement.

1890 – The birth of the automobile industry

In the history of the petrol-engined automobile, we should regard the year 1890 as the start of the automobile 'industry' proper. There were now six pioneers on whom the necessary further development of the automobile rested: Karl Benz, Gottlieb Daimler, René Panhard and Emile Levassor, Louise (now also Levassor) and Armand Peugeot. One could describe Benz and Daimler as the 'brains trust', and the French as the 'doers', the marketing men who brought a professional approach to promoting the gasolene-driven automobile.

The internal combustion engine with its then still unknown potential entered the public consciousness relatively slowly. It would be incorrect to talk of a technical revolution, although the French reacted more sen-

sitively to the first automobiles than did the Germans. They realised that this brilliant invention could give their *savoir vivre* a new dimension, and would create a completely new form of personal freedom. The Germans had nothing comparable to the teams of Panhard, the Levassors, and Peugeot. Karl Benz and Gottlieb Daimler never even met, let alone discussed the future of their work, even though they lived only about 60 miles apart – a fact that would be inconceivable today. Both were loners, each working out his own dreams backed up by his own technical knowledge, in almost complete isolation. It would have been more in their interest, both personal and national, if they had cooperated to prevent France reaping the major benefits, but the idea obviously never entered their heads.

Curiously, most present-day literature on the history of the period still ignores the first tentative steps of the early automobile industry and their consequences in 1890, a year that marked an important turning point in its progress. History takes more note of the facts that in 1890 free education became established in England, Wilhelmina was crowned Queen of the Netherlands, Ernst von Behring discovered diphtheria serum, Paul Cezanne painted his 'Landscape at Aix', Rodin unveiled his sculpture 'Danaid', and workers for the first time celebrated 1 May as International Labour Day.

France drives ahead

However one regards history it must be admitted that the first automobiles did not seem to be milestones of progress. In Germany Benz and Daimler found it very difficult to attract any attention at all; their automobiles were nowhere when it came to contemporary technological research for the future – although there was little enough of that at the time. Even Daimler's business partners did not consider the light high-speed engine at all suitable for road vehicles, and instead concentrated on stationary power units. The Germans wanted nothing to do with this smelly, rattling 'substitute horse carriage'. Benz and Daimler received only ridicule or amazed disbelief when they showed their new machines on their home ground. It was the French who, with tricolors flying, overran the Daimler and Benz camps; the German *moteurs* were soon the great caprice of the adventurous French, firm believers in progress.

Elsewhere in Europe there was more solid resistance. The emergence of the gasolene-driven carriage brought sharp protests from craftsmen and small businessmen, from blacksmith and coach builder, haulier, coachman and horse breeder. They all feared for their livelihood. There was a massive outcry from the first environmental protectionists, a conservative group who warned against too rapid technical progress and who feared that man would be subjugated by noisy machines. The rural population protested by erecting barricades against townspeople making trips into the country in their smelly motor carriages. Those who had invested in railways were, predictably, with the protesters. It seemed that the whole world was against the new machine – except France.

One of the greatest French intellectuals, Anatole France, wrote in *L'Ile des Pingouins*: 'In order to prevent the motor car becoming harmful, and so that it may be beneficial, we must build roads that are adapted to its speed. Roads that cannot be destroyed by rapidly revolving tyres, roads the dust from which cannot gather in our lungs like some dreadful poison'. France, with its exemplary road network, was an ideal testing ground for the young French automobile industry.

By the middle of the 19th century France had a road network of some 74,000 kilometres, a legacy that gave the French a great mobility advantage compared with other industrialised nations, an advantage that led directly to France becoming the first country with a genuine automobile industry.

Towards new shores

On a cold January day in 1891 an engine-driven carriage drove spitting and popping through urban Paris streets. Emile Levassor was at the wheel of a Panhard on its first test drive. He had set himself the target of covering ten kilometres in the experimental fourwheeler, built painstakingly in a tiny workshop in a corner of the main factory by eight dedicated mechanics. A contemporary French report states that 'Levassor piloted the car without incident' but somehow one doubts it. That engineer Levassor *a poussé avec succes* to Versailles a few days later is well documented and it can be taken that the account did not mean that he pushed it for the 55 kilometres there and back.

At the end of July 1891 a longer run was made; a drive in a modified two-seater to the resort of Etretat on the channel coast, 25 kilometres north of Le Havre. Madame Louise Levassor passengered on this occasion; the enterprising couple had planned on two days for the 220 km journey. Short meal-breaks were taken during the day, and they stopped overnight in Rouen. There were one or two unscheduled stops due to some problems with the hot-tube ignition, but Levassor attributed these breakdowns to the poor quality fuel sold by the chemists' shops, not to his vehicle's mechanics. He calculated his average speed on arrival in Etretat – 10 km per hour; not bad, he considered, for his first long-distance run.

This pioneering activity of Levassor did not disturb Peugeot, who had already built three such carriages. The fourth, which he started building in 1891 was, in his own words, to 'get Panhard et Levassor and France excited'. This one differed from its predecessors particularly in that the wheels on the front and rear axles were almost the same size, and the vehicle was equipped with rubber tyres and semi-elliptical spring suspension on the rear wheels. The two-cylinder Panhard/Daimler engine gave an output of some 2 h.p. and was mounted transversely more or less in the centre of the car, with chain transmission to the rear wheels. In contrast to the heavy two-seater in which Levassor had driven to Etretat, the Peugeot was a lightly-built four-seater, from which chief engineer Rigoulot could coax a speed of up to 20 kilometres an hour.

Levassor and Peugeot thus became competitors, though this did not affect their long-standing friendship. Armand Peugeot had decided some time earlier that participation in reliability trials and races (for cyclists only at that time, of course) could help further development of the automobile, and when in 1891 *Le Petit Journal* announced a long-distance race for cyclists from Paris to Brest and back, Armand announced that he would accompany the event in his automobile as an unofficial competitor. Most of the pedallers – some on Peugeot cycles – passed him and the car finished way down the field. However, apart from a damaged differential he was pleased with his automobile; it had covered 1200 kilometres.

Levassor greeted his competitor's success with mixed feelings: the Daimler engine in Peugeot's automobile had, it was true, been prepared for the long-distance race in the Panhard & Levassor workshop, but the glory belonged to Armand Peugeot. Panhard & Levassor had received ten orders for cars, due to the Etretat trip publicity. How many would Armand capture with his marathon tour?

The engine moves to the front

Emile Levassor realised that the serious battle to win the goodwill of the automobile customer had now begun, and he built several more prototypes, with seating to accommodate four passengers comfortably. The automobile was in the process of becoming a family conveyance; there should be room for father, mother and at least two children. The previous arrangement had been *dos-a-dos* – back-to-back – with two passengers in the front facing the direction of travel, and two passengers on the rear seat, facing in the opposite direction; but that conformation had been necessitated by the centrally-placed power unit on the earliest prototype.

'What innovation can we come up with in order to beat Peugeot?'. This was the burning question at the workshops of Panhard & Levassor in 1891. The partners departed from their original principle that the engine had to be at the centre or the rear to avoid inconveniencing passengers with its noise and smell. The engine would now be moved to the front. The added weight at the front end would improve steering – which had been rather vague on the early cars. This innovation passed into automobile history as the legendary *Système Panhard* and gave the automobile the power-train layout that still exists today in front-engined, rear-drive cars. However, on closer examination the epoch-making image of this design is seen to be slightly tarnished, for in reality it was the constant complaint from Levassor's wife Louise that the underseat central engine heated her own rear-end uncomfortably that finally made him think again . . .

One can fully sympathise with those devotees of steam engines who complain, perhaps with some justification, that historians belittle the role of steam propulsion in the history of the road vehicle – although in France, particularly, there are some first class examples of how the transition from steam engine to gasolene engine occurred logically. Amedée Bollée's steam carriage *La Mancelle* (Maid of Le Mans) was in many ways the forerunner of the early Panhard and some of the designs of Benz and Daimler: its engines were mounted at the front under the 'engine' hood with chain drive to the rear wheels. Several other Bollée principles constituted important links with later automobile builders.

Herr Makulatur, a German banker, acquired a licence to build the Bollée steam carriage, and planned to set up an extensive coach network in Germany, Russia, Austria and Sweden. Unfortunately for him, the Wohlert engine and locomotive factory, which was to have built the steam coaches, went bankrupt in 1883. His plans collapsed, and Bollée also lost some large potential licence revenues. The Le Mans company was rocked to its foundations. Nevertheless, the demise of steam was delayed for a time by a person who, some years later, was to give his name to a rear axle construction that has remained viable to the present day; Count Albert de Dion.

In a toyshop in Paris de Dion discovered a working model of a steam engine that had been built by two skilled craftsmen of some repute, Bouton and Trepardoux. Count Albert, an aristocrat from the 'Old Order', contacted the mechanic George Bouton (and this was in the days when de Dion senior, who was typical of the *ancien régime*, would still not recognise those whose families had been ennobled by Napoleon, so rigid were the class divisions!) and suggested they cooperate to build a steam engine for road use. George Bouton agreed, and by 1883 the first de Dion steam automobiles were trundling over the roads of France. However, Count de Dion was a true progressive,

and ten years later he realised that the age of steam propulsion for road vehicles was gradually drawing to a close. He converted his plant to the production of gasolene-driven automobiles and in 1895 he and his partner Bouton introduced their first model.

It was an astonishing unit, a light tricycle driven by a tiny one-cylinder air-cooled engine, that could run, mainly due to the new type of electric ignition, at speeds of up to 3,000 rpm, when most other 'high-speed' engines – notably the Benz and Daimler products – turned at a leisurely 500-600 rpm. The power and efficiency from this frenzied little 137 cc buzzer made it a popular light vehicle and by the time the 20th century was ushered in French urban roads were beginning to sound like beehives.

The birth of motor sport

While Benz and Daimler in Germany were beset by petty complaints and other obstacles of prejudice and ignorance, French manufacturers were already planning the first rallies and races, which they naturally treated as publicity campaigns for their products. *Le Petit Journal* (daily, 5 centimes, with Sunday Supplement) sponsored and organised a Paris-Rouen reliability run on 22 July 1894, the first-ever motor sporting event.

The entry list included 102 vehicles, many of which only existed on paper and boasted outrageous types of propulsion, such as 'gravity carriages', 'compressed air automobiles', 'lever-driven carriages', none of which turned up on the day. Finally, 21 vehicles started, driven either by internal combustion engines or steam power.

The 1894 reliability trial, which was not a speed contest (that is, until the cars were round the first corner, out of sight of the judges), was basically a match between five Panhards and five Peugeots, if one discounts a steam-driven de Dion which was disqualified – a triumph for Gottlieb Daimler more than anyone else, for all ten were fitted with his engines. A carburettor developed by Wilhelm Maybach had put new life into the victorious Panhard and Peugeot cars. Emile Roger reached the finish in Rouen at the wheel of a Benz 'Viktoria', at an average speed of 12.6 km per hour – not far behind the winners, Panhard and Peugeot, who shared first place.

Although this reliability run represented a very modest beginning, the success of the Daimler gasolene engine marked the end of steam power, and brought the French motoring côterie to a higher pitch of enthusiasm. Next year, they said, there must be a genuine race.

The learned journal *Le Génie Civil* wrote: 'The Paris-Rouen event has, with an impact like a clap of thunder, drawn the attention of the public at large to the possibilities of the automobile driven by a combustion engine.

If used sensibly and wisely, the automobile will fundamentally alter our mobility and our whole concept of transportation.' Although the Paris-Rouen reliability run had not yet caused panic in the ranks of the steam and horse-drawn carriage builders, the gasolene-driven automobile had nevertheless left behind its first indelible mark on history.

The world's first automobile race, from Paris to Bordeaux and back, was held 11-13 June 1895. It started at the Place d'Armes in Versailles, continued through the Chevreuse valley via Limours, Etamples, Orleans, Tours, and then on the Route Nationale 10 to Bordeaux, and back the same way, some 1,200 km. Emile Levassor competed in a Panhard two-seater driven by a new Daimler engine. Designed by Wilhelm Maybach, Daimler's technical colleague, it was an in-line two cylinder engine which proved considerably more powerful and lighter than the previous V-twin unit. Levassor himself had modified this unit to his specification and, weighing only 80 kg, it had a speed of 800 rpm, producing more than 4 h.p. from a piston capacity of 1206 cc.

'It's rough but it works!'

Levassor's car with its new Daimler-based engine had a friction clutch operated by a pedal and a gear-change which he had earlier described in a typically laconic way: 'C'est brusque et brutal mais ça marche!' (It's rough but it works!). Levassor's two-seater did not comply with the rule that only four-seaters were allowed to compete, but the intrepid automobile pioneer nevertheless took part in order to subject his carriage to this rigorous test. Levassor's progress was so rapid that he reached the small town of Ruffec, about a third of the way to Bordeaux, three hours before the time at which he had arranged to pick up his relief driver there. The driver was still asleep and Emile Levassor could not find his lodgings; he took his place behind the wheel again and continued, so wide-awake and excited that he did not even ask his 'riding mechanic' to relieve him. Early farm-workers must have been astonished to see the strange device, dimly lit by two candle lamps, trundling through the darkness, its solid rubber-tyred wheels unmercifully jolting the two occupants every time they hit a pothole. The people of these outlying regions could never have seen an automobile before and would certainly be apprehensive of the noise, the unfamiliar smell and the sheer horselessness of the vehicle . . .

The 53-year-old engineer had long ago left all the other competitors far behind, and cheering thousands crowded round the car when he entered Bordeaux at daybreak. Levessor briefly refreshed himself with a glass of champagne, ate a frugal breakfast, and set off on the return journey to Paris. On the way the engine faltered several times. D'Hostingue, the riding mechanic, discovered that the centrifugal governor was sticking, and repaired the damage on the spot. Levassor utilised the brief break to take a nap. As he was travelling back towards Ruffec he met the rest of the field coming in the opposite direction, still on the outward journey to Bordeaux! Among them was a rumbling Bollée steam carriage. The sophisticated interior appointments of this monster included a *toilette*, which was in constant use by the seven occupants of the carriage for the simple reason that the jolting and shaking affected their stomachs so much that they frequently had to answer the call of nature!

A winner by six hours

There was a further curiosity in this race, a small Peugeot motor carriage with André and Edouard Michelin at the wheel. They were testing their new 'pneumatic' tyres for the first time in a race, and had more than 50 punctures, finally retiring from the race after 90 hours. Levassor, who in many ways had a sixth sense for anything new and innovative, didn't think much of the future prospects for air-filled tyres . . .

When Levassor once more reached Ruffec the relief driver was waiting to take over the wheel for the rest of the journey to Paris. However, Emile was adamant. He would continue to drive – and enjoy the rewards of the single-handed victory that was now imminent.

He arrived at 1 p.m. the following day at the Porte Maillot in Paris, after 48 hours and 47.5 minutes behind the wheel, completing the race in one enormous 'lap'. His average speed was 24 km per hour, discounting scheduled (and unscheduled) stops. The victor had already spruced himself up and was on his way to the champagne reception when the second carriage, a Peugeot with engineer Rigoulot at the wheel, arrived some six hours later.

As his two-seater did not comply with the regulations Levassor was relegated to third place behind two Peugeots that claimed the honour of official victory. Nevertheless, he obtained his just rewards: he received 12,000 francs, and a memorial was erected in his honour at the Porte Maillot in Paris. Levassor had achieved what he wanted and indeed it is his name that echoes down the corridors of history. He proved that automobiles driven by internal combustion engines were capable of withstanding the stresses (unimaginable under normal conditons in 1895) of such mammoth journeys.

The historic Paris-Bordeaux-Paris long-distance race of 1895 was the prelude to many similar spectacles. A new carriage with a 4-cylinder engine (with an output of 8 h.p.), designed by Levassor and with Emile again at the wheel, ran for the first time a year later in the Paris-Marseilles-Paris race, a distance of 1728 kilometres. Sadly the great French automobile pioneer was injured in this race, and died the following year.

By the end of the 19th century the firm of Panhard & Levassor was the undisputed leader of the automotive world, and in most cases also led the winners' lists in the great long-distance races, most of which generally lasted at least ten days. In 1899, nineteen carriages, including eight Panhards, were at the start in Paris of the 1350 miles long 'Tour de France' for automobiles, sponsored by *Le Matin*. The course included Cabourg, Nantes, Périgueux, Vichy, Aix-les-Bains and Nancy, and back to Paris, a route that included some daunting mountain country in the Auvergne, a severe test of cars and *pilotes*. Stray dogs, unaccustomed to these roaring quick-as-the-wind objects on the roads, caused a number of accidents, and breakdowns littered the highways. The big 16 h.p. Panhard of Chevalier René de Knyff led a start-to-finish victory at an unprecedented average of 48 kmph. Motor sport had entered its Heroic Age, which would last for some fifteen years.

France remained the premier automobile manufacturing country in the world till 1906, and until 1913 the largest car exporter. The seeds sown by Karl Benz, Gottlieb Daimler, Louise and Emile Levassor, René Panhard and Armand Peugeot had grown into the might oak of a new industry . . .

3

Previous pages: 1. 1905 Dufaux. 2. 1938 Bugatti 57SC 'Atlantic'. 3. 1933 Rolls-Royce Phantom II.

4

4. 1929 Rolls-Royce Phantom I.

5. 1936-1938 Rolls-Royce 25/30.

6. 1929-1935 Rolls-Royce Phantom II. Following pages: 7. 1938 S.S. 100. 8. 1905 Dufaux Gordon Bennett.

THE IMMORTALS

The pacemakers for the 20th Century had a thorough sense of the practical. When Gottlieb Daimler married for the second time, after the death of his first wife, his honeymoon trip with Lina Hartmann in 1893 led him to Steinways in New York, a company that not only built pianos but had taken over the sales of Daimler products. Technology and the muses went hand in hand, and the German engineer's pleasure and private affairs were combined with business matters. Karl Benz too had an eye for a market. As early as 1888 he had informed his customers in an advertisement that his motorised carriages were 'Patented in all industrial countries. Always ready for operation! Comfortable and safe! Complete replacement for horse-drawn carriages! Dispense with the coachman and the expensive accessories, care and upkeep of the horse. No special training necessary...' and other somewhat optimistic claims....

KARL BENZ AND GOTTLIEB DAIMLER –
FATHERS OF THE AUTOMOBILE

On the last day of 1879, as people were remembering the achievements of the year that was just ending and hoping for a happy and prosperous 1880, there was an air of deep gloom in the Mannheim home of engineer Karl Benz. A few years previously his company had got into financial difficulties and his creditors had pursued him so hard that he was made bankrupt in 1877. Fortunately, he was able to prevent his property being sold off, but the economic boom of the years immediately following the end of the 1871 war had passed the small business by.

Karl Benz pinned his faith on the future. In order not to be left out of the now inevitable industrial revolution, he began to develop an internal combustion engine. Automobile technology was now on the move following the development of the four-stroke Otto engine in 1877, a patent application for which (German Reichspatent No. 532) had been filed in 1876. The heyday of steam and electricity as motive forces was already past, due not least to their extremely poor power-to-cost ratio. However, anyone who wanted to use the Otto principle had to take out a licence; the thrifty Karl Benz shrank from this step and chose instead the two-stroke principle.

This was the situation therefore when Karl and Berta Benz wandered disconsolately over to their workshop on New Year's Eve 1879 to examine, once more, their little bench-bolted two-stroke engine, which was still beset by problems. After supper that evening, Berta had said 'Let's go to the workshop again and have another try. I've got something on my mind that doesn't give me any peace'.

They strolled over to the workshop, and without much hope, Karl turned his engine over. He recalled later: 'Tat, tat, tat! answered the engine. The beats of the music of the future followed one another in a beautiful, regular rhythm. We listened, deeply absorbed, for more than an hour to the steady song. The two-stroke engine could now do what no magic flute in the world had been able to accomplish. We were able to ignore the merrymaking in the outside world on this New Year's Eve. We experienced true happiness in our small workshop, which on this evening saw the birth of a new engine. We heard the bells ringing, bells welcoming in the New Year! And for us they rang in not only a new year, but a new epoch.'

Nikolaus Otto's great gamble

In Cologne, some 160 miles away, Otto, Daimler and Maybach were already ahead of Benz. The two engineers Gottlieb Daimler and Wilhelm Maybach, who had struck up a friendship that was to last until Daimler's death, were employed in 1872 by the Deutz gas engine factory in Cologne, where they worked on stationary internal combustion engines. However, in 1875 the future of the company seemed threatened by a sudden unexpected slump. Nikolaus Otto's historic moment had arrived. His notebook of experiments shows, in an entry dated 9 May 1876, the diagram of an apparently workable four-stroke engine, and as early as October 1876 the finished prototypes were being tested. Production models ranging from a half horsepower up to eight quickly followed. Not only was the future of the Deutz gas engine factory thus ensured, but the march of the modern internal combustion engine had begun.

It was originally intended that Daimler should take over the Vienna branch of the Deutz Gasmotorenfabrik. However, he was first sent on a trip to Russia to explore sales and marketing possibilities in the giant empire of the Tsar and the detailed report that he prepared of his investigations there reinforced the intention of the board of directors to set up a branch in St Petersburg.

A photographer's advice

Daimler was offered the position of branch manager; a safely distant posting for a difficult person. He refused but realised that his time at Deutz was now up: he had been extremely successful during his years with the company, but this blow to his pride meant that there was now only one choice open to him. Daimler was forty-eight when, in July 1882, he moved into a villa in the spa park at Cannstatt, a suburb of Stuttgart. The greenhouse of the property was converted into a workshop, and here he built his 'high-speed' four-stroke engine. Wilhelm Maybach followed him, and on 1 January 1883 they began their mutual collaboration. (The greenhouse, by the way, is still there in its original state, with Daimler's early engines and tools left as he would have worked with them.)

What had happened to Benz in the meantime? The technical success of his two-stroke engine, which continued to work impeccably, could not disguise the fact that he was once more in financial difficulties. There was too little time left to prepare for series production and obtain orders – cash was running out fast. While Benz was in this precarious situation, court photographer Emil Buhler entered automotive history. He needed a smooth-polished steel plate for his glazing machine, which the ingenious Benz was able to produce, exactly as required.

Benz showed his engine to Buhler. The photographer was enraptured: 'My dear Benz, there's a future here! I'll help with some finance!' The photographer went even further. He advised Benz to set up a limited liability company in order to spread future cash risks more widely. The Gasmotorenfabrik Mannheim was founded on 14 October 1882, nine shareholders putting up the capital of 100,000 Marks. Benz's own business was valued at 45,000 Marks and was taken over by the company.

After only three months, however, Benz asked for his contract to be revoked. He joined two acquaintances, Max Kaspar Rose and Friedrich Wilhelm Esslinger, and founded Benz & Cie, Rheinische Gasmotorenfabrik in Mannheim, on 1 October 1883. The objects of the enterprise were 'Production of internal combustion engines according to the plans of Karl Benz'. The Benz two-stroke engine was soon a best-seller both at home and abroad, and larger production workshops, covering an area of 40,000 sq feet, were built in 1886.

Now that his engine was so successful, Benz decided to concentrate on building a vehicle to be driven by it, although his business partners still hesitated. Then, in January 1886, the Imperial German Supreme Court declared Otto's patent invalid, on the grounds that French engineer Beau de Rochas had already demonstrated the four-stroke principle (in theory) in 1862, and the construction technology that Otto had specified was now accessible to everyone. Benz had already started to develop a four-stroke unit, with the result that he was now (unknowingly) neck-and-neck with Daimler in the race to develop the gasolene engine. Otto and Daimler had both chosen incandescent (hot-tube) ignition, whereas Benz opted for the so-called 'trembler' ignition which the Frenchman Lenoir had invented — a difference that was to prove significant.

The year 1886 became an important turning point in road transport history – the first practical motor vehicles were built: Karl Benz's three-wheeler and Gottlieb Daimler's motorised carriage. At first Karl Benz was in the lead with his Patent No 37435 of 29 January 1886. The conveyance, described as a 'vehicle with gas engine drive', was the first roadworthy automobile in the world. The Benz three-wheeler, its structure visibly influenced by available cycle material, was driven by a relatively light, open-structure four-stroke engine with a maximum output of 0.8 hp, which chuffed away at the considerable speed (for the times) of 250 revolutions per minute.

The first public excursions of the new machine through the suburbs of Mannheim caused a sensation among the astonished population. The public, who had previously failed to recognise that the bicycle had inaugurated a new technical age, considered it a nine-day

wonder. Luckily for Benz the press was well-disposed towards the novelty, and at the Munich Machinery Exhibition in 1888 the reception was positive, although an article in the *Annual Of Natural Sciences*, which dealt with Benz's new motorboats, cast some doubt on the road vehicle's success: 'Benz has also built a gasolene carriage, which has created something of a sensation at the Munich Exhibition. This application of the gasolene engine might well, however, turn out to be just as impracticable as that of steam in highway transportation.'

The world's first long-distance drive

Karl Benz was not discouraged by such criticism. In his prospectus – the first automobile brochure in the world – the three-wheeled carriage is described as 'an accommodating carriage as well as a hill-climbing machine'. It was able to take a six per cent gradient when loaded, and an eight per cent gradient unloaded, at a speed given as 16 km/hour (10 mph). An attractive proposition in 1888 when road travel was a plodding, clip-clop progress punctuated by meals of hay or oats. Sadly no great crowds beat a path to Benz's door. In fact nobody at all came to his door. . . .

The fact that purchasers were not forthcoming did not disturb either Karl or Berta Benz. On the contrary, his plucky wife continued to convince her husband that they were right in pinning their hopes on the future of his 'self-propelled' carriage. One August morning in 1888 she set out, accompanied by their young sons Eugen and Richard, on the first car journey in the world. Their aim was to reach Pforzheim, some 50 miles away. Karl Benz, sleeping late, knew nothing of this risky expedition. It was a journey full of surprises and calamities. The vehicle had to be pushed up hills, village blacksmiths helped in numerous breakdowns, gasolene was bought from chemists' shops on the route. The intrepid trio were able to solve many problems themselves – chains which became detached from the gearwheels, blockages in the flow of petrol to the carburettor, short-circuits in the electrical equipment (Berta had to sacrifice an elastic suspender to rectify this) and several renewals of the brake linings. Excited passers-by burst out laughing: 'Now we can get rid of our old nags!' Karl Benz was informed by telegraph of the success of the expedition. He was proud of his three test drivers, amused by their secrecy, and asked for the chains used for the journey to be sent back by express delivery as he needed them for an exhibition car. . . .

By the second half of 1886 Gottlieb Daimler's engine was ready to be installed in a carriage. The single-cylinder unit produced 1.1 hp at 650 rpm had a 70 mm bore and a 120 mm stroke. Wilhelm Maybach was at the wheel as the first Daimler carriage was driven on its first test run in the courtyard of the Esslingen engine factory. Daimler, now fully in the picture concerning Benz's work, had once more caught up.

The fact that the two men never met was no accident. Daimler was a proud, self-confident man, who fully expected that the introspective and shy Karl Benz would have to come to him for information or advice – and now the situation was just the opposite – Benz could have helped Daimler, particularly in ignition matters. One can imagine how much these two engineers would have had to say to one another if they had ever met!

What's the use of an engine?

Daimler was not primarily interested in self-propelled road transport as the successor to horse-drawn carriages. He envisaged his engine as a universally mobile power, propelling ships, locomotives, airships, coaches and wagons.

Fire-fighting vehicles were particularly dear to his heart – too slow with steam drive, losing vital minutes in starting.

Benz on the other hand had long been fascinated by the idea of a motor vehicle in which the drive unit and structure would form a single unit, right from the initial design stage. For him a 'road conveyance' meant an organic entity – not a traditional light carriage with the shafts removed – a fact reflected in the light construction, rack-and-pinion steering and differential gears.

Whether Benz, or Daimler/Maybach, should be honoured with having invented an automobile driven by a petrol engine is relatively unimportant in the history of the automobile. Of far greater significance is the fact that the Germans had no idea of the immense significance of the development work of their brilliant fellow-countrymen, Benz, Daimler and Maybach, and left it to the French to act as trail-blazers for the age of the motor, with engines from Mannheim and Cannstatt installed in vehicles with Gallic names like Peugeot and Panhard. . . .

LOUIS RENAULT –
THE MAN WHO BANISHED CHAINS

In 1891 the Paris fashion industry mourned one of its most important accessory suppliers: Alfred Renault, the well-known button manufacturer, had departed this life. His three sons Fernand, Marcel and Louis inherited the thriving business on the Place des Victoires.

The youngest, Louis, was 14 when his father died. He was an average schoolboy, something of a loner, and his head was full of fanciful technical ideas. His brothers had been drilled in business and commercial skills by their strict father, but Louis was more interested in the first automobiles that were then beginning to be seen in Paris streets.

That year Louis had seen a Peugeot motor carriage for the first time, had been taken for a spin in a steam-driven Serpollet, 'piloted' by its inventor, and had read with barely concealed excitement that a Peugeot had accomplished a fantastic feat: a long-distance journey over 1200 kilometres. Louis followed the route of the automobile in minute detail on his father's ordnance survey maps: from Beaulieu-Valentigney to Paris, then on to Brest and back.

Tinkering around with all kinds of tools and instruments had already become a mania, coupled with an academic ineptitude at school, a fact that had caused his father to let out a heartfelt sigh on more than one occasion: 'This block-head with his dirty hands will never make a businessman!'

When the time came for 16-year-old Louis to begin his apprenticeship in the family business, he rejected

family advice; it went against the grain to have to earn a living making buttons – to spend a whole lifetime with these trivial fashion accessories. Besides, in 1893 news came from across the Rhine that Karl Benz had built a four-wheeled motor carriage, the Viktoria, and it was clear that if he was going to move into the automobile business he would need to start as quickly as possible.

Young Renault had no luck when he applied for a job with the De Dion-Bouton company. He would have been particularly interested in this firm since it had smoothly undergone the transition from steam carriages to gasolene engined automobiles. However, a relative obtained an apprenticeship for him with the locomotive-and-ship-boiler manufacturers Delaunay-Belleville. But it was to be some time before Louis could start his apprenticeship, for he was called up for military service.

In the army he immediately made his mark with his extensive technical knowledge. This manufacturer's son, with his calloused and always-dirty hands, impressed his comrades. The fact that his father had indulgently given him a second-hand Panhard engine, with which Louis had experimented in a shed at the bottom of the garden of his parents' home in Billancourt near Paris, now paid off. He was in demand for his mechanical skills, constructing a field searchlight, a collapsible bridge, and an electric generator.

In 1898 Louis, aged 21, became a civilian once more and bought a second-hand De Dion-Bouton three-wheeler. A small high-speed unit drove this automobile/cycle hybrid and it was this 273 cc engine, weighing only 18 kg, that caught Louis Renault's trained eye. When he added a fourth wheel to the ensemble, and had radically changed the transmission system, the little 'trike' became an automobile in the true sense.

Decision in favour of 'direct drive'

In November 1898, the games of *pétanque* beneath the plane trees of Billancourt were suspended for a time as the youngest Renault son chugged up and down the avenue in his minuscule automobile, ceremoniously dressed in black bowler, wing collar and dark business suit, his calloused hands hidden in elegant gloves.

Louis Renault gave influential friends of the family rides up the hilly road to the Butte Montmartre and by Christmas Eve had a dozen orders for the car in his pocket, at 40 gold Louis each. Enquiries from other interested persons started coming in. What should he do? He was well aware that his technical concept was the right one: four wheels, two seats side by side, the engine in the front (following the 'Système Panhard') and advanced gearing and transmission. It was in fact his transmission that was the great technical advance. In contrast to the still conventional floppy belt or chain drive system of getting power to the road wheels he had designed a 'box' of gears, with a drive shaft to the rear wheels via bevel gears. Renault's three-gear drive arrangement was for decades the standard system.

After his initial success Louis Renault developed the entrepreneurial foresight and skills that his father had always accused him of lacking. He not only engaged two workers to help in the construction of the car (apart from gear-cutting he made all the parts himself), but he also patented everything connected with his transmission system that was capable of general use in other power applications. The two elder brothers had first of all watched Louis' progress with goodwill, and then with amazement – and finally joined him, forming the company Renault Frères in 1899. At the Paris *Autosalon* of the same year some 60 orders were taken for their production model with the 273 cc De Dion-Bouton single-cylinder engine under the tiny 'meat-safe' hood....

A price had to be paid for the rapid progress and proliferation of the automobile. These were the years of dusty and noisy streets, smelling now of gasolene fumes instead of the horsey aromas of yesterday. Anyone who travelled in a motor-carriage in the country had to be muffled and wrapped until almost unrecognisable, a vital protection against swirling dust, spraying mud, lashing rain and wind. Dogs, frightened by the menacing bark of a

motor, would jump up on to the running board; in rural regions, passers-by would throw stones. Automobile travel still had a long public-relations task ahead! Accordingly, Marcel and Louis Renault (Fernand still ran the button factory) built a box-like housing on top of the chassis – and called it a *conduite intérieure* (a 'drive-from-the-inside'), a term the French still use today for a sedan or saloon car; it was the first all-weather car in automobile history. Those citizens of Paris who were able to buy a gasolene-driven carriage could now drive to the Opera House without being soaked, muddied or covered in dust. Now the well-brought-up Frenchman could sit in just as dignified a manner in his car as at home in his salon. To be able to *teuf-teuf* through the Bois de Boulogne in an elevated shoe-box with two horse-power under the bonnet was becoming the height of elegance – thanks to the Renaults. The canny brothers had discovered a gap in the market. Curiously it was almost 25 years before the closed automobile was popularly accepted as a normal bodywork style.

Louis Renault, the mainspring of Société Renault Frères, had earlier decided on the method of promoting the company's products; he entered the long-distance races that usually started in Paris, and scored some spectacular wins under the banner of the family business. He then publicised these successes in large advertisements.

The Paris-Madrid 'suicide race'

By 1903 the Renault works occupied an area of 13,000 square metres, employed some 600 workers, and had already produced some 3000 cars, but great business success was overshadowed by a tragic event: Marcel Renault was killed in the Paris-Madrid long-distance race. This competition has entered into automobile sporting history as the 'suicide race'. It had been organised jointly by the French and Spanish automobile clubs, and was to take place over three stages: from Paris to Bordeaux, Bordeaux to Vitoria, and Vitoria to Madrid. The organising committee had attempted to introduce regulations to protect both the drivers and spectators, and to improve the timekeeping. When a competitor entered a town he was stopped, his arrival time recorded, and then a cyclist accompanied the vehicle to the town exit (towns were non-racing areas), where the departure time of the vehicle was also recorded.

However, these measures made little sense since the greatest dangers to both drivers and spectators existed on open stretches, where some of the cars could touch speeds up to 150 km/hour on the unfenced, rutted, dust-fogged roads. It is said that about three million people were present on the Paris-Bordeaux lap, cheering on the 275 competitors who had started from the capital. In addition to many private drivers some works teams had been formed. Panhard et Levassor fielded 15 cars, Mors had 14 on the line, De Dietrich 12, and Renault entered four vehicles. The start in Paris was teeming with bizarre vehicles – 70 h.p. racing cars cheek to jowl with light voiturettes, and steam carriages that should have been pensioned-off years earlier.

Dawn was rising over the Place d'Eau Suisse when, at 3.46 a.m. on 24 May 1903, the first vehicle set off. Charles Jarrott in a De Dietrich was the first to be flagged away. His car had an innovation which greatly intrigued the experts – electric headlights. Louis Renault at No. 3 shot away at an observed speed of 110 km per hour and had managed to take the lead by the time he arrived in Chartres. Questioned by reporters, he stated that he was terrified by the conditions on the route: the dust thrown up by the two preceding vehicles had impaired his vision, and the further back one was in the field the thicker the fog! The other serious danger was the behaviour of the spectators who, uncontrolled by the police, ran over the road in the path of competitors and allowed their children and dogs to wander about. A third handicap was inefficient brakes, which at the speeds the cars were doing were about as effective as a pair of reins.

The end of road racing

On the first day of the race Marcel Renault became a tragic victim of the blinding dust. On entering the small village of Couché-Vérac he ran into a thick white cloud raised by another car a few metres ahead, when taking a right-hand curve. He lost control of the car, spun off the road, and crashed into an embankment. His co-driver Vautier sustained a serious head injury; Marcel was killed instantly. When Louis learnt of the death of his beloved brother, he withdrew the Renault team from the race and never personally drove in any further competitions. The Paris-Madrid race was stopped by ministerial decree, as it had already caused ten fatalities and many injured on the Paris-Bordeaux stage. The vehicles were not even allowed to return to Paris under their own power, but were loaded onto railway carriages for onward despatch. Open road racing was abandoned for nearly a quarter of a century afterwards...

After several prototype shapes Louis Renault finally arrived at his famous 'coal-scuttle' hood, which, with a little stretch of the imagination, could be called the first aerodynamic line. The problem of the location of the radiator was a teaser, however. In 1900 he had mounted the radiators alongside the hood, but from 1902 on it was placed between the engine and the dashboard – an un-

likely site, but one that was copied by several others, and remained there, a characteristic of Renault cars for three decades. The astute young Frenchman patented this unorthodox arrangement of the radiator with its (then) reasonably efficient thermosyphon circulation. By 1903 a market-orientated range appeared, the first blossoming of a new Renault empire. Five different models vied for the customers' attention.

Although Louis had sworn never again to sit behind the wheel of a Renault in a race, he did not restrict the company's racing activities, and a 90 hp 12.8 litre Renault won the French Grand Prix in 1906. The Renault works driver, Hungarian Ferenc Szisz, won the race largely due to the fact that his car was equipped with special quick-change wheel rims. Most of the other competitors had to spend considerable time on the slow business of mending punctures and laboriously replacing tyres.

Louis Renault did not rest on the laurels won by his sales and racing efforts; he was constantly looking for new, untapped markets. In 1905 he began building the AX and AG models, both with 1100 cc 2-cylinder engines developing some 8 horse-power. From these Louis developed a short-chassis taxi suited to city traffic conditions, which soon changed the street scene in both Paris and London. These taxis, 'Deux Pattes' as they were called, became part of the story of the first world war, earning the name 'Taxis of the Marne'. When the conflict was scarcely a month old the German 1st Army under General von Kluck was driving hard towards Paris. Only a quick counter-attack could save the French capital from being taken by the invading troops. Desperately General Gallieni, Military Governor of Paris, gave the order to requisition 600 Renault taxis to be used to ferry five infantry battalions – 6,000 soldiers – to the front. The daring venture succeeded and the French counter-attacked at Nanteuil. The German high command was taken completely by surprise, and the troops were forced to retreat. The taxi drivers, with typical French care about money matters, charged double fare for this trip to the front line plus a small extra charge for their trouble!

In 1907 the Renault company had developed its first aircraft engines, and delivered the first Renault omnibuses to customers. When elder brother Fernand Renault died in 1908, Louis reorganised the business and in 1909 it became a joint-stock company under the control of its management, Société Anonyme des Usines Renault. Louis Renault led his company confidently for decades through stormy times to prosperity and, amazingly, never once borrowing a single sou from bank or financier in a period when most other manufacturers were deep in debt.

He was always careful to ensure that, as well as the production of basic, run-of-the-mill utility vehicles,

Renault representation in motor sport did not suffer. In 1926 a 6-cylinder Renault 40 cv of over 9 litres held the world 24 hour record at the Montlhéry racing track at an average speed of 176.6 km/hour.

Louis Renault had been made a Chevalier of the Legion of Honour as early as 1906 and was the undisputed master of his empire, captain of the French motor industry. After World War II, although he had been literally compelled to produce material for the German war machine in order to save his employees from starvation or forced labour in Germany, liberated France regarded him as a collaborator and imprisoned him. It is probable that he was beaten up by the prison warders, rough treatment that finally broke him. Louis Renault, the man 'with the face of a poet' to quote writer André Maurois, died in 1944 at the age of 67. On 16 January 1945 Charles de Gaulle signed the order to nationalise France's greatest automobile factory.

CHARLES AND FRÉDÉRIC DUFAUX – THE QUIET PAIR FROM SCHLOSS BALEXERT

When Europeans think of Switzerland, the first things that come to mind are banking, skiing, and watchmaking. Few people would think of looking for an automotive industry in the history of the Alpine Republic, and yet up to the present day there have been no less than 70 Swiss automobile marques!

From 1888 the Swiss firm of Saurer, well known for its outstanding textile machinery, manufactured stationary gasolene-driven engines. In 1896 Adolphe Saurer incorporated one of these engines in a vehicle, and was able to announce that the experiment was a success. Historians consider 1895-1896 to be the birth year of the Swiss automobile industry; author Ernest Schmid in his book *Swiss Automobiles* lists no fewer than twelve firms, mainly small operators, that were founded between 1895 and 1900, including such resplendent names as Dufour-Ballabey (1897), Egg (1893), Helvetia (1898), Henriod (1886), Hercules (1900) and Kaufmann-Millot (1896).

Technical delicacies from Switzerland

The period from 1900 to the First World War is regarded as the heyday of the Swiss industry. More than 30 firms were founded during these years, including Ajax (1906), Berna (1902), Ernst (1905), Fischer (1908), Gmür (1914), Garbaccio (1913), J.M. (1913), Lucerna (1907), Pic-Pic (1906), Safir (1906), Sigma (1909), Tribelhorn (1902), Turicum (1904), and Yaxa (1912).

Swiss manufacturers did not seem to make a great fuss of their, sometimes highly significant, technical innovations. Fritz and Charles-Edouard Henriod, for instance, built air-cooled engines and, as early as 1896, a carriage with front wheel drive. The Berna 'Ideal' of 1902, with its 'square' engine (100 mm bore and 100 mm stroke, a very modern conformation) and a De Dion style rear axle, were other technical 'delicacies'. The Turicum of 1907, built by Martin Fischer, had a so-called friction wheel drive, an embryo automatic system. The Pic-Pic, made by the Geneva firm Piccard, Pictet & Cie, also enjoyed a high reputation. After the company had built racing cars for the Dufaux brothers (of which more later) they started producing their own automobiles in 1906. The then still unknown engineer Marc Birkigt designed the first models, dubbed 'Swiss Rolls-Royces' for their meticulous workmanship, high performance and silent running. Pic-Pics were among the first racing cars to have four-wheel brakes, fitted for the 1914 French Grand Prix. Only Isotta-Fraschini had previously entered a four-wheel braked car in competition – in 1913 – and Pic-Pic's two-car entry also had the considerable advantage of hydraulic shock absorbers. The firm's valveless 4.5 litre engines produced 150 h.p. and accelerated the vehicles to a maximum speed of 170 km/hour. There is no doubt that Swiss manufacturers were well in the van in those youthful days of the automotive industry. . .

Aged only 22 and 24 respectively, Charles and Frédéric Dufaux appeared like birds of paradise against the contemporary 'nuts-and-bolts' scene when they opened their workshop in Geneva in 1904. Earlier they had given full rein to their intoxication with speed in a number of competition events before they decided to build a serious contender for the 1904 Gordon-Bennett race, a car that would meet the 1,000 kg weight-limit regulation imposed by sponsor James Gordon-Bennett, publisher of the *New York Herald*. Any country could enter up to three automobiles, which however had to be completely manufactured in that country. The races were held in the country of manufacture of the previous year's winner. Since Camille Jenatzy had won in Ireland in 1903 in a Mercedes, the 1904 Gordon-Bennett race was to take place at Hamburg in the Taunus region of Germany. Frédéric Dufaux wanted to be there too.

As they lacked the necessary machinery, the Dufaux brothers gave their engine block contract to the firm of

Piccard & Pictet for the preliminary work. Charles Dufaux's 12,756 cc design included no less than eight cylinders, cast in pairs and surrounded by aluminium water jackets. This titanic machine produced 90 h.p. at 1200 r.p.m. However, scarcely had the Dufaux brothers arrived in the Taunus when their dreams of victory were shattered. On 16 June 1904 Frédéric discovered that the car was not responding fully to the steering wheel. Ernest Schmid describes the situation: 'The steering arm and swivel connecting the steering knuckle arm to one of the front wheels was broken, after it had obviously been deliberately damaged by a hacksaw. . . .'

The Dufaux brothers hurried to re-build the sabotaged piece – but did not race in the Gordon-Bennett Cup. Instead the car was entered in the Coupe Monod, a sprint race over one kilometre from a flying start, held at Eaux-Mortes near Geneva. Frédéric travelled the distance in 31.2 seconds and achieved an average speed of 115 km per hour, a new Swiss record. He was also very successful in France in speed trials; during 1904 he came second in a kilometre race, and in a one-mile race in Paris.

The giants from the Alps

In 1905 Switzerland's first automobile exhibition opened in Geneva. As the highlight of their exhibition stand, the Dufaux brothers showed a huge engine whose bucket-sized cylinders had a capacity of 26,400 cc, and a claimed output of 150 b.h.p. The stand also held a 35 h.p. Dufaux limousine with a 4-cylinder engine, and a racing car with an 8-cylinder in-line engine which the constructors termed a 'Coupe Gordon-Bennett' car, capable of developing 80 h.p.

The Dufaux did not take part in the 1905 Gordon-Bennett race, held in the Auvergne, largely because of a dispute with the Automobile Club of Switzerland. Their hearts must have leapt when the Honourable Charles Rolls politely enquired whether he could drive their 150 h.p. giant in speed trials on the smart promenade at Brighton. The knowledgeable English aristocrat, whose Rolls-Royce car had arrived on the international automobile scene like a mechanical monarch, was staggered at the size of the Dufaux colossus (which, with a bore of 225 mm and a stroke of 166 mm, had truly the first 'under-square' engine), but entered it in the trials. However, trouble with ignition and cooling spoilt its performance. Thick cooling water tubes of copper coiled round the four giant cylinders, and English motoring journalists were amazed that the Swiss designers felt confident enough to be able to dispense with a conventional radiator.

Frédéric Dufaux had the giant 4-cylinder car transported to Provence in France to make an attempt on the world speed record over the flying kilometre. In 1904 the French driver Baras had achieved an average speed of 168.2 km/hour on the beach at Ostende, driving a Darracq. On 15 November 1905 Frédéric Dufaux drove over a measured road section between Salon and Arles; the rules called for a two-way run. The Swiss covered the kilometre twice at a mean speed of 23 seconds, an average speed of 156.522 km/hour. The attempt on the world record had failed. Later the same year Victor Hémery pushed the world record speed to 176.43 km/hour, again on a Darracq.

The disappointment of their world record failure in Provence did not however discourage the brothers. At the 1906 automobile exhibition in Geneva they proudly unveiled some elegant models – a 4.1 litre 16 h.p., a larger 40 h.p. model and a *berline de voyage*, a luxury six-seater touring limousine in the grand style, housing an 8-litre unit developing some 90 h.p. In addition, two 8-cylinder racing cars from the Dufaux stable also appeared at the Marchairuz mountain races, one with a 12,760 cc 80 h.p. engine, and the other with a 14,449 cc 100 h.p. unit. The judges were somewhat irritated by the fact that the Dufaux cars did not carry exhaust silencers (when the engines were started up the local fauna fled in panic), and since the Dufaux only took part in the race for fun they were not placed – 'a car not qualifying cannot be disqualified' argued the brothers with the type of logic that seemed to rule their lives. Unofficially they had beaten all the previous records for this mountain section with a time of 9:34:4 minutes, so they departed content.

A sad end to a brave story

In 1907 Frédéric and Charles Dufaux were compelled to realise that their small organisation was not financially strong enough to be able to hold its own in the 1907 Grand Prix, which the Automobile Club of France had organised in Dieppe. They joined forces with the Italian automobile firm of Marchand in Piacenza to develop jointly a radically new 14,700 cc, 120 h.p. Grand Prix racing car, using a redesigned 8-cylinder in-line engine. From 1907 onwards the cars produced by these two firms (Marchand had been a bicycle and sewing machine manufacturer) went under the name Marchand & Dufaux. The end for the Italian-Swiss co-production came in the seventh round of the French Grand Prix on the closed-road circuit at Dieppe. Frédéric, in the 8-cylinder car, was in 24th place when he had to withdraw in the seventh lap owing to engine damage. A sad end to the brave attempts of the two brothers from Switzerland, small master craftsmen, who had tried to conquer the world of motor sport against the might of the powerful automotive companies.

10

Previous page: 9. Lorraine Barrow at the wheel of a De Dietrich driven in the Paris to Madrid race in 1903. The four cylinder engine, with a 10 litre cylinder capacity, developed 45 bhp.

10. The first car in the world with air-filled tyres – Peugeot's 'L'Eclair' – with a 4 bhp Daimler engine. This took part in the Paris-Bordeaux race in 1895, with André and Edouard Michelin as its drivers.

11. A 1905 Peugeot 'Bébé', with rack-and-pinion steering, driven by a single cylinder engine, with a modest 785 cc cylinder capacity.

12. Karl Benz with his wife and daughter and friend Fritz Held on an excursion in the Benz 'Victoria' in 1894.

13. Twelve elegant gentlemen put the load-carrying capacity of a Mors to the test in London in 1900.

Following pages: 14. Opening of the Bellinzona-Carena (Ticino) mail car line in Carena in 1927. The local dignitaries all gathered in the village square.

11

12

13

15

15. German racing driver Karl Jörns Opel at the wheel on the day before the Lyon Grand Prix in 1914.

16. The Grand Prix de France, Lyon 1914. Eventual winner Lautenschlager on the roadstone track – shown here on the 'piège de la mort' [death trap] section.

17. Successful lady racing driver of the mid twenties, Ernes Merck, in her Mercedes Benz S.

18. Kay Petre, England's female motor racing idol of the thirties, with a 750 cc supercharged Austin on the famous Shelsley Walsh hill track.

19. Elisabeth Junek in 1926 in her Bugatti 35 (1991 cc, 8 cylinders, 95 bhp) on the 'Ecce Homo' section of the romantic Praděd mountain in Czechoslovakia.

Following pages: 20. Idyllic conditions at Brooklands in 1937 – boating to the race. The river Wey flowed through the famous oval track to the south west of London.

17

16

18

19

MEN AND MARQUES

The men who made the first cars came from many strata of society. From the farm and from the court, from industrial city, from locomotive factories, from the world of finance and the drawing office. Some were the sons of the aristocracy, like the Hon Charles Rolls, others were as far from the gilded life as one could be – his partner Henry Royce for instance, whose job as a boy was that of a crow-scarer. They all had similar goals – to provide a means of transport more efficient than the horse at a time when the world was ripe for the sort of development that mobility would bring. For good – and for ill – their collective dream was fullfilled, and some of the pioneer names are still with us in marques such as Daimler, Renault, Opel, while others, no less influential in the long and sometimes painful technical progress of the automobile, are now shadows of history, evocative only to those who still cherish some of the finest automotive products of the past. . . . Mark Birkigt of Hispano-Suiza; Henry Leland, creator of Cadillac; René Panhard, responsible for the 'shape' of the modern car; the Duryea brothers who ignited the spark of motoring in the United States. . . .

THE ELECTRIC HIGHWHEELER – FIRST AMERICAN CAR?

The *Des Moines Register and Leader* made a startling statement some time ago. It ran: 'The first automobile in the world was invented by a Des Moines man, manufactured in Des Moines, and ran on Des Moines streets.' That statement would have been hotly denied by every motor manufacturing country, but in fact it was not all that far from the truth. However, there is a catch in it. The automobile that William Morrison of Des Moines built was an electric vehicle and it does not really belong to the great upsurge of gasolene-driven transport that occurred around the turn of the century.

Iowa-born Morrison, chemist and vegetarian, who had dabbled in electricity since a youth, built a high-wheel carriage (he claimed his first was constructed in 1887, a declaration which if substantiated would put him among the earliest of pioneers, ranking with Benz and Daimler, and way before Duryea or Haynes of the US) which was first seen publicly in 1890.

The first highwheeler was tested on the streets of Des Moines 'but was turned aside too easily by obstacles on the road.' His second vehicle was officially recognised by the respected journal *Scientific American*, which published a technical description of the electric carriage. The vehicle was used several times for displays and for public rides, and seems to have operated without much trouble – and indeed was one of the entries in America's first motor race in 1895.

The first years of the century saw many attempts to put America on wheels. Some cars were built on Benz or Daimler lines and looked like straight copies, a fact that did not escape the notice of those two worthies, who began to export their *motorwagen* to the States. Others showed their domestic buckboard and buggy ancestry. Most were ironshod or used solid rubber tyres and almost all ran on slender wheels of large diameter. Thus the USA spawned a generation of vehicles that were some ten years behind Europe in structural design – even to the position of the motor (which Panhard of France had for good reasons established at the front end of the car), which was often under-floor or at the rear.

However, late entry into the automotive world was not the sole reason for the early design of American cars. America's roads, where they existed, demanded much of wheels and suspension. Large wheels eased out the bumps and potholes of the road, while anything less than 3-feet diameter could sink in the winter mud, never to be seen again.... A flood of highwheelers began to be produced in a number of different states – this was before Detroit had become the crucible of the motor industry – until

some 8000 automobiles were struggling over the dirt roads and town streets of America at the turn of the century. Daimler had shown his 'Steelwheeler' at the 1893 Columbian Exhibition in Chicago, and Benz had achieved considerable publicity in the press the same year. Automotive transport was beginning to move, even though the continent of America could not boast more than a mere 150 miles of paved roads outside city limits...

Three different sorts of propulsion

Elwood Haynes was one of the first men in the field after the Duryea brothers had demonstrated their gas-buggy. Haynes had built a single-cylinder vehicle in 1894, formed a company with the Apperson brothers, and sold his first car in 1898 – another skeletal highwheeler designed to meet US conditions. By 1900 road-wagons, hunting traps, and 'petroleum carriages' were *de rigueur*, equipped with engines of various astonishing designs and dubious reliability, gasolene competing on about equal terms of popularity with steam and electricity. The Stanley brothers, former photographic-plate makers, made their first steam car in 1897, a highly successful highwheeler that sold some 200 in the first year of production. They sold the rights to Locomobile of Westboro, Mass. – and designed another steamer that was to remain on sale, in increasingly sophisticated form, until 1927. Electrics were in demand – Riker of Brooklyn NY made two and four-seaters in 1900, followed by runabouts and a hansom-type coach, in an attempt to appeal to every market. Baker Electric cars could be seen in the streets of New York, often driven by madame, with her small child at her side. These town cars had a top speed of 17 mph and a range of around 50 miles on one charge – quite enough for the lady to visit her friends for tea and do a little shopping at Maceys.

Hundreds of small car-makers, most of them backyard blacksmiths, produced one or two highwheelers, and then faded out of the automotive picture. But there were others such as Oldsmobile whose efforts brought lasting renown.

Ransom Eli Olds was always a woodshed engineer. He had been a steam buff, then built a few electric cars before moving on to gasolene vehicles. In 1897, when Theodore Roosevelt was police commissioner and the Klondike Gold Rush was in full spate, Olds formed his first company and built his first gasolene vehicle, a wagon-like highwheeler, at Lansing, Michigan. Olds's early claim to fame, the Curved Dash, is described elsewhere in this book, but it is interesting to observe that he was the first exponent of genuine mass-production and high annual sales. The Curved Dash sold just 11 examples in 1900, but rose to a peak of 5,000 by 1904 – an enormous success by the standard of the day. But this was about the time that most American carbuilders decided 'If you can't beat 'em, join 'em!' and began, like so many European manufacturers, to copy some of the best designs available, which usually meant Mercedes or Panhard. Engines moved to the front, wheels and suspension became more sophisticated and US automobiles started to look like automobiles...

To return for a moment to our pioneer electrician William Morrison. His 1890 six-seater highwheeler made the rounds of Des Moines regularly and reliably, and was sold commercially for some six years, from 1890 to 1896. So was America really so far behind the rest of the world in the early automotive stakes? And would Des Moines have been the automobile capital of America if Bill Morrison had found wider backing for his company? Perhaps the USA will celebrate a Motoring Centenary in 1990....

THE DURYEA BROTHERS –
FATHERS OF THE AUTOMOBILE

America's first automobile race, on Thanksgiving Day, 28 November 1895, was almost snowed off. The *Chicago Times Herald* had announced this competition in order to popularise the new technical phenomenon, known as the 'motor road wagon', 'motocycle' or 'automobile' in the USA. News had arrived recently from Europe that Frenchman Emile Levassor, driving a Panhard-Levassor gasolene vehicle, had won the first-ever race for motored road transport, from Paris to Bordeaux and back. Americans naturally did not want to fall behind Europe in such innovations, but although it was known that an automobile industry was already starting to take shape in Europe designers and constructors in the USA were still very much in the 'woodshed' experimental stage, and found it difficult to envisage such a spectacle, since there were in America no long-distance or inter-city roads such as existed in Europe. Dusty tracks or mud-rutted trails began just twenty miles outside even the great capital city of New York, and cynical travellers would joke that it was easier to sail round the American continent than to drive over it. Americans had perforce concentrated on the railroad as the transportation best suited to the size of their country.

The route chosen for the first automobile race in the New World was consequently partly urban, and short; from Chicago to Evanston and back, a total of 54 miles. It had snowed heavily the day before the race with the result that, of the 83 original entries, only six appeared at the start; two electric cars, three Benz cars, and a Duryea as the sole American car driven by an internal combustion engine. Only two cars finished the race, which was won by Frank Duryea at the wheel of the car he had built himself, a 2-cylinder 4-stroke machine, already equipped with own-make pneumatic tyres. Second was a Benz, driven by Oscar Mueller. Beside both drivers sat an observer – Duryea drove with Arthur Whitte from Toronto and Oscar Mueller with Charles B. King (who the following year was himself to build automobiles in Detroit).

Frank Duryea's driving time was, according to his own records, 7 hours 53 minutes. He reached the finish in Chicago 1 hour and 35 minutes before the Benz and collected the victor's prize of 2000 dollars. Frank Duryea informed inquisitive reporters that he had incorporated a number of new technical components of his own invention in his car, including an engine with electric ignition, water pump, jet carburettor, power transmission with three forward gears and reverse, petrol pump, ball bearing-mounted transmission shaft, and rear axle shafts, engine cowling, and pneumatic tyres – the latter presumably developed independently of the Michelin brothers, who were using air-filled tyres that same year, and of John Dunlop, who had invented them as far back as 1888. Compared with the Benz the Duryea indeed bristled with innovations – the Benz had only three of the American horseless buggy's modern components, namely electric ignition, a ball bearing-mounted transmission shaft, and a partial engine cowling.

The Duryea of 1893 was the first successful American automobile, and the brothers Charles and Frank Duryea may justly be described as the American Fathers of the automobile. Their firstborn, a single-cylinder model, would have been ready in the autumn of 1892 but for the fact that Frank fell ill and temporarily had to stop development work on the car. And truly the Duryea was the first US automobile to be the basis of a company making and selling cars. However, as in almost every sphere of technical development, there are other names that could be put forward as even earlier pioneers. Designer and constructor John Lambert from Anderson, Indiana, appears only occasionally in automobile history – but he built a self-propelled 3-wheeler in 1891. And Henry Ford, who was already living in Detroit in 1893, where he was regarded as a highly talented mechanic, was conversant with Otto engines, and had experimented with his first engine in 1893, although he did not build a vehicle until about a year after the Duryeas had demonstrated their automobile in practical form.

A patent agent tries to stop history

Why, in a country so proud of its pioneering spirit, was the progress of the automobile not as rapid as in the old world? The innovations of the Duryea brothers, and the arrival of the German Daimler engines, which were introduced from 1891 by the American piano manufacturer William Steinway, should have provided a good starting base. One is surprised to learn that in 1895 there were at most 100 mechanically-driven road vehicles in the whole of the USA, half of which were equipped with gasolene engines and the others with steam or electric drive systems. When we examine the reasons for this astonishingly low figure, we come up against a man termed by historians 'the brakeman of the American automobile industry': patent lawyer George Baldwin Selden, from Rochester, New York.

This Yale-educated advocate hit upon an ingenious, if perfidious, idea. He had become acquainted very early on with the advantages and future prospects of the internal combustion engine, and was one of the comparatively few men of his time who seriously considered the long-term future of motor transportation. As a patent attorney, he was able to find his way through the legal jungle and calculated that, with some well-documented far-sightedness, any Otto-cycle engined vehicles manufactured in the future could be a never-ending source of licence fees under his own patent. In 1877, just one year after Nikolaus Otto had patented his four-stroke principle, Selden drew up plans for a motor-driven carriage, in which it was possible to incorporate an engine.

George Selden filed his patent on 8 May 1879, after making and testing a half-completed engine which in itself had no new features but in which, Selden argued, the *combination* of these features constituted a new principle. He had been most ingenious in this early application, quoting the Brayton stationary engine of 1871, a great clumsy 1,160 lbs machine (but America's first) which, the specification said, was to be operated by liquid hydrocarbon (i.e. gasolene), and which, on the drawing-board at least, he had much improved. But the road vehicle which was the overall purpose of his 'invention' was in fact not built at all, merely set out in his drawings.

Under US law all patent applications were protected for only two years after filing, but the Rochester lawyer, by altering details of his pending patent every couple of years,

kept his rights alive and exclusive – until on 5 November 1895 the Selden Patent No 549,160 was finally issued.

Selden, in brief, claimed to be the inventor of the automobile, a claim that was officially confirmed in the 1895 patent. In 1899 Selden assigned his patent to the Electric Vehicle Company – who immediately decided to build gasolene cars, paying Selden a royalty of $15 for each one. The company then demanded royalties from any manufacturer who built vehicles 'within the scope of the Selden patent'.

It was Henry Ford who, after a long and costly legal battle in co-operation with other American automobile manufacturers, was successful in 1911 in having the Selden patent annulled by the Supreme Court in New York. But for more than a decade carmakers had paid up or risked legal proceedings. The Selden Patent effectively put the brakes on many a budding enterprise.

America's first working automobile

Like many other automobile pioneers, the brothers Charles and Frank Duryea had been involved in bicycle manufacture: they were full of bright ideas, though their many technical inspirations and more fanciful notions sometimes got in each other's way. And it could not be said that the two brothers always worked together in perfect harmony. Both could be described as 'unsteady and volatile', but despite some acrimony they had nevertheless introduced a number of significant improvements in the basic concept of the bicycle – a spring-mounted front wheel fork, a 'hammock' saddle, a frame suitable for ladies' dresses – all still used in cycle design. In 1891, they decided to build an automobile.

Their first automobile, America's first practicable motor vehicle, was a rickety vehicle, a 'horse buggy' with friction drive powered by a 4 h.p. single-cylinder engine. This was of course an automobile within the meaning of the Selden patent, but when it proved to be more or less a non-starter Charles dropped the project and instead concerned himself with exhibiting his bicycles at the 1893 Chicago World Fair. Many years later he recalled in a newspaper interview how, after the World Fair, he returned to his home town of Peoria, Illinois, where he dealt in real-estate, during which time he found a partner, Monroe Seiberling, with whom he founded the Duryea-Seiberling Company to build automobiles. But the company collapsed before it had got off the ground.

Charles Duryea was obsessed with the idea of what he termed the 'unicontrol system' – one-handed control of the car by the driver. His dream was to be able to steer, accelerate and stop by means of a single lever. His argument: 'so that I can hold my umbrella up with the other hand...' Frank Duryea, whose designs followed much the same principle, had in the meantime found his own business partner, Erwin F. Markham, with whose money he built the second Duryea car. American historians give 20 or 21 September 1893 as the birthday of the first American 'working' automobile. Decades later Frank Duryea could still remember vividly how his jubilation at the building of this vehicle was overshadowed by many mechanical faults and breakdowns. Although the engine operation caused no difficulties, the 'motor road wagon' was no great mover, due to the poor power transmission of its friction drive; this he realised, would not attract investment from a potential financial backer. The very first unsuccessful attempt of a few months earlier had proved Charles's engine design a flop; this time it was the friction drive, which had also been designed by Charles. After a few weeks of trials and tests Markham, the sponsor, lost patience; Frank asked for a last chance, offering to build a new gear-system and install a new friction clutch at his own expense. The car was thus finally finished, and the *Springfield Union* reported on 19 January 1894 that a Mr Frank Duryea had made a successful trial run with a self-built engine and new drive. It may be seen today in the National Museum at Washington DC.

Frank approached financier Henry W. Clapp in March 1894 with plans for a two-stroke two-cylinder car. Clapp was impressed by Frank's ideas and put up some hard cash, and work began in April 1894. The car was tested in December 1894 on the top floor of the factory, but the engine timing was unstable, due to a faulty electric spark ignition. Frank converted the two-stroke to a four-stroke unit and installed it in a chassis in February 1895. The first road trials took place in March 1895, and after numerous test runs (the local newspaper enthusiastically estimated 'several thousands of miles') more financial backers were found, with the result that the Duryea Motor Wagon Company was founded in Springfield, Mass., in September 1895. In November that year, Frank won the first automobile race on American soil.

No future for the car?

The victor of the Chicago–Evanston race was the second Duryea automobile to be built. After the founding of the company Frank designed a third model, thirteen of which were built up to 1896. The Duryeas – a repentant Charles had in the meantime returned – now owned the first automobile factory in the USA.

'Carriages, not Machines' they proudly advertised in the press. 'The whole control of the car is effected almost by a thought,' claimed the brothers. And indeed their 'one-hand control' concept was not too far from that

claim, although the journal *Horseless Age* was perhaps a little over-enthusiastic when it stated: 'The variable speed ranges from three to sixteen miles an hour ... and to obtain greater speed than ten miles an hour the pressing of a button at the front of the seat will increase the speed of the motor. A brake drum of peculiar construction placed under the seat is connected with a thumb-button located at the front corner of the seat and by pressing the thumb upon this button the carriage, if running at twelve miles an hour, can be stopped within a distance of a few feet.' Some button, some thumb!

Perhaps 30 May 1896 was one of the happiest days in the working life of the normally squabbling Charles and Frank Duryea. It was the only occasion when they competed against each other in a race – from New York City Hall to Irvington-on-Hudson and back, a distance of some 83 km. The race was sponsored by *Cosmopolitan* magazine and was to some extent a later version of the Chicago race that had taken place in November the previous year. However, this time the weather conditions were considerably better. To show the thousands of spectators that the Duryea Motor Wagon Company actually produced something, four Duryea cars were entered for the race, to compete against the inevitable Benz cars. Frank beat his brother and won the 3000 dollar prize.

The end of the 'Red Flag Act'

After this great triumph Frank Duryea decided to venture into Europe. On 14 November 1896 he competed in the London-to-Brighton 'Emancipation Run', organised to celebrate the repeal of the 'Red Flag Act' and the lifting of the speed limit on English roads from 4 to 12 miles an hour. (The internationally famous London-Brighton Veteran Rally held annually in November commemorates this event). The reports of the day were confused, and investigations by various historians in later times have failed to unravel the mysteries of the event. Dependent upon the partisanship of the writer, we learn that the Duryea arrived first, second, third, or was disqualified – although the consensus of opinion is that it acquitted itself with honour. The American circus, Barnum & Bailey, rented another car from the Duryea factory and presented it as a great sensation in the ring between their brown bears, flying men, clowns and Arab stallion acts.

However, although they attracted excellent publicity, these bizarre activities were of no avail. In 1898 the Duryea Motor Wagon Company came to the end of its brief life as the paths of the brothers parted once more. After several changes of jobs, Frank became head of the development section at the Stevens Arms & Tool Company in Chicopee Falls, Mass., where in 1902 the first

Stevens-Duryea car was wheeled off the production line. He had a successful career, becoming chief engineer and vice-president of his company, building fast and luxurious touring cars. In 1915 the owners sold the company, then at the peak of commercial success, for a large profit. The company itself produced and sold cars up to 1927.

And what of Charles, the 'wild one'? After Frank had left, he too produced automobiles, now under the Duryea Power Co. name, vehicles that were somewhat smaller than the heavy touring cars designed by his brother. Charles Duryea died in 1939 aged 78; Frank was 97 years old when he died in 1967.

HENRY M. LELAND – 'MR. CADILLAC'

In March 1901 a fire destroyed the Detroit workshops of the American automobile pioneer Ransom E. Olds. Although there was no loss of life, the results of many years' development work, electric and combustion engines, accessories, drawings, as well as precision tools – all were destroyed. Only a prototype of the Curved-Dash Runabout, a single-cylinder carriage standing on spidery bicycle wheels, could be saved from the flames.

When he had finished cleaning up after the fire, Olds dismantled the small runabout and prepared new structural working drawings. He contacted specialist workshops in Detroit asking them to supply him with parts which would cost too much time and money in re-tooling and fabrication. The firm of Leland & Faulconer was asked to supply engines, John and Horace Dodge made transmission gears, Benjamin and Frank Briscoe provided the cooling system, while C. R. Wilson, Fred J. and Charles T. Fisher made the lightweight superstructure. Only the foundry remained as a working factory unit at the Olds site.

Olds was thus the first automobile manufacturer to adopt the principle of 'farming-out' work to outside suppliers. With his partners, Ransom Olds provided the impetus for the first experimental mass-production and conveyor belt assembly systems, which Henry Ford was to develop to near perfection some seven years later. Thanks to his far-sighted planning, Olds very quickly raised the production figures of his Curved-Dash model to a staggering 4000 in 1903 – this in a year when the vast majority of Americans had never even glimpsed a car.

Highest possible precision

When Olds ordered engines from the firm of Leland & Faulconer, Henry Leland had already earned a reputation in the USA for the highest possible precision and strictest quality-control in the engineering industry. Leland had trained as a gunsmith in the Springfield & Colt Weapons Factory, and later worked at machine-tool manufacturers Brown & Sharp, where he built up a team dedicated to producing parts with tolerances of the order of one millionth of an inch. Up to then automotive engine parts

of all types had been thrown together by rule of thumb, assemblers matching individual pieces manually by trial and error. Now Henry Leland, with missionary zeal, brought undreamed-of accuracy into the workshops of American automobile manufacturers. He developed lathes on which even unskilled workers could machine parts with a minutely precise degree of accuracy.

Leland himself owned one of the first Curved-Dash Runabouts, its engine produced in what remained of the Olds works. Leland had insisted that Olds should himself try to turn the stubborn engine with the hand-crank; it seemed it just would not fire at the first attempt. Olds had murmured an apology about the characteristics of the automobile ... but when Leland installed one of the engines produced by his factory into his Oldsmobile, there was no more engine trouble.

Leland's modified runabout led directly, with a little help from Henry Ford's designs, to the first Cadillac production model. In 1902 there were acrimonious disagreements within the Detroit Automobile Company, then nearly four years old, in which a number of prominent people including William C. Maybury, mayor of Detroit, influential dealer William H. Murphy, Ellery Garfield from the Fort Wayne Electrical Company, Leland and a dozen others were involved. Henry Ford, Detroit Automobile's managing director, resigned to start his own company, and Leland amalgamated the Detroit Automobile Company with his own firm, the result being re-named the Cadillac Motor Company. Its first car, the Model A, was exhibited with great success at the New York Automobile Show of January 1903, tangible evidence of the Leland maxim 'Craftsmanship a creed, accuracy a law.'

The Model A Cadillac, though simple in concept, was considerably superior to most competitors' cars at the exhibition. The single-cylinder 1.6-litre engine was mounted horizontally amidships, under the seat, providing an even weight distribution on all four artillery-type wheels. The drive was via a 2-speed planetary transmission, with centrally mounted chain, and spur differential. The air-cooled engine produced 6.5 horse power and there was even a steering wheel in place of the then still-customary steering tiller. A not-so-curious fact of history is that the car showed a marked resemblance to that other Henry's Model A, which appeared the same year, 1903.

Since Leland wanted, not only to build reliable automobiles, but to sell them in large numbers, he engaged William E. Metzger, who had operated a flourishing automobile trading business in Detroit as early as 1898. Metzger, well acquainted with the range of engines produced by American manufacturers, knew that Leland was using the best engines, structural items and workforce available at the time. He agreed to establish a flexible and efficient dealer-organisation from Maine to Colorado. He also thought up some spectacular publicity stunts: a Model A was harnessed to a fully laden horse-drawn vehicle to demonstrate its tractive power; it was driven up and down the front steps of important municipal edifices (for the benefit of local newspapers), and it was driven, fully laden with sixteen strapping students, to the top of the steep Shelby Hill in Detroit, without faltering.

A gruelling test

In February 1903 the British importer F. S. Bennett read of the new Cadillac. In the *Cycle and Automobile Trade Journal* he discovered an impressively long list of American Cadillac dealers, and some informative and forceful advertising material. He ordered an example to be shipped over. Bennett subjected his new car – the 530th Model A to roll out of the Detroit works – to rigorous tests in hill-climb trials and other events organised by the Automobile Club of Great Britain. The British *cognoscenti* were extremely impressed by the ruggedness and durability of the hitherto unknown marque, and Frederick Bennett soon became the exclusive dealer for Cadillac, setting up business at Orchard Street in London's West End.

However, many Europeans still held some reservations about technical products from the USA. Bennett travelled to Detroit in 1907 to become acquainted with Cadillac production methods and Leland's quality principles. There he was astonished to discover that each individual part of the car could be freely exchanged with any similar part from any other Cadillac.

Bennett dreamed up a brilliant promotional idea on the return journey, which he implemented with the help of Britain's Royal Automobile Club. In January 1908 the RAC announced a standardisation test open to all marques. The rules stipulated that officials of the Club could select any three cars from the existing stock of a dealer and completely dismantle them after several laps on the Brooklands racetrack, after which they would select any parts from the components of the three cars and exchange them for new replacement parts. Next, they would 'scramble' the three cars' component parts and assemble three completely 'new' cars. The condition placed on the reassembly was that only screwdrivers or spanners could be used. When the work was completed, the cars would be driven another 500 miles over the track.

All other companies shied away from the test, and finally only Cadillacs were entered. The result of this spectacular event, which took place during the icy February of 1908, was that Leland's machines worked perfectly. His dictum that standardised parts of a car must be interchangeable had been proved beyond any doubt. Leland was awarded the first Dewar Trophy for the outstanding automobile innovation of the year.

Cadillac – founder member of General Motors

Over 16,000 single-cylinder Cadillacs (4-cylinder models were also made from 1905) had rolled off the production lines when, in 1908, production of the Model A was stopped. A harsh wind of competition was sweeping the USA. In the same year Henry Ford announced his coming assault on the American market with his Model T, and William Durant founded the holding company General Motors. Leland and many other independent automobile producers were in danger of being ground between the millstones of the two giants and when General Motors offered Leland 4.5 million dollars for his Cadillac Company in 1909, he accepted, joining Buick, Oldsmobile, Oakland-Pontiac and Chevrolet.

In 1912 Cadillac models were equipped with electric lights and electric starters, the first automobiles to have these innovations, for which the Dewar Trophy was again awarded. In 1915 Leland lured English designer McCall White away from Napier in England. White was asked to develop a V-8 cylinder engine based on a De-Dion Bouton design dating from 1910. He produced an extremely smooth-running 5.1 litre V-8 engine, the unit built to power the first left-hand drive vehicle of the Cadillac marque. Some 13,000 V-8 Cadillacs were sold in the first year alone, and the engines were also supplied in large numbers to the army. V-8 engines were not new, but Cadillac installed this engine as the standard power unit for 1915, and that was a severe jolt for competitors.

During the First World War Henry M. Leland and his son Wilfred were involved in building Liberty aircraft engines. In 1917, after they had left the Cadillac Company, they founded their own Lincoln marque, named after the assassinated American President Abraham Lincoln. However, in 1921 they ran into financial difficulties and Henry Ford took over the company. Lincolns were to be his luxury products.

AMERICAN ARISTOCRATS – THE THREE Ps

Packard, Peerless and Pierce-Arrow were the top of the pile in pre-First World War America, the height of engineering quality, performance, comfort, appearance – and cost. Those with long purses – and there was a rapidly increasing number in the emergent America of the time – hired a uniformed chauffeur, bought one of the Ps, and hobnobbed with the mighty. Such an automobile was a necessary adjunct to life in high society...

In 1898 a 35-year old enthusiast purchased a twin-cylinder Winton, one of the earliest American cars to be made commercially. On his drive home the car broke down half-a-dozen times and had to be hauled to his house by a team of horses. He was understandably annoyed, and called on Mr. Winton at his office in Cleveland, Ohio. He made several suggestions, and Winton, stung, snapped back 'If you're so smart Mr. Packard, why don't you make one yourself?' So James Ward Packard did just that.

In fact Packard and his brother Bill had made plans for a new car back in 1893 and had just needed a push in the right direction. Within a year he had built his first car – and by 1900 had set up a manufacturing company producing a traditionally American single-cylinder buggy-type quadricycle. However, it had three forward speeds and reverse – an innovation that few US cars possessed in those days, and one that gave the new Packard a considerable sales boost. Packard sold one of his first automobiles to entrepreneur Henry Joy, who bought up the Packard company as a major investor – while a somewhat shortsighted James Packard went back to making cables in Warren, Ohio....

In Detroit the Packard line continued to thrive, with larger, high-quality products, and by 1904 the Model L had been launched, a landmark in that it was the first of this marque to appear with the famous 'shouldered' radiator and hood, a feature that distinguished Packard until the late thirties. In 1907 the famous Packard 30 appeared; with its 7 litre engine giving 60 hp it was perhaps the model that secured the lasting success of the company. Packard cylinder displacements continued to increase until in 1913 the Twin-Six was unveiled, and the motoring world saw its first series-produced 12-cylinder car which, priced at a modest $2600, was a bargain that filled the order books in a remarkably short time. Personal recommendation was the Packard maxim. If you wanted an opinion, just 'Ask the Man Who Owns One' as the Packard advertisements said....

Early American cars were either built light to avoid being swallowed in the mud of the unpaved roads – or weighty and strong to avoid being shaken to pieces by potholes and bumps. The Peerless was one of the latter.

A move from washing machines (more accurately clothes-wringers) to quality cars may not seem an auspicious start, but the Peerless Manufacturing Company, another enterprise from Cleveland, Ohio, offered its first model in 1900. It was powered by the inevitable De Dion Bouton buzzbox, and built in the American idiom, buggy-style. Designer Louis Mooers arrived on the Peerless scene in 1901, and by the following year had re-designed the car and the company, applying his European-based engineering knowledge. Mooers had in fact produced a car that looked very like the Mercedes from Germany, with luxury 'Roi-des-Belges' seating.

Two years later Mooers presented the sport with the 'Green Dragon', an 80 hp racer with full pressure lubrication, that was entered in the Gordon Bennett Trophy of 1903. The car later passed into the hands of cigar-chewing ex-showman Barney Oldfield, who won several races and set several records in it. The car itself became so famous in the USA that it starred in a Broadway musical, driven on to the stage every night....

The White House garage accommodated a Pierce-Arrow when William Taft was in office, three of them when Woodrow Wilson was President of the USA, and at least a couple when Franklin Roosevelt occupied the position. The great families of America followed suit.

The car had started humbly enough in 1901, as the Pierce Motorette, brainchild of one George Pierce of Buffalo, New York, who had been in business as a birdcage maker. His experience with wire-drawing had led him into the bicycle industry, for whom he made spokes, and then complete (shaft-driven) bicycles. The Motorette was a lightweight buggy-type runabout powered by the then ubiquitous De Dion unit. It sold very well, encouraging Pierce to move into larger vehicles, and by 1903 he produced his first 2-cylinder tonneau. Credit must go to its designer, David Fergusson, from Yorkshire, England, who had arrived in the US with the automobile promoter and charlatan Edward Pennington – but had proved that he was cast in a different mould. Fergusson continued to design the cars and by 1909 the company's product was so well established as a top marque that when the first Pierce-Arrow was launched the car was made in strictly limited numbers, to be sold only to selected clients.

The car grew in size with the years until in 1914 (with a 13.5 litre engine) it was claimed to be the largest series-production car in the USA. At various times, its sedan was built with a bulge in the roof to accommodate the large floral hats of the day, its headlamps were fared into the wings, and it had the supreme snob-appeal of eschewing an identifying badge....

THE
PERSONAL TOUCH

In 1919 Henry Ford bought up in one mighty deal all the shares still in the hands of minority shareholders of the Ford Motor Co, and by this single step became the sole ruler of his 500 million dollar empire. In sixteen years, by meticulous attention to detail, coupled with a fierce personal devotion to the growth of the company, he had set his mark indelibly upon the history of the automobile. Marc Birkigt, too, in a very different way added his personal touch to the story....

HENRY FORD – 'TIN LIZZIE, I LOVE YOU'

In 1907 the lights would frequently burn late into the night in a small room on the third floor of a house in Piquette Avenue, Detroit. Ford's engineers Joseph Galamb and Harold Wills were putting the finishing touches to the latest design of the Ford Motor Company, the Model T, and their director would pedantically go through each technical detail yet once more before he growled: 'All right, boys, let's go home.'

In 1893 Henry Ford, then just thirty years old, built his first engine. He called it 'the second highpoint of my life' – the first had been the birth of his son Edsel some weeks earlier. As a typical 'natural' engineer, Henry had little time for ceremonial or festivities. It was on Christmas Eve, of all times, when his wife Clara was fully occupied preparing the meal, that he walked into the kitchen, placed a metal device in the sink, and said 'Finished at last; come and help me start it!' After a few false starts, the single-cylinder engine fired, puffed and banged, and began to beat a rhythm.

In 1896, Ford's first vehicle, a quadricycle, was produced in his backyard workshop in Bagley Avenue in Detroit. Gaps had to be knocked out of the brick walls so that the vehicle could be rolled into the daylight. Ford, at that time a mechanic at the Edison Illuminating Company electricity works in Detroit, was sent as a delegate to the firm's seventeenth annual convention held in New York in 1896. There he exchanged a few words with his boss, Thomas Alva Edison. He drew him the outlines of an automobile, as it would one day be built, on the back of a menu. The great inventor, with his feel for brilliant ideas, was a man of few words. He simply said: 'Young man, that's it! Stick with it!' When Henry returned to Detroit he gently warned his wife what she would have to expect: 'You won't see much of me in the next year'.

From A to T in easy stages

Henry Ford jumped eagerly into the race with other early American automobile builders. In 1899 he left Edison's company, and by June 1903, after a few false starts, had made such progress that he was able to set up his own business, the Ford Motor Company. He had already made his mark by some spectacular racing successes and in this way he attracted several shareholders. On 10 October 1901 he had beaten the well-known American racing driver Alexander Winton on the circular track at Groose Point, Michigan, and in 1904 he set a new speed record over one mile, achieving an average speed of 91.37 mph (subsequently recognised by the American Automobile Association) in his Arrow on the ice at Lake St. Clair.

The first of Henry's cars to appear on the market was the Model A, launched in the summer of 1903. It was driven by a two-cylinder horizontally-opposed engine with large dimensions for the conditions of the time – 100 mm bore and 100 mm stroke. It was priced at $850, and sold in relatively high numbers. Ford continued to design a large range of subsequent models, tagged with sequential letters of the alphabet. Type B, in the $2000 bracket, was produced, parallel to the development of the Model F. Models G, H and I went no further than the drawing board, and Models K and N appeared on the market in late spring of 1905. The Model K was a powerful six-cylinder car in the luxury class, built at the insistence of one of Ford's backers, former coal merchant Alex Y. Malcolmson, so that the company could also offer the market a prestige automobile; the Type N was a modest four-pot car which was to become the direct forerunner of the 'Tin Lizzie'. Ford bought out the constantly pestering Malcolmson in 1906 for 175,000 dollars, and was finally rid of him. The K was not a success, though the Type N, a more solid utility car, was highly marketable.

Tin Lizzie takes a bow

However, for quite some time Henry Ford had been contemplating something other than this rapid succession of different models and sizes. His dreams of a universally popular low-priced automobile had come closer to fulfilment with the success of the Model N. A small automobile produced in large numbers makes higher long-term profits, he calculated, despite the smaller unit profit margins, than an expensive model that is produced in small numbers. This, his prime principle, was followed by principle No. 2 which was deeply and sincerely held: 'I shall put the world on wheels. The times are past when the small, hard-working man, farmer, artisan, craftsman, commercial traveller, midwife, priest, country doctor . . . cannot afford an automobile.' And principle No. 3: 'In the final analysis no factory should be so large that more than one model can be manufactured in it'. Accordingly, from 1908 onwards Ford made a radical swing towards a one-model policy, as Britain's Rolls-Royce company had already done a year before with their majestic Silver Ghost.

The model that Henry Ford's team had ready for production in October 1908 was a simple automobile with all the charm of a blacksmith's hammer. The Ford T was gawky, lanky and awkward, as ugly as sin, and sounded like a tin can. Its characteristics earned it the nickname: 'Tin Lizzie'. The opposition laughed loudly. However, the laughter soon turned to envy. The Tin Lizzie created the first real mobility, apart from the railroads, and thanks to it the pulse of this great nation beat faster; the USA experienced a new awareness of life, a social and commercial change, the enormous significance of which was not at first realised.

The car of the century was of captivating simplicity. As there were still virtually no highways in the United States and scarcely any permanent metalled country roads, the Ford T had to run on wagon-wide rigid axles (better to run in the ready made ruts than have a wheel jumping in and out!) which were attached to leaf springs. The chassis and suspension was not unduly disturbed by pot-holes and the car tolerated twisting and torsional forces, since everything was constructed according to the motto: 'What's flexible can't break'. The four-cylinder engine had a capacity of 2.9 litres and produced 25 hp at a compression of (at first) 4.5:1. This caused a little trouble; later the compression was reduced to 3.9:1 and Tin Lizzie behaved perfectly satisfactorily with 5 hp less. The engine was a genuine all-purpose workhorse. It could be used, with a belt take-off, for logging, milking, hauling – almost any work for which a farmer could use extra muscle.

Legends are woven

Many enterprising Americans changed rapidly from the horse-drawn carriage to the 'sheet metal conveyance' – and often tended to treat the Model T like a stubborn rodeo horse. The operating instructions took into account the widespread technical innocence of the buyers. A lighthearted booklet explained it thus: 'You have three pedals in front of you. On the right is the foot brake. Put your foot on that pedal when you want to stop. Then you have the reverse pedal. However, only press this when the car is no longer moving in the forward direction. Then you have the most important pedal. When this is in the middle position, the engine is idling. The engine is then completely disengaged from the wheels. When you press this pedal firmly as far as it will go, your Ford is in first gear. That is the power gear. When you want to disengage the clutch, i.e. the engine should no longer pull, move the pedal to the middle position again. When you want to drive smoothly, the pedal must be fully at the top. And now, let's go boys'.

The hands, it seemed, had little to do. They could remain on the steering wheel, from where they could adjust the manual accelerator throttle and the carburettor jet. The adjustability of the jet had other, very practical, reasons: when it was blocked up by dead insects, its opening could be enlarged.

A driver could 'step turn' from the forward gear to reverse gear in a split second, without having to engage and disengage, a feat that proved to be particularly advantageous when a Model T got stucky in muddy tracks or in snowdrifts. It could then be 'rocked' out of trouble. A single turn of the steering wheel produced full lock and a turning circle of less than 30 ft increased the manoeuvrability of the Ford. It very quickly became everybody's darling. Farmers would drive with their family in a Model T to church on Sundays, and on weekdays transport their pigs, calves, potatoes and cabbages to market. They equipped the car with sidewheels so that it could draw a plough. It hauled seed drills and planters over the giant fields of the mid-west, and powered lathes, water pumps and generators. Very soon legends began to grow and a host of Model T jokes were generated.

The car's starting handle broke many a driver's wrist – it kicked like a mule.

Owner-drivers were extremely proud of their Ford but were rarely careful of its welfare. Anyone who lived in hilly country would have to use first gear for hours on end, keeping his foot constantly flat down on the pedal. Often, due to the shaking of the engine, the 'change' pedal jumped out of the neutral position and the car shot forward without the driver's intervention. Alternatively, the applied hand brake disengaged, with similar results. Several starting tricks were recommended by those in the know: pour boiling-hot water on the induction manifold and heat the spark plugs on the hearth until they are glowing, then screw them in as fast as possible. Not a bad idea for some of us – even today!

Teeth begin to chatter at 20 km/hour

The Model T Ford came from the works plain and unadorned. It was sufficient that Henry Ford had approved a horn as an extra for his 'people's car' – he didn't find it necessary to supply one fitted! The accessories industry made efforts to smarten up the basic products. During the period of Model T production (1908 to 1927) over five thousand accessories for the car were developed and marketed. Early in the game were the Non-Kick-Start Company from Kansas City, who offered a handbook for $2.50, with the slogan 'How to avoid a broken arm when starting the Tin Lizzie!' A tachometer was said to cost $7.25, which prompted a Ford driver to write to the company at the Highland Park plant in Detroit: 'What do I need a speedometer for? When the mudguards on my Model T begin to flap, I know that I'm doing 6 mph. When my teeth start to chatter, I know that I'm going at 12. When the gears jump out, I'm doing 15 . . .' Henry Ford loved such jokes: 'Every joke sells another Tin Lizzie' he told all those who laughed.

Ford operated a flexible pricing policy. The first Ford T cost $850, and in 1910 $950, but then prices fell. A tourer could be bought for $360 by 1916, and at a bargain price of $260 in 1925.

Ford also introduced a discount system which would leave our present-day car salesmen speechless; from coast to coast he announced in 1914: 'Anyone who buys a Model T in 1914 gets $50 back if more than 300,000 Tin Lizzies are sold in 1915!' To be exact, 308,213 Tin Lizzies were finally sold, and the nation-wide repayment promised was promptly honoured. Henry did not make that offer again.

The manufacturing methods that were gradually gaining acceptance also contributed to this bold and consumer-friendly pricing policy, although Ford was not the inventor of the conveyor belt system. America's automobile industrialists had earlier studied this production system in the Chicago meat trade centres, where thousands of dead pigs and calves hung from moving belts, but Ford was certainly the man who first made extensive use of the method. In August 1913 it took 12 hours and 28 minutes to assemble a Ford T; by December that year it was a 2½ hour job, and then it was cut to only 93 minutes – mainly due to improved assembly systems. In the 1920s a car left the works every 1.6 minutes. It is clear that the pace of work was tough and demanding. On the other hand, Ford was lavish with his praise for the speed and nimbleness of his conveyor belt workers. On 5 January 1914 he astonished his competitors by announcing that his company would pay a minimum wage of $5 per day – twice as much as any other American automobile manufacturer. A shorter 8-hour day was also introduced.

Had the Ford works now become transformed into something approaching a workers' paradise? Not exactly. The factories in Detroit were managed with tight discipline by two of Henry Ford's close friends, Charles Sorensen and Harry Bennett. Sorensen was so disliked by the workers that he used to dash through the factory halls to avoid presenting an all-too-easy target for missiles! Bennett, a former professional boxer, was responsible for the internal security in the works and his friendly relations with the underworld were overlooked, but the ex-boxer kept two pistols in his writing desk 'for all eventualities'. On one occasion he shot a lighted cigar out of the mouth of a labour union official. Even the boss's shy son Edsel had to suffer under the outrageous Bennett.

Ford's empire building brought a series of problems in its wake. The problem of material procurement was immense. In order not to be dependent on foreign suppliers, he bought up woodlands, coal and ore mines, glass factories, Brazilian rubber plantations and, as his master stroke, built his own railroad, the Detroit-Toledo-

Trenton line. Nothing could halt the victorious progress of the Ford and the Model T. In 1922 the profits of the Ford Motor Company were $119 million, and more than half of all the cars in the world bore the name of Ford. The car had, however, not become any more beautiful in the meantime. If buyers expressed a preference for a particular colour, Henry Ford would boast: 'You can have any colour you want so long as it's black' – happily one of the few doctrines to which he did not adhere. In 1916 the Tin Lizzie got electric lights; up to then carbide lamps had been sufficient. In 1919 one could purchase an electric starter as an optional extra, and bodywork variants appeared on the market – 'Runabouts' and 'Sport Tourers' were now available.

Henry Ford's tough, forward-looking commercial policies altered the social climate of America – the monumental changes that the Model T introduced into the industrial landscape and infrastructure of the United States constituted a silent revolution in the life-style of Americans, rich or poor. There was an automobile for Mr Everyman at the beginning of the second decade of this century, although there were few proper long-distance roads to run it on!

The old lady retires

In 1919 Henry Ford bought up in a single mighty $105,820,894 deal all the shares still in the hands of minority shareholders, and became the sole ruler of his $500 million empire. In 1922 he acquired the ailing Lincoln Motor Company and so was able to offer, in addition to a low-cost automobile, a luxury model. However, he persisted stubbornly in his one-model policy, even though it had not escaped his notice that the Model T was gradually losing ground to other makes.

Henry Ford had achieved his life's aim: to put America and the world on wheels and to 'democratise' the automobile, formerly the toy of the rich man. The Tin Lizzie became part of American culture, immortalised in many shows and musicals as the great love of the American male, for whom a new, more beautiful world was opened up in which men could still be adventurous.

The Ford T grew from a drawingboard scheme to an American institution in a few short years, adding a new dimension to life, as American as Coca Cola, as Kodak, Hoover and the Brooklyn Dodgers.

It became the butt of a thousand jokes – and Ford laughed with the jokers. Knocking copy was hidden in many but 'The guy who owns a secondhand Ford may not have a quarrelsome disposition – but he's always trying to start something,' and mock-proverbs like 'You can't get to heaven in a Model T Ford', were meat and drink to the ever-growing Detroit company. The Ford flivver influence on poetry may not have generated immortal verse but some of it contained a strong plug for the Tin Lizzie:

> Let me move from the bustling highway,
> A lonely road will do,
> Through a land of swamp and quicksand,
> Where only Fords get through...
> In a cottage there in the maples,
> Contented I'll be evermore;
> For I feel the world's growing better –
> Where the Fords go by the door...

...and much more in the same mood, which could not be called the muse's finest product but served its purpose well. And take a look at John Steinbeck's *Cannery Row*, where you will find the strangest, but truest, eulogy to the Model T that ever found its way into modern American literature. . . .

The proliferation of the Model T (whatever we may think today of its influence on our way of life for good or ill) certainly took a heavy load off the back of emergent America, and played no small part in the prosperity that the citizens of that country enjoy today.

THE A TEAM – FROM FORD

By the early twenties the old Ford Model T was on its way out. Half-a-dozen new models from rival companies were competing for the custom that was formerly Ford's, and many technical advances were now on offer to the buyer, improvements that were nowhere to be seen on the old Tin Lizzie. Ford's son Edsel (who played a vital part in the success of the company, although he is usually associated only with the unsaleable Edsel car of 1957) finally convinced father Henry that he should modernise and launch a new car.

Most damage was done to the image of the Model T by Chevrolet, with factories just down the road at Detroit; as part of General Motors they were growing fast, and beaten in the sales-graphs only by Ford and Dodge. Ford's sales had been declining right through the twenties, mainly because buyers were searching for a better-looking vehicle, and for a few dollars more could buy a smart Chevvy 490. By 1923 Chevrolet were offering the 'Superior', again at a little over the price of a Ford T. It was just what the customers wanted – modern lines, more comfort, more accessories – worth paying that little extra.

Edsel was right. Ford desperately needed another world-beater to follow the great Model T enterprise. They buckled down to the daunting project. Designed in 1926-7 by the company's top design team, the new car was called the Model A.

On 31 May 1927 the last Model T rolled off the assembly lines, and the works closed down for six busy months of re-organisation and retooling at the enormous plant everyone simply called 'The Rouge'.

Never had there been such secrecy surrounding the introduction of a new car – and America was bursting with curiosity. Other makers were dropping their prices in anticipation, dealers were running out of Model T stock, the country was held in a sort of automotive suspension. On 2 December 1927 Henry and Edsel announced the Model A.

Launched at the end of the year, the 'New Ford' was the result of superb design coordination and forward thinking. Ford's ambition had been a car with speed, power, comfort and safety – and the Model A had it all. The power unit was a 4-cylinder 200 cubic-inch (3.3 litre) side-valve L-head engine, only slightly larger than the Model T's but developing a full 40 hp at 220 rpm compared with the earlier car's 20-plus. The engine had light alloy pistons and head, a three-bearing crankshaft and battery ignition. A 3-speed sliding-gear type transmission completed the power-drive updating. New features were hydraulic shock absorbers, safety-glass windshield, bumpers, automatic windshield wiper, Bendix self-starter and a dozen other innovations.

In any colour you like – even black

The bodywork was in the modern idiom and was also offered in five different styles and, to the joy of the new breed of female drivers, in almost any colour they could dream up. Women's tastes had become a strong factor in the planning of interior trim and the general appearance of the automobile – and here again the Ford Model A was right on the button. The late twenties was a period of open cars, tourers, roadsters, phaetons (some said that an open car offered a wider field of fire for the Thompson sub-machine-gun, the boot-legger's favourite weapon), but the Model A offered a weathertight, roomy seating arrangement, with almost as much luxury as the lady could find at home – and without being effete.

In fact the Model A was designed by a team comprising experts with considerable knowledge of motor sport and safety at speed, in addition to engineers of traditional background, resulting in a car that could move at a genuine 65 mph, at around 20 miles to a gallon.

Eulogies appeared in the press as soon as the Model A was seen in metal. This, it will be appreciated, was one of the most dramatic unveilings in the automotive world since Henry's Model T – and it appeared at a time when the world still knew little of the potential of the car.

'Strong and sturdy – just what the market needs,' crooned one report, 'and close on 400,000 eager customers have put down their deposits on it in the first two weeks of its preview.' Not a bad start even for the late twenties, the salad days before the great financial blizzard. In that first production year, 1928, some 820,000 Model A Fords were built, so many that Henry Ford had to abandon his former policy of total self-sufficiency and buy-in such items as wheels, body panels, piston rings, pumps and distributors.

'The remarkable thing about the new $450 car is its quality', said another magazine . . . 'It would be difficult to build a better car at *any* price!' Rather far-fetched, perhaps, but it illustrates the mood of both the press and public when the first showroom model was revealed – an event attended by huge crowds hoping to get a glimpse of the mystery automobile of the year.

Ford's Model A knocked Chevrolet's ambitions of scooping the market right on the head – for a while. Although the Model A sold about 4½ million during its years of manufacture – including the troubled years of the depression – its life was to be far shorter than that of the old T. The world was moving faster in more ways than one, and designs became out-dated much sooner. Although Ford sold twice as many cars as arch-rival Chevrolet in 1930, from then on sales began to wilt. Total car production in the USA dropped from the then all-time peak in 1929 (the depression did not strike until 24 October) of 4,587,400, to 2,784,745 in 1930, and a desperate 1,973,090 the following year, dropping yet again to just over a million in 1932.

Model A production shut down in August 1931, but Henry Ford was by no means defeated. Another model was on the drawing board, and by 1932 69-year-old Henry Ford unleashed an automotive lion once again – the powerful Ford V-8, a prestige car for the man-in-the-street.

MARC BIRKIGT –
HISPANO-SUIZA, MON AMOUR

Some automobile marques attract fans like moths to a candle. Thus for many, unquestioning loyalty to a marque becomes almost a substitute religion, and names such as Rolls-Royce, Ferrari or Porsche are honoured as mystic deities. Curiously, although Hispano-Suiza featured for more than a generation as top-of-the-pile Grand Tourer (in the proper sense of the term) and even in almost every thriller-novel of the 'tween wars period, its following has been small, if necessarily exclusive.

Hispano-Suiza is an elegant and stylish marque that hides the identity of an ingenious but modest Swiss engineer-designer who has left indelible marks on the French and Spanish automobile industries since the beginning of the century – Swiss-born Marc Birkigt. He shunned publicity to such an extent, and immersed himself so selflessly in his work, that even up to the present day he is greatly underrated in specialist literature. So it is a relatively small band of automobile 'gourmets' who belong to the Hispano-Suiza 'cult' and who consider the cars of this marque to be the best in the world, rivalling the claim of the aristocratic Rolls-Royce.

Hispano-Suiza devotees refer, not without pleasure, to an important event at the beginning of the 1920s: Rolls-Royce were desperately worried. The rear wheel brakes of the luxury conveyance were no longer up to the mark on Europe's fast roads. Rolls-Royce had never been one of the most progressive automobile manufacturers,

and the fact that British companies such as Argyll and Arrol-Johnston had successfully tested a four-wheel braking system even before the First World War merely provoked a disdainful sniff from Derby. But now that the hour of the four-wheel anchor had obviously arrived, how could His Lordship be expected to apply enough force to a pedal on which four brakes depended? This problem inevitably forced the Rolls-Royce engineers to consider a servo-system, to relieve the driver's foot of the brunt of the necessary braking force. In their search for a suitable servo-mechanism the Rolls-Royce engineers finally picked on Marc Birkigt's ingenious concept – really positive four-wheel brakes actuated by a gearbox-driven servo, which he had developed in 1919 for his Hispano-Suiza H6B model.

The model to copy

A magnificent 6-cylinder engine and a really efficient brake, these formed the basis of Birkigt's fame. The 6-cylinder engine of the H6B was, in effect, one 'half' of the V-12 engine that Birkigt had built during the First World War. It had a capacity of 6597 cc and produced 135 h.p. at 3000 r.p.m. It had a seven-bearing crankshaft and the overhead camshaft actuated two valves per cylinder. The engine was an oversquare unit with a 100 mm bore and a 140 mm stroke, and proved to be unusually flexible: it could accelerate from 10 to 50 m.p.h. in 21 seconds – in top gear. The *pièce-de-résistance* of the H6B, the bit which chipped the 'best in the world' reputation of Rolls-Royce, was Birkigt's four-wheel servo-braking system, first-ever to be incorporated in a production automobile.

The fact that Hispano-Suiza enjoyed a high popularity just after the end of World War I and experienced a huge wave of goodwill was partly due to recent patriotic fervour, and earlier military development. Some 50,000 of Birkigt's water-cooled 200 h.p. overhead camshaft V8 aircraft engines had been built during the First World War, more than all the other aircraft engines of the Allies put together. No fewer than 24 firms in France, England and the USA had produced the Hispano-Suiza engine under licence. It proved itself a winner, particularly in 8,500 French Spad S13 fighter planes and British S.E.5a fighters, and this legendary engine had helped significantly in the Allied victory.

The Hispano-Suiza radiator mascot, the 'flying stork', also dates from this period. During the war it was the mascot of the squadron led by Captain Georges Guynemer, who had flown Spad fighters.

Training grounds for automobile manufacturers

Born in 1878, Marc Birkigt went, at 21, to work in a Barcelona factory making electric buses. During his military service in the artillery the hardworking young Swiss had carried out some metallurgic studies on the properties of materials used in the armaments industry. By the turn of the century the munitions factories with their giant arsenals had become the 'high schools' of the science of military engineering, demonstrating among other things that a ballistics expert should also be an aerodynamicist. Weapons production with its emphasis on high precision was an excellent training ground for budding automobile manufacturers, and Marc Birkigt always acknowledged the high regard in which he held the production methods of the armaments industry. Perhaps it was logical that in addition to building touring cars and luxury limousines he also developed aircraft engines, and was responsible for a 20 mm cannon, which proved one of the most effective weapons of the allies in the air battles of the Second World War.

In 1901 Birkigt joined the Spanish industrialist J. Castro, who was looking for a talented automobile designer following the reorganisation of the La Cuarda combine. The first Castro automobiles were still strictly modelled on the earlier 4.5 h.p. chain-driven 'La Cuarda' model, but between 1902 and 1904 10 h.p. 2-cylinder and 14 h.p. 4-cylinder shaft-driven cars were produced. Strikes intermittently plagued production, and in 1904 a group of businessmen – including some Swiss – took over the Castro automobile company, calling their new organisation the Hispano-Suiza (Spanish-Swiss) enterprise, with the Swiss Marc Birkigt as chief technical designer.

The first Hispano-Suiza car of 1904 was really only an increased-h.p. Castro with a new name. However, succeeding models bore Marc Birkigt's unmistakable imprint. One of the earliest developments – water-cooled brakes with hollow aluminium brake shoes, connected to the cooling system by flexible hoses – proved much more sophisticated than the brakes of the much-vaunted Mercedes cars of 1902 to 1904, in which water trickled onto the drums as the brakes were actuated.

The King is enchanted

The technical refinement of the automobiles from the drawing board of Spaniard-elect Marc Birkigt made a great impression on the young King Alfonso XIII – who later acquired some 30 examples of the luxury marque and became one of the greatest auto-enthusiasts among Europe's rulers, and a great friend of the ingenious Birkigt.

A 4-cylinder, 2.6 litre capacity car bearing the company name and driven by Paul Zuccarelli won the 1910 Coupe des Voiturettes and with this victory Birkigt successfully gained a foothold in voiturette racing of the day, which had previously been dominated by French cars sporting massive single or twin-cylinder curiosities. From this development sprang the sports tourer introduced in 1912, the car that entered into the genealogy of the automobile as the now-famous Hispano-Suiza 'Alfonso'. The 4-cylinder pressure-lubricated engine had a capacity of 3620 cc, and an extremely flexible performance due to its long stroke of 180 mm (with a bore of 80 mm), delivering 65 h.p. at 2300 r.p.m. A Hotchkiss three-speed gearbox was mounted in unit with the engine. The Hispano-Suiza Alfonso had rear-wheel brakes and Whitworth detachable wire-spoke wheels.

The company needed to break into the lucrative French market, and in 1911 Hispano-Suiza built production workshops in France where the demand for the more expensive automobile was considerably greater than in Spain. Besides, political and social tensions in Spain were increasing. The branch office in the Catalan capital was retained, but increasing activity was centred on the Levallois-Perret plant on the Seine, and in 1914 a new factory was built in Bois-Colombes. It was here that Marc Birkigt began building the legendary lightweight 150 h.p. V-8 aircraft engine which was to be the Allies' great hope against the new, frighteningly efficient Mercedes 4½ litre being fitted to German planes, soon to be testing their relative qualities in a life-and-death struggle.

Andre Dubonnet's victory in the 1921 Georges Boillot Cup in Boulogne encouraged Birkigt to modify the H6B basic model of 1919 for sporting use. In 1922 Dubonnet drove a rebored 6.9 litre H6B at Monza, and a year later an 8 litre car (H6C) appeared, which since then has also been known as the 'Boulogne'.

The Spanish-French automobile company no longer sponsored works teams, and participation in sporting competitions was left to private initiative. Thus, for example, when the celebrated 'Indianapolis wager' was made in 1928, and Fred Moskovics, vice-president of Stutz, asserted that he could beat a Hispano-Suiza H6C with one of his own 8-cylinder, 4.9 litre models in a 24-hour race over the fast Indianapolis circuit, the French bodywork firm Weymann took up the challenge and built a light two-seater superstructure on a H6 chassis. C. T. Weymann won this wager and returned home across the Atlantic with a $25,000 cheque.

Marc Birkigt in fact kept fairly quiet about the sporting successes of his cars; it was more important for him to solve the problem of muffling the engine noise of the H6, about which 'converts' from Rolls-Royce constantly complained. The power of the 8-litre automobile was reduced to 144 h.p., only nine horse power more powerful than the 6.5 litre automobile dating from 1919. At the end of the 1920s the 6.5 and 8 litre models were re-named 46bis and 56bis respectively, though the reason for this still remains a mystery.

Hispano-Suiza began the thirties with two sensational moves. In 1930 they bought up the Paris automobile company Etablissement Ballot, which had attracted a great deal of attention after the war at many races in France and abroad with their high-performance sports cars and tourers. Birkigt designed a smaller 6-cylinder, 4.6 litre engine, mounted it in a Ballot chassis, and named this model the Hispano-Suiza 'Junior'.

Marc Birkigt's largest and most costly model, first seen in 1931, was the Hispano-Suiza V-12 Type 68, a 9.5 litre two-cylinder which produced 220 h.p. The Swiss automobile constructor, who was constantly experimenting with different engine capacities, designed the V-12 engine 'square', with a 100 mm bore and stroke for, although he adhered to his general principle of the 'blessing of the long stroke', he was also prepared to stimulate developments that, for him, represented new technical ground. Thus, in the Type 68 V-12 engine he dispensed with the overhead camshaft and instead adopted a push-rod mechanism. Although some automobile historians consider the V-12 with its 220 h.p. 'the finest car that was ever built', collectors who own this car occasionally express reservations. They feel that the model had still not been fully developed by the time production began, so that the clutch was inadequate for the engine power and the transmission was underpowered.

In 1934 Birkigt up-engined his luxurious masterpiece, presenting a 11.3 litre version in which the stroke was increased to 120 mm. The engine now produced 250 h.p. This did not mean, however, that he had decided to live exclusively in the world of the grandiose. On the contrary: at the beginning of the 1930s he also produced a so-called 'government, administration and army' car of modest performance, which he powered with a four-cylinder 2.5 litre engine. Another simple design, produced in 1928, had been a six-cylinder 3-litre pushrod engine developed for the American Hudson company, which was also installed in the Hispano-Suiza 60 in Spain from 1932 up to the end of the car's production run in 1943.

'Only an engine-builder'

Marc Birkigt, modest to the point of self-effacement, knew his limits, which he once outlined thus at a banquet to celebrate the introduction of a new model: 'I'm only an engine builder'. In his famous V-8 aircraft engine he developed the twin overhead-camshaft system that was to influence engine technology world-wide. In 1928 he was the first to use a durable metal alloy (now known as nitralloy) for cylinder liners. In the cooling system of the Hispano-Suiza Model K6 (1937) thermostats regulated the position of the radiator louvres, keeping the engine at an accurately constant temperature. A dual ignition system and a cylinder-head design in which the valve drive of the overhead camshaft is surrounded by a metal housing are also due to Birkigt.

Marc Birkigt, who had been made an officer of the Legion of Honour as early as 1928 and was later awarded an honorary doctorate from the Zurich Federal Technical Institute, died on 15 March 1945 at the age of 75. In his career he produced just over 8000 cars, nearly 6000 made in Spain and about 2600 in France, each one a gem in its own right.

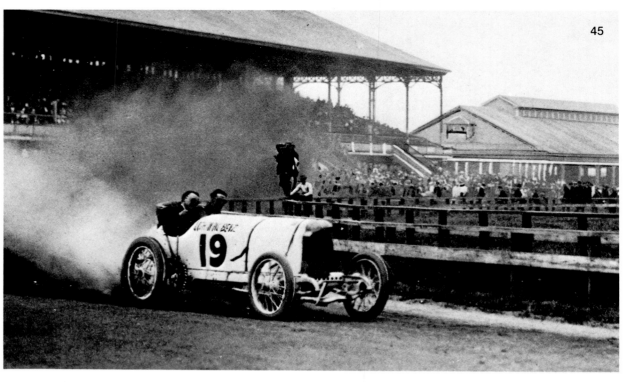

Previous page: 44. Coosimans in a Belgian F.A.B. before the start of the 1913 Belgian Grand Prix.

45. American Bob Burman at the wheel of a Blitzen Benz in 1911.

46. Tommy Milton in the Duesenberg 'Beach Car'. The power unit consisted of two eight-cylinder 5-litre engines. The record he achieved in 1920 was one mile at an average speed of 251.17 kmph.

47. A Lion Peugeot 2-litre car in speed trials on the cement track at Brooklands.

48. Ferdinand Porsche in 1903 at the wheel of a Lohner Porsche 'Mixt' (petrol/electric car). At his side is his bride Aloisia Johanna Kaes, whom he married the same year.

49. Jules Goux at the wheel of a Peugeot at Brooklands in 1913. In the same year, again in a Peugeot, he won the Indianapolis. Goux was one of the best French racing drivers of all time.

47

48

49

50

51

50. Fiat S. 76 – a giant with a cylinder capacity of 28,353 cc, developing 290 bhp at 1900 rpm. Four-cylinder in-line engine bore/stroke 190×250 mm. The car – shown here with Felice Nazzaro at the wheel – was used in a series of record drives.

51. Parry Thomas in his 1925 'Babs' Thomas Special on the beach at Pendine. Rain prevented an attempt at the record on this particular day.

52. Another giant – a Triplex Special with three twelve-cylinder aircraft engines and a total cylinder capacity of 81 litres, sponsored by American manu-facturer White.

53. Englishman Lionel Rapson with his son in 1924 standing in front of his Lanchester Forty, fitted with extra powerful headlights for 24 hour record drives.

54. Count Zborowski in 1921 in his colossus Chitty-Chitty-Bang-Bang, with a six-cylinder Maybach engine, developing a proud 300 bhp at 1500 rpm.

52

53

54

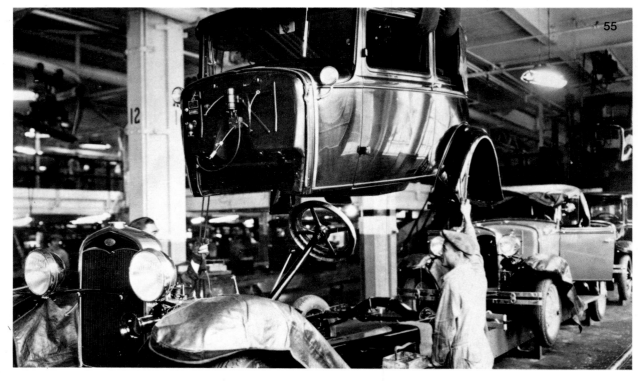

56

55. In 1926, the situation became dramatically critical for the Model T. Tens of thousands of Tin Lizzies lay around unsold at the works and at dealers. It was clear to the more discerning members of the Ford company that inevitable disaster was at hand unless a radical change could be made to a new model. It had to be a trailblazer like the Tin Lizzie 18 years beforehand. Henry Ford's son Edsel and employees Ernest Kanzler and Ed Martin urged their elder to change. Faced with the losses of 30 million dollars suffered by the Ford works in the period from 1926 to 1927, he finally did so. On 26 May 1927 the works were closed for six months. The only production that continued was spare parts for the Model T. Over this period, interest was kindled in the new model Ford A, and the value of pre-ordered cars amounted to an impressive $36 million. In December 1927, the first Ford A left the gates and drove out onto the streets of the USA. It was to prove almost as successful as the Tin Lizzie.

56. Henry Ford in 1904 beside his racing car, the 'Arrow'. A second identical car bore the type designation '999', being driven either by Ford's then sponsor, Tom Cooper, or by Barney Oldfield, an arrival from the sport of cycling. in Ford's eyes, it was merely an experimental car used to demonstrate his know-how – a giant four-cylinder with no clutch and no gear shift.

57. In this workshop in Bagley Avenue, Detroit, Henry Ford's first car, a quadricycle, was born in 1896.

Following pages: 58. French racing driver Georges Boillot (left) and Jules Goux with their mechanics in front of their rustic Peugeot pit at Indianapolis in 1914. The winner of the 500 miles was René Thomas in a Delage.

Coburn Photo
Indianapolis

59

60

61

59. Ettore Bugatti at the wheel of a Deutz car designed by him, at the start of the Prinz Henry run in 1909.

60. Louis Renault in his 8 bhp Voiturette in the 1901 Paris-Berlin race, in which he took eighth place.

61. Ernest Friderich in a Bugatti type 30 'Tank' before the French Grand Prix in Tours in 1923. 30s also ran as single seaters in Indianapolis in the same year.

62. The great Chadwick Six. This was the first car in the world to be fitted with a supercharger.

63. Alfred Neubauer at the wheel of his Austro-Daimler 'Sascha' in which he won the Targa Florio in 1922.

64. A group photograph with 'Sascha'. To the left of the radiator cap, Dr Ferdinand Porsch, managing director of Austro-Daimler. At the wheel of 'Sascha', Alfred Neubauer, and at his side his racing fitter, Auer.

THE GREAT CHADWICK SIX
Winner of the 1910 Fairmount Park Race, Philadelphia
Established a new record and average of

62

4876 J1

63

64

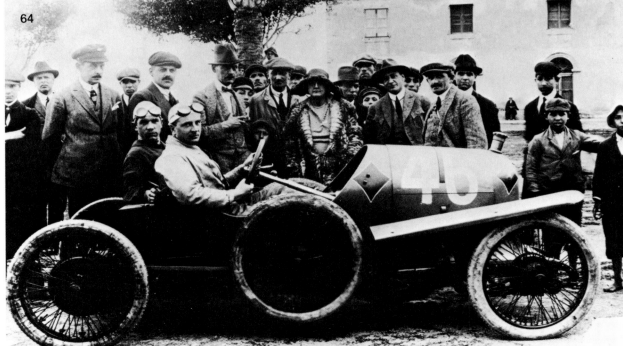

65. 1921 Alfa Romeo 20/30 ES Sport. It developed 67 bhp at 2600 rpm.

66. The winning Mercedes car in the 1914 French Grand Prix, with Lautenschlager.

67. Filling up a Humber for a record attempt over the mile at Brooklands in 1913

68. Renault world record car in 1926. 24 hours at an average speed of 173.6 kmph.

Following pages: 69. A lightweight Rolls-Royce armoured car in 1916, on a Silver Ghost chassis. Lawrence of Arabia attributed his desert victories in the First World War in part to the reliability of the Silver Ghost armoured cars.

70. A Bédélia cycle car used as an ambulance in the First World War.

71. The 1908 Protos with which Lieutenant Koeppen competed in the New York-Paris long distance rally.

72. An 1895 Peugeot type 13 used as a delivery van.

73. The world's first saloon car – a Renault built in 1899. It was popularly known as the 'hatbox'.

67

68

69

70

71

72

GLAMOUR AND GO

The finest cars have always possessed both. For the rich enthusiast of the thirties the epitome of glamour, coupled with almost unimaginable power, was the 'Duesie'; for his counterpart today, there is no name more likely to stir the blood than that of Porsche. The Duesenberg brothers and Ferdinand Porsche were near contemporaries – but while the Duesenberg star burned briefly in the heavens and then was suddenly extinguished, the name of Porsche represents a history of steady growth, the application of revolutionary technical ideas and a continuing willingness to return to the drawing board....

DUESENBERG – THE POWER AND THE GLORY

Duesenberg – for Americans this is still a name as glamorous and nostalgic as Rockefeller, Garbo or Valentino. Brilliant self-taught automotive engineers Fred and Augie Duesenberg built luxury automobiles at the end of the 1920s and the beginning of the 1930s, cars that became part of the American dream; fast, elegant, expensive and reliable. Hollywood star Clark Gable kept four of these magnificent swank automobiles in his garages, and Greta Garbo owned a 'Duesie', as did King Alfonso XIII of Spain, Prince Nikolaus of Bulgaria, Mae West and Randolph Hearst. To own a Duesenberg in the Thirties was a mark of high prestige in American social circles.

Two young lads from Lippe-Detmold

The mystique surrounding the Duesenberg was great, for Fred and Augie built a total of only 650 examples. Nevertheless, this number was sufficient to place the two brothers in the Hall of Fame of American automobile history. Few realised that these masters of their craft came from a small village called Detmold near Hannover in northern Germany.

Fritz was born on 6 December 1874, and August two years later. When the family decided to seek their fortune in America after the death of their father, their mother tongue was still colloquial German. Brother Heinrich had been sent across the Atlantic beforehand to pave the way: he became a 'drummer' for a large horticultural firm – looking after north-east Iowa and neighbouring Wisconsin – and settled in Rockford, Iowa. By the middle of the 1880s he felt secure enough to receive his mother and five brothers and sisters.

Neither Fred nor Augie learned a proper trade, let alone studied formal engineering. However, they were both naturally talented in technical subjects. By the age of 17 Fred was already an extremely busy mechanic, who repaired agricultural machinery and constructed windpumps. In 1893 the Duesenberg brothers decided that the bicycle was the up-and-coming means of transportation for the small man, and began their manufacturing career making two-wheelers. Fred was, from the start, the go-getter, the front man, while Augie, quieter of the two, remained more in the background.

They designed their own bicycles, built in their modest workshop, and Fred entered cycle races as his own works' representative. In 1898 he hit the sporting headlines by setting up two world records over a distance of two miles and three miles. However, the Duesenberg brothers had now begun to watch closely the hesitant but continuing progress of the internal combustion engine. In 1900 they mounted a self-built auxiliary engine on one of their iron steeds. One of the first motorised bicycles (if not quite a motorcycle) in the United States thus came into being.

In 1902 Fred went to Rambler (later American Motors) as development engineer, while Augie continued to build bicycles. Four years later, in 1906, they jointly sold their bicycle factory and designed their first automobile, a flat-twin-cylinder model with chain drive which they built at Des Moines, Iowa. An astute lawyer by the name of Mason recognised the brilliant technical know-how of the two 'new Americans' and financed the project. He insisted however that the first Duesenberg automobile should carry his name.

In 1910 Fred introduced his 4-cylinder racing engine, which immediately scored modest successes on American speedways, particularly at the new course at Indianapolis.

By 1913 the Duesenbergs had saved enough cash to pay off their financial backers and were finally able to start up their own unfettered business, the Duesenberg Motor Company. At first they built only racing cars in their St. Paul, Minnesota, factory.

A macabre consignment

In the years of the First World War Fred and Augie were among those constructors who were to develop engines for American military aircraft. It was in connection with this work that they became involved with a drive unit from the workshops of Ettore Bugatti. He had built a 16-cylinder aircraft engine, which he had smuggled to Paris when war broke out.

Bugatti's American friend W. F. Bradley had a quiet word with Colonel R. C. Bolling, lawyer son-in-law of President Wilson. Bolling had travelled to Europe at the request of the American Government in order to 'collect' engines, engineers and aircraft constructors. Bradley recommended Ettore Bugatti's 16-cylinder engine. American experts such as Colonel J. G. Vincent of Packard, Howard Marmon of the Marmon Company, and E. J. Hall of Hall-Scott considered the Bugatti design and construction suitable, and gave the Duesenbergs the contract to build the engine under licence.

Bradley later recalled a macabre event: 'During a trial run of the first engine, an American soldier was wandering about the workshop. He walked, unsuspectingly, into the propeller and was killed, the first American soldier to be killed in the war. We decided that the engine and two mechanics from Molsheim should be sent back to America – together with the corpse. We accordingly filed an application with the French authorities for one corpse, two German mechanics, and an aircraft engine. One can imagine the reaction of the French officials! When they had recovered from their shock and regained their speech, they talked gently and compassionately to our officer, assuming that he had lost his senses. They told him that what he wanted was quite impossible. We reminded them however of what Napoleon had said, namely that the word 'impossible' does not exist for a Frenchman . . . we then got our permit'.

The automobile pioneer Charles B. King was despatched to the Duesenberg factory in order to get the engines in full running order. However, the first King-Bugatti engine exploded during a test run, and the parts shot like bullets through the roof of the workshop. It was bad luck for Bugatti; none of his engines ran for more than four or five hours. When the contract was cancelled, forty engines had already been supplied.

Entry into Grand Prix sport

The 8-, 12- and 16-cylinder engines developed by the Duesenbergs (they had no connection with the Bugatti engine) on the other hand passed their test runs with flying colours. When they began civilian work again in 1918 after the First World War, the brothers were able to utilise their wealth of new engine experience.

Their new 4260 cc 8-cylinder in-line engine was in effect half a 16-cylinder aircraft engine. Eight-cylinder in-line engines were no sensational novelty: C.G.V. (France) in 1902, Winton (USA) with the 'bullet' model of 1904, Weigel (Great Britain) in 1907, and the Zeppelin engines of Mercedes, had already established the tradition. In 1920 the Duesenbergs coupled two of their 8-cylinder drive units together, engaged Tom Milton as driver, and set a new world record over one mile at Daytona Beach, at a speed of 156.046 mph.

In 1921 the Duesenberg brothers entered four 8-cylinder cars in the French Grand Prix, which took place on 26 July at Le Mans. The entry was for racing cars with engines up to three litres. A special technical feature of the Duesenberg cars was that they had hydraulic brakes on all four wheels, developed by the Loughhead Company (later renamed Lockheed) and a vital factor in the sensational win by American driver Jim Murphy. A Duesenberg also took fourth place, with French aperitif king André Dubonnet at the wheel. Dubonnet had spent a great deal of money to qualify for the French Grand Prix – and to everyone's delighted surprise he also proved to be an extremely good driver. Duesenberg cars also recorded four wins at the Indianapolis 500, in 1922 (with a Miller powerpack), 1924, 1925 and 1927.

A legend is born

By 1925, however, the company was in a state of crisis. Their first production car, the Model A, a costly luxury car, had appeared in 1920 but this was the era of mass production of cheap automobiles. The situation changed radically when former racing driver Erret Lobban Cord crossed the brothers' path. Cord had become a millionaire, owned several car dealerships, and wanted to build automobiles himself. He had bought the car-making firm of Auburn in 1924 and made a fortune selling Auburn Speedster and touring cars, which had a sporting image and were good value for money. In 1926 he suggested going into partnership with the Duesenbergs and bought a majority shareholding in the company.

Cord gave the two constructors a free hand: their task was to build 'The World's Finest Motor Cars'. This they successfully did, in the opinion of many experts of the time. In December 1928 the Duesenberg brothers and Cord presented to the American public their idea of a 'dream car'. The Duesenberg Model J was the most fantastic passenger car that America had yet seen: a 6.9 litre Lycoming engine conjured up 265 hp (twice the output of its nearest US rival) from its eight cylinders and accelerated the luxury car to a maximum speed of 117 mph. Duesenbergs supplied the car in chassis form only, which alone cost close on $8500. Bodywork companies such as Murphy, Bohman & Schwartz, Judkins, Derham and Le Baron tailor-made the coachwork. Not suprisingly the purchase price quickly climbed to $18,000.

The Model J was packed tight with technical refinements: four-wheel hydraulic brakes (vacuum servo-assisted from 1930 on), hydraulic lever-type shock absorbers, and an engine with two overhead camshafts and with two inlet and outlet valves per cylinder. The pistons, con-rods and oil sump were forged aluminium. There were three petrol pumps (two electric and one mechanical) which fed, from 1932 onwards, a Stromberg downdraft carburettor. A double dry-plate clutch transmitted the power to a non-synchromesh three-gear drive and thence to the differential and rear wheels. It also had an altimeter-barometer, a tachometer, a stopwatch chronometer, oilchange warning lights, a brake-pressure gauge. . . .

There were of course critics, those who pointed out that it was all the four drum brakes could do to bring the one-ton car to a stop. Drivers of medium stature complained that they had difficulty in sitting comfortably high on the expensive leather seats; others said the J did not like sharp bends at all, and that a Duesenberg made the greatest impression when it was parked under the Californian sun in front of a film star's villa. . . .

Nevertheless, when the Duesenberg J first appeared, American testers declared this model to be the 'best automobile in the world', which is what Fred and Augie Duesenberg as well as Erret Lobban Cord optimistically had in mind. At last, they said, the luxury cars of the old world – the Rolls-Royce, Isotta-Fraschini, Hispano-Suiza and Mercedes-Benz – had been put in their place. For example, the 1931 Hispano-Suiza T 38 with its 9.5 litre V-12 engine developed only 190 horse power, some 75 hp less than the Duesenberg J. And, claimed the pundits, the Hispano-Suiza was clumsy to drive compared with the American luxury car; and of the 770 K Mercedes-Benz with its 200 hp, their opinion in comparison to this US made car was low to say the least. The Isotta-Fraschini 8 B, the only real competitor in this class was, it is true, easier to drive, which could also be said of the intriguing Delage D 8 model, but neither could match the Duesenberg.

A last mighty effort

In 1932 Fred Duesenberg launched his supercharged version of the J, the SJ, with a claimed 320 hp and a top speed of 129 mph. Usually built on the shorter J chassis, it was sold to Hollywood stars like Gary Cooper and Clark Gable as the SSJ, a superb monster with a 0-100 mph time of just 17 seconds. The enormous power of the Model SJ was Fred Duesenberg's undoing: on 2 July he crashed in one of his cars and died twenty-four days later.

Times were bad for luxury cars like the Duesenberg during the Depression. A qualified skilled worker or technician would have to work some fifteen years in order to earn the price of a Duesie. In the end, no more than 650 J, SJ and SSJ examples were built. In 1937 Cord's group of companies folded and the Duesenberg marque came to an end. August Duesenberg survived until 1955.

FERDINAND PORSCHE – BACK TO THE DRAWING BOARD

The 1900 Paris World Fair. Ferdinand Porsche, a young Bohemian engineer, impresses French experts with an electric vehicle which, according to contemporary reports is 'the epoch-making innovation in the production of the very first existing transmissionless carriage'. As early as 1897 Ferdinand Porsche, then 23 years old, had built the first electric vehicle with his own wheel-hub motor for the Lohner Company. It was one of the most bizarre forms of drive ever dreamed up. In the Lohner-Porsche vehicle an electric motor was mounted in each front wheel-hub, drawing energy from huge batteries stowed in the boot. Technically the idea appeared convincing; the vehicle was driven directly by the motors, an early form of front wheel drive. The braking system was also ingenious – the hand brake acted on the rear wheels, while there was an electric short-circuit system braking the front wheels. In the documents in the Porsche archives the power of each motor is given as 2.5 hp at 120 rpm, while over short periods the power could be increased to 7 hp.

Why did Porsche build electric vehicles?

Porsche's electric vehicle rapidly became a best-seller in Vienna as a silent town carriage, purchased not only by members of the nobility but also by the regional authority as utility vehicles. Panhard & Levassor in Paris were interested, and ordered several Lohner-Porsche vehicles for sale in the French capital. The inventive designer even developed a racing car with wheel-hub motors, in which the batteries alone weighed 4000 lb, and in which he rushed round the Semmering to achieve his first track speed record.

One is often puzzled, looking back at this electric vehicle episode in the life of Ferdinand Porsche. Surely the successful progress of the gasolene engine over the past decade, especially in France, then the leading automobile nation, must have impressed him? Had he never done a cost-benefit calculation for the electric motor on the one hand and the internal combustion engine on the other hand? Porsche was a dynamic person, one who constantly looked ahead to the future, which makes his original preference for the electric motor all the more puzzling. Had he not understood the signs of the time, or had he consciously rejected them?

The answer, if there is one, lies perhaps in the Vienna of the day. Transport was for wafting elegant ladies home from the Operahouse, for conveying them to coffe-and-cakes at Demel's Cafe, for delicate urban travel. Not for them the 'rattling, stinking monsters, with their risks and fires'. And as Porsche himself said: 'The trouble with most horseless carriages is the complexity of their transmission. All this fuss of shafting, bevel gears and chains could be done away with if we used electric cables to carry the power direct to the driving wheels.' Which is exactly what he did.

Ferdinand Porsche was well acquainted with developments in automobile construction, but at first he was satisfied with the success of his electric vehicles. In 1903 the Vienna Fire-Fighting Service converted its mobile units to Lohner-Porsche fire engines; soon Berlin,

Hamburg and other cities followed suit. In 1909 London too equipped its City Council Fire Brigade with the new-style fire-fighting vehicles. Gasolene-driven vehicles would have reached the scene of a fire more quickly, but firemen were naturally apprehensive of a fuel that was itself highly inflammable.

At Lohner, where doubts had been raised about the electric motor, there were no illusions regarding its efficiency. Porsche's electric vehicles had a short charge-range, and their motive source, the batteries, reduced the useful load of the vehicle they were meant to drive due to their large weight. Flat batteries meant that the vehicles often had to be towed away, which was a time-consuming process, as charging stations for electric vehicles were few and far between....

Gas engines in electric automobiles

Porsche was forced to come up with something new. He installed gasolene engines in his electric automobiles, not in order to drive the vehicle directly but coupled to a generator, to produce the electrical energy with which the wheel-hub motors were supplied. Why opt for simplicity when you can opt for complexity? In 1901 the *mixt* transmission system was born – one further curiosity from the early years of the designer and constructor Ferdinand Porsche – although, to be historically fair, the system was adopted and built under licence by none other than the great Daimler company.

In 1905 Porsche decided to change companies, when Emil Jellinek invited him to join Austro-Daimler in Vienna. This company had existed since 1899, and built Canstatt-designed Daimler cars under licence.

The company had been searching for a successor to Paul Daimler, who wanted to retire, and in 1906 Ferdinand Porsche was made Technical Director. He assembled a team of skilled and loyal collaborators and began to build several different types of automobiles, including among others the 30 hp Maja which the autocratic Jellinek, a shareholder in Austro-Daimler, had virtually commissioned him to build in order to please his young daughter Maja – as he had previously done for the elder daughter in 1900, when he had persuaded the firm of Daimler to call their vehicle Mercedes. The Maja was Porsche's first genuine gasolene-powered car; it was not however particularly successful. In 1909 he produced the substructure for a car for the Prince Henry Tour, which although it was very reliable was too slow to play any role in the reliability trial. However, in the following year, 1910, Austro-Daimler cars occupied the first three places in the event, Ferdinand Porsche personally driving the winning car.

During the period before the First World War nothing very exciting came from Ferdinand Porsche's drawing board; his work tended to be conventional and solid, mostly side-valve T-head power units – with the exception of the o.h.c. 86 hp 'Prince Henry' car. More interesting is the fact that during the period 1906-1909 he was turning his attention to air travel and the production of more efficient airship and aircraft engines – a facet in the life of the constructor which is considered only marginally in most accounts.

When Porsche was already working towards powering various types of aircraft (airships, airplanes and even primitive helicopters) there were scarcely a dozen aircraft in the whole of Austria, and the Emperor's army did not possess a single one. In contrast to this, Austrian airship pioneers Stagl and Mannsbarth had created a sensation with their dirigible airship, which at 91 metres long was the largest in the world. Its two Austro-Daimler engines, each delivering 150 hp, were designed by Ferdinand Porsche. Some of the non-rigid inflatable airships of the German constructor August von Parseval were also equipped with Austro-Daimler engines, and when on 28 November 1909 *Parseval I* began its sensational flight over Vienna, Porsche himself was at the controls of the two 150 hp units. The airship, which carried four persons and 200 lbs of ballast, circled serenely around St. Stephen's Cathedral, and the Emperor Franz Joseph observed the flight through binoculars. After the landing the airship pioneers informed the Hofburg that they had successfully performed their task for the honour and glory of Austria. What Herr Porsche did not tell the Emperor Franz Joseph was that he had very nearly disappointed His Majesty. A gas-valve had jammed while they were aloft – and whose job was it to unjam it? Porsche climbed the rigging and unplugged the valve just before the whole envelope burst. A few moments delay and our modern world could have been without its 20th century fantasy car....

A dainty morsel for the military

Sometime in 1910 the paths of Ferdinand Porsche and aviation pioneer Igo Etrich crossed. Both were chips off the same block, technically ahead of their time, never lost for solutions to difficult or tricky problems, and prepared to throw caution to the wind when it was a question of implementing their own ideas. Porsche developed a 60 hp 4-cylinder aero-engine for Etrich, followed by 6-cylinder aircraft engines delivering 90 and 120 hp; all massive, solid long-stroke units. However, the upper limit was not reached even then: in 1918 he conjured up 400 hp from twelve cylinders in V-form with four valves per cylinder. Particularly prominent among the fascinating catalogue of

Porsche propeller engines is an air-cooled 60 hp 4-cylinder near-flat engine, with two pairs of cylinders in a slight V-arrangement – possibly the progenitor of the VW engine.

In this way Porsche became a great pacemaker of Austrian aircraft construction through his engine development work before and during the First World War, and also became one of the most successful and progressive engine designers and constructors of his age. The Hansa-Brandenburg D1 fighter plane, designed by Ernst Heinkel and built in Austria, was powered by a 160 hp Austro-Daimler engine, while a 200 hp unit from the same factory was installed in the most commonly built Austrian fighter plane, the Aviatik D1. Porsche worked in close collaboration with the engineer Joseph Mickl in designing this range of more efficient aircraft engines, and the latter also became a member of the Porsche team some time later.

Porsche's military Juggernaut

The renowned M17 mortar carrier, which performed almost unbelievable feats of transportation during the First World War, should not be omitted from the list of activities in which Porsche was engaged. The carrier was a 12 ft high colossus with a compressed-air self-starter and solid rubber tyres which, equipped with a 80 hp 6-cylinder engine, hauled the huge Skoda mortars (a single round weighed a ton) to the European theatres of war. Another of Porsche's significant achievements in the military technology field was the development of the C-tractor. This was a huge 'snake' transporter formation, in which the *mixt* drive system was used. In the transporter train the tractor, with its 150 hp gasolene engine, constituted the power unit. A 300 volt 270 ampere dynamo was driven at 1000 rpm on this generator wagon, and transmitted its energy via a cable to up to ten trailers. The generator thus produced the current for the tractor drive unit as well as for the wheel-hub electric motors driving the wheels of the trailers. The great advantage of this system was that each trailer was in effect self-propelled, independent of the tractive power (but not the generated electric power) of the C-tractor itself. Porsche increased the efficiency of this war machine still further by enabling the train to be easily converted for tracked operation. He was decorated with the Order of Franz Joseph for the construction of his C-tractor, but the awarding of an honorary doctorate by the Vienna Technical College for his work in the war probably brought him greater satisfaction.

In 1916 Dr. Porsche became general manager of the Austro-Daimler Works. Liaison between the vehicles department of the Austrian War Ministry and Austro-Daimler Motoren was maintained by a young artillery officer, Alfred Neubauer, who joined the Porsche team in 1928 and became famous during the 1930s as the Daimler-Benz racing team manager.

After the First World War the Austro-Daimler armaments foundry fell on hard times. Some 6500 workers still had to be kept busy, and the company could hardly afford to rely on the pre-war fame of Porsche-designed cars. A new Austro-Daimler car, the AD 617, Porsche's first post-war design, was introduced at the 1920 Brussels Autosalon. It had a 60 hp 6-cylinder in-line engine of 4.4 litres (80 mm bore×130 mm stroke), and a single overhead camshaft. From its launch this elegant touring car sold well both at home and abroad. The AD 617 became the basic model for all 6-cylinder cars produced in Austria during the 1920s, and was later to be equipped with 4-wheel brakes as the ADV 617.

Ferdinand Porsche had long set his heart on another model however, one which was to become an important turning point in the history of sports car construction. He wanted to build a 'people's sports car', and such was his influence that he was able to go ahead with his plan despite the resistance of some of his colleagues in Austro-Daimler. In this project he was supported by a sponsor, Alexander Count Kolowrat, who had made his millions in the film business, and was known familiarily as 'Sascha.' The first prototypes had a 50 hp, water-cooled 4-cylinder engine with a 1100 cc capacity, twin overhead camshafts, and 4-wheel brakes. With a weight of 420 kilograms, the Porsche 'baby' weighed only half as much as the Mercedes racing cars. Four 'Saschas' driven by Alfred Neubauer, Count Kolowrat, Lambert Pocher and Friedrich Kuhn competed in the 1922 Targa Florio. Neubauer, whom Porsche had named as chief driver, won the race in the Voiturette (light car) class.

Smaller, lighter, faster

The Austro-Daimler Sascha was to be one of the highpoints of Porsche's life as a designer and constructor. In 1922 Austro-Daimler entered the diminutive sports car in fifty-two races, and won 43 of them. With the Sascha Porsche had departed from the conventional path of all other sports car builders who, in order to increase the available power, built cars that were as a rule larger-engined, heavier, and hopefully faster. Porsche on the other hand built cars that were smaller-engined, lighter and certainly faster.

In order to consolidate the growing reputation of his sports car, Porsche entered a vehicle for the 1922 Monza Grand Prix. The driver, Friedrich Kuhn, was killed during trials when his car overturned due to a fractured wheel.

Porsche had already antagonised the board of directors of Austro-Daimler, who were in any case somewhat sceptical of their general manager's plans for a small car. Added to this, Dr Porsche had quarrelled with a shareholder in Austro-Daimler, one Camillo Castiglioni – and one thing led to another . . . Porsche was removed from office and forbidden to enter the works. A hard blow for one used to success. However, he might just have had an inkling that at that moment Daimler in Stuttgart needed a chief designer with director status. . . .

First of all Porsche sorted out Daimler's incomplete supercharger projects. The problem child in 1922 was a two-litre Mercedes sports car with a very fickle super-charged engine revving up to 8000 rpm, and designed to produce 160 hp – which it sometimes did. Porsche solved the problem and in 1924 entered three 16-valve blown 2-litre cars for the Targa Florio, with Alfred Neubauer, Christian Werner and ex-champion Christian Lautenschlager as drivers. Under Porsche's team management Werner won the race on 27 April 1924 in record time (distance: 268 miles, time: 6:32:37 hours, average speed: 41 mph). Joy was unconfined in Stuttgart, and the Wurttemberg Technical Institute awarded Porsche an honourary doctorate of their own. Despite this impressive success, the two-litre supercharged car remained a problem and after Count Zborowski was killed in 1924 in the Italian Grand Prix the car earned a reputation for unreliability.

Mercedes Benz is formed

Porsche turned to the high-performance touring cars of the Daimler Company, which British car builder W. O. Bentley called 'the long-legged cars', a range of models with fascinating variations. There were two basic types, a 6-cylinder, four-litre car and a 6-cylinder, six-litre car, which Daimler-Benz, in a subsequent history of the company, dubbed the 'Stradivarius of the road'. In 1926 these models were upgraded in power and the wheelbase short-ened, which was reflected by the addition of the letter 'K' (for *kurz* – short) in the type designation. They were the fastest tourers of their time, developing 140 hp unsuper-charged, and 150 hp with supercharger. From these K types Ferdinand Porsche then created one of the most breathtaking sports car series in the history of the auto-mobile, first the S type (S for sport), with a 6.8 litre engine and engageable supercharger, whose six cylinders devel-oped 180 hp. The SS (super sport, 200 hp) the SSK (225 hp), and in 1931, the SSKL (L for light, 300 hp), followed as model variants. All had a 7.1 litre engine capacity. For the *afficionado* these sports cars, which appeared after the merger between Daimler and Benz in

1926, represent outstanding highlights in the career of their uniquely brilliant designer, a career which extended over more than fifty years. The S Class represented the peak of automobile construction, a decade ahead of its time, and a list of its racing victories would fill pages. After five years Ferdinand Porsche left Stuttgart with an illus-trious record, and in 1929 became Technical Director at the Steyr Works in Austria. However, a 'guest appear-ance' with this company was only short-lived. Never-theless, the technically advanced 'Austria' model was produced, with an 8-cylinder engine of 5.3 litre capacity producing 100 hp, before Steyr too were overtaken by the world economic crisis.

A team of enthusiastic collaborators

So, on 23 April 1930 Ferdinand Porsche was once again out on the street. This time he chose to set up on his own. Now he could make use of his talent for gathering skilled collaborators around him and enthusing them with his ideas, workers like his son Ferdinand Anton Ernst (nick-named 'Ferry'), Karl Rabe (chief constructor), Karl Fröhlich (gears and drive mechanisms), Josef Kales (engines), Josef Zahradnik (front axle, rear axle) and Josef Goldinger (chief driver). The small team of those early days grew to 98 by the beginning of 1938. At first the company lived from hand-to-mouth, although a wide variety of ideas and concepts were developed for other firms: six- and eight-cylinder engines for Wanderer, a swing axle for Horch, and (in conjunction with a body-work design which clearly pointed to the later VW Beetle shape) an air-cooled 5-cylinder rear-mounted engine for Zundapp. The Porsche team modified this engine for the Phänomen works, which wanted to fit them into trucks. Porsche turned down an offer in 1932 from the Soviet Government to reorganise their automobile industry for personal reasons – and even the offer of a blank cheque failed to make him change his mind.

For some time now plans for a 'people's car' had been forming in Porsche's mind. The general manager of Zundapp-Motorrad-Werke, privy councillor Fritz Neumeyer, persuaded Porsche to consider the possibilities of designing such a model. The plans laid out on the drawing board between December 1931 and April 1932 were already moving toward the later Beetle mechanics: engine mounted behind the rear axle, streamlined body-work, and the spare wheel in front. However, Zundapp rejected the planned air-cooled engine. Porsche yielded, and incorporated a water-cooled 5-cylinder rear-mounted engine.

The test drives with this Type 12 were beset by trouble. The engine overheated, and the oil boiled after only 10 km. Fritz Neumeyer resigned, and Porsche was paid off. In 1934, following a commission from the NSU Works, an attempt was made once more to design and build a people's car, this time with a 1580 cc flat-four engine (two pairs of cylinders arranged opposite one another) and a Porsche invention that alone would have ensured him a place in the Automobile Hall of Fame: a torsion bar suspension, that, with its ingenious and simple mode of action, fundamentally revolutionised the driving comfort of automobiles. However, this experimental model, designated the Type 32, was also ill-fated. In the first place the torsion bars flew off, past the heads of the testers in the first trial runs; and in 1934 the massive re-arming of the German Third Reich began, during which private initiatives like that of the NSU Works were no longer permitted. The prototypes of an 'official' People's Car (later to be called the KdF-Wagen and known to us as the Volkswagen Beetle) were built by the Porsche team in Stuttgart in 1934. However, that is quite another story, which lies outside the scope of this book.

When the era of the 'Silver Arrows' arrived and the ground was cut away from under the feet of the hitherto leading racing cars of Bugatti, Maserati and Alfa Romeo in the 1933/34 season, Ferdinand Porsche was ready with his Type P Grand Prix car which he had developed for Auto-Union. This was a 4.4 litre supercharged single-seater, whose engine, with its sixteen cylinders in V-arrangement, had been mounted as a rear unit. The engine produced 295 hp at 4500 rpm. Porsche thus re-entered his beloved high-performance engine field once more. It must have been rather like a man who, after some lean years, returns to eating apple pie after dry bread.

When Ferdinand Porsche died on 30 January 1951, he had been involved for 54 years in the development of the automobile, and had left behind a distinguished legacy in the technology of our century.

V.C.C.
1898
BENZ

A-220

Previous page: 74. 1898 Benz. 75. 1893 Benz.

76

76. 1912 N.A.G. Speedster.

77

77. 1907 Napier. Following pages: 78. 1912 Bugatti 19.

79. 1914 Mercedes

80

80. 1901 Decauville.

81

81. 1914 Mercedes. Following pages: 82. 1907 Métallurgique.

83. 1902 De Dion Bouton.

84. 1903 Mercedes.

85. 1907 Itala.

86. 1905 Dufaux. Following pages: 87. 1909 Ford Model T.

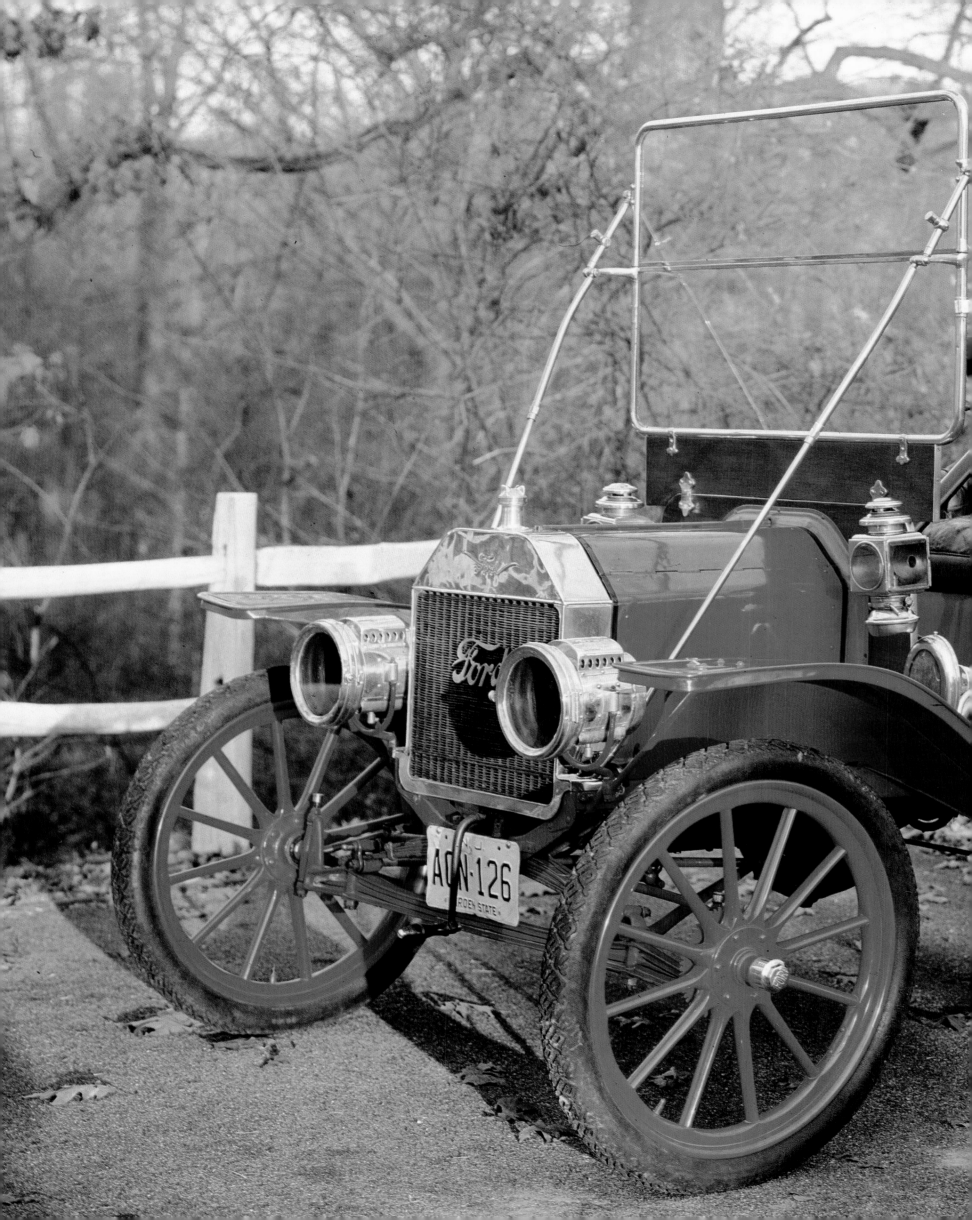

88

88. 1900 Clément-Panhard.

89

91

89. 1905 Dufaux

90

o. 1910 Panhard-Levassor.

91. 1905 Dufaux. Following page: 92. 1895 Gladiator.

THOSE WERE THE DAYS

When the American constructor Harry Miller and the German-born Duesenberg brothers were developing their first high performance engines in the middle of the second decade of our century, they were unable to obtain the necessary alloys from any of the leading American steel companies. They had to travel, often many hundreds of miles, with their designs and blueprints, to small skilled handcraft foundries to satisfy their quality requirements. Those were the times when other up-market American automobile companies had the most important precision components for their cars 'custom built' in Europe. The cylinder blocks and crankshafts of Packard, Peerless and Pierce-Arrow vehicles were for example cast in France; others bought their valve gear from the other side of the Atlantic. The US company Simplex specifically referred in its advertising to the fact that they used steel made by Krupps, a fact they hoped had snob appeal. This was the heyday of individualism, when custom-built automobiles were very much in vogue.

ONE MAN AND HIS OPEL

Thousands of sport-mad Frenchmen danced away the night of 3 July 1914. They were getting themselves in the right mood for the next day's race, the French Grand Prix. Confident that their idol, Georges Boillot, would win in his Peugeot they were full of the joys of imminent victory. However, history took a different turn that sun-drenched day; after 7 hours and 8 minutes German driver Christian Lautenschlager in a Mercedes was first past the line followed by two of his Mercedes team-mates.

In complete contrast to Peugeot and other competing marques, preparations for the great event had been made with Teutonic military precision at the Mercedes Works in Stuttgart-Unterturkheim, their racing cars and drivers learning the circuit, the gear-change and braking points and the optimum speeds over months of intensive work. Mercedes entered five cars in the Lyon Grand Prix; all of which were driven to a concerted tactical plan.

While the 1914 race was recorded as a day of triumph for the Mercedes organisation, it was a black day for the German Opel team. Drivers Emil Erndtmann and Franz Breckheimer were forced to withdraw in the 12th lap of the 20-lap race; Karl Jorns (elder son of Adam Opel himself) came only tenth. There was great dismay at Opels over this bitter defeat at Lyon, for Opel were counted among the German pioneers in motor sport. . . .

The range of popular sports cars and specialist racing cars bearing the Opel marque in the years up to the First World War ranged from 1.5 litre cars up to 12 litre racers. These and other best-selling models were strong factors contributing to Opel's high reputation, resulting in the company becoming the largest German automotive manufacturer in later years.

The next racing event for Opel was the Bank Holiday Race on 3 August 1914 at Brooklands, the racing circuit south-west of London. Karl Jorns wanted to beat Percy Lambert's speed record of 100 mph established in 1913 in a 25 hp Talbot. He was already acquainted with the high speed track: he had come third in Easter 1914 in a 100-mile event, with an average speed of 99.4 mph. However, as the Opel team arrived in England the impending shadow of the outbreak of war was already upon them. Drivers and mechanics decided to return to Germany the quickest possible way. The two Opel racing cars remained in London, however, confiscated as enemy property. They were moth-balled and spent the duration of the war in a garage in Halkin Street, just off Hyde Park Corner.

After the war Captain Alistair Miller tracked them down and bought them. He was a car connoisseur and belonged to that branch of the British upper class who spent their lives in the stern pursuit of pleasure – in this case, motor racing. When Brooklands was re-opened after the First World War the two Opel cars appeared at the starting line, with the Karl Jorns Opel piloted by a talented young driver, Henry Segrave. During the Whitsun race one of his rear tyres burst at high speed. The coolness and efficiency with which Segrave controlled the dangerous situation greatly impressed Sunbeam team chief Louis Coatalen, who made a note of the name of the young daredevil, and Segrave later became world-famous as a Sunbeam driver.

Hard times for a racing car

After Brooklands came a sad day for the Opel Grand Prix car. Who finally sold it, Segrave or Miller, is even now not clear, but the car ended up with a Miss G. Curlie in Yorkshire and, as an English automobile historian wrote with some justification: 'One would dearly love to know what induced the lady to purchase a pre-war racing car. . . .' The Opel was next heard of in Hampshire, where it served as an advertising car for a pub in the small town of Fleet. It is said that the landlord's daughter sometimes used to go shopping in the car; a strange fate for a racing car of historic fame. . . . All trace of the Opel was then lost again for some years, until it reappeared in 1931. The publican from Fleet, now in retirement, wanting to get rid of this worthless 'old crock', had given it to BMC Motors in Brick Street, London. However, they too had little luck with the veteran racer, and offered it for sale.

Brooklands fan and amateur racing driver Noel Mavrogordato now appears in the story. He bought the car for £40. As chance would have it, an article on famous old-timers, including the Karl Jorns Opel, appeared at the same time in the journal *Motor Sport*. The pensioner landlord at last understood what a valuable car he had given away for a song; he wanted to buy it back, but Mavro (as he was known among racing enthusiasts in England) could not be persuaded.

Thus began the second, and by far the more interesting and glamorous, career of the 1914 Karl Jorns Opel. It played a major role for over half a century in the fascinating life of engineer, racing motorcyclist, pilot, driver and car restorer Mavrogordato. At first the car was used as a 'bread and butter' automobile for small daily journeys, and as a towing car for the trailers on which Mavro transported his motor cycles from race to race. It was resprayed white, and equipped with electric lights and fenders.

Initially the Opel ex-racer was just a trusty beast of burden in the various escapades of the eccentric adventure-seeking Mavro. A damaged con-rod was the reason for a first thorough restoration, beginning in 1932 and taking more than four years to complete. As the personal pilot of Lord Nuffield, head of Morris Motors, Mavro had a lot of spare time, which he used (when he was not competing in motorcycle races) to work on the Opel. No instruction manuals or structural drawings existed, so he learnt about the car the hard way, by stripping it down and rebuilding it, fabricating new parts where necessary.

In the meantime he studied the car's history, which reinforced his decision to preserve this memorable car for posterity. If it is possible for a man to fall in love with an engine, Mavro did – his eyes would light up at the very sight of the drilled, milled, polished 4-cylinder, 4411 cc engine block. The valve gear is still a work of art: the four valves per cylinder are actuated by an overhead camshaft, which in turn is driven by a vertical shaft at the rear end of the engine. The splash-type centrifugal lubricating system was also something special for a Grand Prix car of 1914. The engine power is estimated to be about 100 hp, and the car itself is a featherweight for the time. At around 130 lb lighter than other contenders, the three Opels entered in the 1914 French Grand Prix were well under the 1,000 kg upper limit.

At the beginning of the Second World War Mavro-gordato became a flying instructor in the RAF, and the old Opel racer was mothballed once more. Mavro changed the oil, ran the engine for a few revolutions, and then locked the car away in the garage of his cottage in Oxford. Only in 1956 did he tow it from there to his country estate on the south coast of England, and the Opel was to remain like a sleeping beauty for another ten years in the workshop among the world record-breaking motorbikes, Bentleys and Rolls-Royce cars before emerging once more.

Noel Mavrogordato, now retired from most of his wilder escapades, set aside ten years for the Opel's second major restoration, which he began in 1966. His ambition was to manage as far as possible without outside help and to limit the use of new parts to a minimum. However, the tyres were specially made by an Australian firm, and the distributor, three crankshaft bearings, the Bosch ignition coil, and the mudguards, were also new. The fascinating exterior of the car is largely determined by the shape of the original parts, such as the four-arm exhaust system – which terminates in a pipe that looks like a pepper pot – or the Zenith carburettor. The protective stone-guard is also original. The tachometer was first installed in 1920 and was adjusted to the new tyre size during the second restoration. The three brakes – the transmission brake and the brake on each rear wheel – were refurbished as near to modern standards as rear-wheel-only braking allowed.

The petrol tank together with its gauge are located (somewhat disturbingly) behind the two seats, now resplendent in expensive new leather upholstery. A petrol pump is mounted to the right of the driver, in a handy position on the dashboard between the radiator and cockpit. Even the respray was done in Mavro's own workshop. 'The cost of the restoration was kept within reasonable limits', he has said, 'by doing almost everything myself, although it certainly took several thousand working hours, which are not included in the cost calculation. The ten years that I devoted to restoring the Opel have been among the most interesting of my whole life. To see a famous old car come alive again, item by item, from a pile of hundreds of individual parts, which in many cases were broken or corroded, has been absolutely fantastic'.

Mavro estimated that the Opel, now over 70 years old, can scarcely have done more than 5000 miles. The car runs happily on normal grade gasolene and fuel consumption is extremely low – about 25 miles to the gallon. The car is still capable of over 105 mph, and its present-day value is a king's ransom. . . .

AUGUST HORCH – AUDI WAS THE WORD

The spectre of dissension plagued the early, slow-moving days of the German automobile industry. Brilliant but frustrated designers and constructors would, dissatisfied, part company with their employers or leave the companies that they had founded to seek a new employer or even to go it alone. In 1882 Gottlieb Daimler left Deutz in order to become independent. In 1903 Karl Benz resigned from the board of directors of Benz & Cie. Rheinische Gasmotorenfabrik, became a member of the board of trustees, and three years later, with his sons Eugen and Richard, founded the firm Benz Sohne in Ladenburg. In 1907 Wilhelm Maybach left the Daimler company in order to become a partner with Count Zeppelin in Friedrichshafen. From 1921 on he helped his son Karl as the latter was establishing the exclusive marque of Maybach. Ettore Bugatti had to leave Deutz in 1909, and from 1910 began to build his own cars.

This nomadic list must also include a person whom many consider unjustly confined to the footnotes of history: August Horch. His life is an example of how difficult the early years of the German automobile industry were for a brilliant designer.

Horch finished primary school when he was thirteen and took an apprenticeship as a blacksmith under his father. In his memoirs he describes the fascinating life a journeyman could lead during his time if he were adventurous, inquisitive, and believed in the future. After two and a half years apprenticeship his father pressed 20 Reichsmarks into his hand and said 'Now, my son, take to the road and see something of the world!' August, who set off with his friend Hermann Sunner, recalls: 'In those days you could recognise the wandering journeyman by the knapsack that he hung round his neck on a strap. Blacksmiths and locksmiths carried their personal belongings in a leather apron. Cartwrights and tinsmiths used to keep their effects in rolls of cloth. Each of us had a shirt in his apron, two pairs of stockings, some basic tools, and a pair of shoes buckled on the outside. We used to hold the traditional walking stick or stock in our hand'. Those were days when European working men looked like something out of Grimm's *Fairy Tales*.

His first automobile

What we nowadays unromantically call 'job-hunting' was for young seekers of work like August Horch a carefree, optimistic wandering over Europe's silent, dusty byways. Horch walked via Bratislava to Budapest, learnt watch and clock making on the side, then worked near the border between Serbia and Bulgaria on a road-building project, and in 1887 returned home to Vienna in order to study engineering as a second string. As a student, Horch kept on the alert for engineering developments, especially in the shipbuilding and marine engineering industry. He was present when, in the middle of 1896, a motorcyle of the firm Hildebrand & Wolfmuller was demonstrated at the Leipzig racing track. As early as 1889 Hildebrand had attempted to install a small steam engine in a so-called 'single-track vehicle'. However, it was not until 1893 that the company obtained their first four-stroke engine which they installed in one of their own bicycle frames. Horch points out in his memoirs that Hildebrand & Wolfmuller obtained commercial protection for the technical term 'motorcycle' in the same year.

Deeply impressed by this two-wheel vehicle, he went up to the demonstrating officials, and enquired whether practicable carriages with engines were also being built. Yes they were, by Daimler in Stuttgart and Benz in Mannheim – and didn't he know? August Horch wrote to Karl Benz – and in May 1896 became works manager at Mannheim.

There were difficulties with the boss however. Karl Benz was an autocrat. He rejected any proposals for technical innovations that were not his own, particularly if they questioned the basic principles of his overall design and construction. August Horch felt inhibited and under-

valued by his somewhat heavy-handed employer, left Mannheim in 1899, and founded his own firm, A. Horch & Cie. at Cologne, repairing motor vehicles. Then in 1900 he introduced his first own car, a 2-cylinder 5 hp vehicle. Horch did not make any world-shattering contributions to automobile technology with his first car, but he was the first German automobile producer to adopt Louis Renault's shaft drive combined with Panhard's principle of the front-mounted engine, a layout that later becamne almost universal throughout the world.

In 1902 Horch moved his to Reichenbach in Germany's Voigtland, and two years later moved again to Zwickau in Saxony, where the firm was formed into a limited company.

Horch put up an impressive number of wins in motor sport competitions with his newly-developed 4-cylinder cars, and in 1906 the marque won the first Herkomer Trophy with a 2.7 litre 22 hp machine. This encouraged Horch to build a 6-cylinder car, which he entered for the Prince Henry race in 1908. This time however he was unsuccessful, although the low-profile line of his cars was historically significant as the precursor of the 'torpedo' shape of a decade or more later. He realised that this setback would be held against him – and at a meeting of the board of directors he was held responsible for the failure of the car. Tempers were lost, and Horch recognised that his time at the firm he had founded was over. He was compensated with a payment of 20,000 Marks and in June 1909 left the motorworks in Zwickau. Just one month later he formed, together with some friends, the August Horch Automobilwerke in the same town, with a share capital of 200,000 Marks. This resulted in his former company successfully suing him and denying him the right to call the new firm 'August Horch'.

A new name by translation

Action now had to be taken with speed. A crisis meeting was held at the home of shareholder Franz Fikentscher, and a new name discussed. Fikentscher's young son was following the exhausting discussion of the new company name; he sat quietly in one corner of the room, pretending to do his homework. In fact he was listening to the conversation of the group of adults, and finally burst out: 'Why not use the word *Audi* (listen!)? it's the Latin translation for *Horch*!'

Horch announced proudly in his new advertisements that Audi branches had been opened in Hamburg, Wiesbaden, Argentina, Uruguay, Paraguay, Brazil, St Petersburg, the Tauride (in southern Russia), Milan, Zurich, Vienna and Salatiga (Java). The first Audis built by Horch, the Type A, a 4-cylinder producing 22 hp, could be seen on German roads just one year after the launching of the company. While the original Horch company continued to live for years off the ideas of their former chief, the Audi Managing Director was busy testing his brand new generation of cars himself, often under severe competition conditions. Thus, he won the 1911 and 1912 Alpine Races in a 28 hp Type B and in the two following years in a Type C, following which these models, with their stylish, streamlined bodywork, were also known as 'Alpine Victors'.

During the First World War Audi virtually ceased automobile production and produced shells, grenades and trench mortars. August Horch – who was excellent at delegating – was to be seen only rarely in the firm. His advice was sought in armaments and war commissions, in which the question of motorising the army was examined, and he contributed substantially in the capacity of consultant to the development of German armoured vehicles.

In 1919 Audi switched back to civilian production, largely based on its pre-war models. In 1920 August Horch retired from the management of the business and became a member of the supervisory board, and from then on he was little involved in the day-to-day running of his firm, becoming more active in industrial associations and economic organisations; such far-sighted entrepreneurs were urgently needed in Berlin, for the 1920s were to become a period of desperate economic pressures for the German automobile industry.

Four companies shelter under one roof

The automobile industry, which was already a long way along the road to producing transportation for the broad mass of population, was in an extremely shaky state at the beginning of the world economic crisis in 1929. What Daimler and Benz had demonstrated by their amalgamation in 1926 became unavoidable for most of the rest of the industry by the end of the decade, and Auto-Union, which included Horch of Zwickau, Audi (also of Zwickau), DKW (owned by Danish-born J. S. Rasmussen) and Wanderer of Siegmar, was formed. After Hitler's takeover of power in 1933 Ferdinand Porsche began to build the Auto-Union Grand Prix 'Silver Arrow' racing cars (which bore the symbol of four interlocking rings) and greatly enhanced the image of the new co-operative.

The Auto-Union members divided up their market according to specific target groups: the powerful, fast and elegant 8-cylinder luxury cars bore the name Horch, Audi epitomised sporting and elegant front-drive cars with 2 or 2.3 litre 6-cylinder engines for individualists, while Wanderer was classified as embodying 'middle market' cars. DKW, which until 1938 was also the largest motorcycle factory in the world, contributed the unmistakable small cars of the two-stroke king, Jorgen Rasmussen. They were attractive for their low price and their unconventional technology – a transverse-mounted two-stroke engine, front drive, plus front and rear wheels mounted on transverse springs.

August Horch had greatly welcomed the formation of the new concern. He was elected to its supervisory board in 1933, in his own estimate the high-point of his life's work, and he could look on his two 'children', Horch and Audi, which had once caused him so much heartache, with pride and with a sense of reconciliation. He died aged 83 on 3 February 1951 in his adopted town of Munchberg in Upper Franconia.

THE BIRKIN-BENTLEY SINGLE SEATER

'To fit a Bentley with a supercharger goes against the principles by which my cars were built and, what's more, affects their driving behaviour' (Walter Owen Bentley in his autobiography *W.O.*). The designer and constructor of the legendary Bentley automobiles, which became the embodiment of the classical English sports car, shared this antipathy to 'engine doping' in common with Ettore Bugatti, who had reluctantly familiarised himself with this method of increasing engine power, a method which he, too, considered 'unnatural'. The first to benefit from this treatment was the Bugatti 35B, the supercharged version of the 35 T. However, the power developed by his supercharged engines pleased the Alsatian automobile king so much that he fitted blowers to some of his touring cars.

Bentley on the other hand steadfastly disapproved of superchargers and from 1921 until his first financial crisis he did not build any cars with supercharged engines, and during this period expressed the view that performance must come exclusively from engine capacity. It was left to private drivers to fit Bentley engines with superchargers in their own workshops if they were determined on such a modification. Bentley owner Henry 'Tim' Birkin was one who took the risk. He belonged to that species of wealthy Englishmen who used to buy racing and sports cars 'just for fun'. Birkin came 'from the top drawer' and, if one is to believe reports, must have exuded considerable charm. This is certainly how he managed to persuade a rich woman friend to finance his racing ambitions.

The Honourable Dorothy Paget was a millionairess, patriotic, and considered to be eccentric. She lived in a vast mansion with an army of servants with whom she never communicated, save by written notes carried by her secretary. In 1929 she paid for the fitting of superchargers to several 4.5 litre Bentleys at Birkin's workshops in Welwyn, north of London. Charles Amherst Villiers, who had already designed the Vauxhall Villiers supercharger for Raymond Mays' racing cars, was engaged as consultant.

On 13 July 1929 Birkin entered his 'blown' 4½ litre Bentley in the Irish Grand Prix, a 300-mile handicap race for sports cars held in Phoenix Park, Dublin, and run over two days. Birkin challenged a 6.8 litre 36/220 Mercedes supercharged car driven by 'Scrap' Thistlethwayte so hard that the latter had to withdraw after 115 miles with valve trouble. 'Tim' Birkin's own car also dropped back on account of radiator damage and passed the flag in third place behind a normally aspirated Bentley Speed Six, and a supercharged 1759 Alfa-Romeo. For the Ulster Tourist Trophy Race held on 17 August the same year, W. O. Bentley offered his services as co-driver and mechanic. Even this didn't help however – Rudolf Caracciola won in a 7.1 litre supercharged Mercedes.

This prompted some further modifications to the Birkin-Bentley. A streamlined two-seater body was tried out and the car was entered in various races, including Brooklands events, although by the end of the 1920s the salad days of Brooklands were already past. Cautious drivers no longer ventured without special shock absorbers on the increasingly rough track, and the Birkin-Bentley leapt a yard into the air several times over one or two of the bumps in the surface despite the impressive two-ton weight of the car. Three hydraulic shock absorbers on each side were installed to prevent even more dangerous flights.

Heyday of a thoroughbred

The Birkin-Bentley acquired its definitive, one-seater bodywork in the winter of 1929-30. The engine now delivered 240 hp in contrast to the 110 hp of the standard version of the unsupercharged 4½ litre Bentley. In 1930 Birkin was able to convince his patroness Dorothy Paget and the diamond millionaire Woolf Barnato that the Bentley single-seater had a good chance in the Le Mans 24-hour race. W.O. therefore received a commission to build 50 Bentley supercharged cars in order to comply with the regulations. However, in the event, two unsupercharged Speed Sixes took 1st and 2nd places.

During the brief heyday of the Paget racing stables the Birkin-Bentley was constantly being modified. The front wheel brakes were removed, on the grounds that brakes did not play any essential role at Brooklands – there

was enough space to coast to a stop! Birkin also experimented with various types of carburettors and superchargers, had the car painted bright red, and bored-out the engine to 4442 cc. Although the sporting successes of the single-seater were not exceptional, Birkin (by now Sir Henry Birkin, following the death of his father) nevertheless set a new circuit record of 137.96 mph at Brooklands in 1932.

The 1930s saw the end of the original Bentley Company. Dorothy Paget withdrew from motor sport in October 1930 in order to keep up her horseracing activities, and Bentley Motors were so deeply in debt that W.O. had to seek refuge under the Rolls-Royce flag, withdrawing from the management of the business.

Dorothy Paget had in the meantime offered her 'Blower' Bentleys for sale, and most of them were quickly snapped up by enthusiasts. Surprisingly, however, she was left with the single-seater, presumably because it was too costly to maintain and was unsuitable for everyday use. Finally, the millionairess mothballed the red racer in a coach-house. Birkin drove it for the last time in August 1932 at Brooklands in the so-called Lightning Long Handicap, achieving a lap time of 136 mph.

Henry Birkin died on 22 June 1933 of blood poisoning. His arm had come into contact with the red hot exhaust pipe of his Maserati at the Tripoli Grand Prix, and severe burns resulted in a fatal infection.

Single-seater up for sale

The Birkin-Bentley languished in Dorothy Paget's garage until May 1939 when she sold it to young wine merchant and amateur racing driver Peter Robertson Rodger. He had wrecked the engine of his current 4.5 litre supercharged Bentley, bought from the Paget racing stables, on the Melbourne hairpin bend at Donington Park and needed a replacement unit; he transplanted the Birkin-Bentley engine into his 4.5 litre car.

During the Second World War the single-seater was seen, minus important parts, at various London garages and workshops. The firm of Chalmers in Redhill built a two-seater body for it after the war, for joint owners Peter Robertson Rodger and John Morley. When Rodger died John Morley became sole owner of the Birkin-Bentley, but in fact he was more enamoured of the Alvis marque and considered disposing of the Bentley. Soon the rumour that the single-seater was on the market was heard at the Bentley Drivers Club. Devotees of this famous car trusted that the single-seater would remain in its homeland. John Morley turned down a good foreign offer, and in 1964 the car, in a dilapidated state, was sold to Bentley fan B. M. Russ-Turner.

The reconversion to the classical single-seater body, the painstaking overhaul and reconditioning of the engine, the installation of hand-made 4.5 litre Bentley parts, cost a fortune (today a new cylinder-head for the Birkin-Bentley costs around $3000 without fitting).

In April 1966 – 34 years after the car had been laid up – Russ-Turner took part in a Vintage Sports Car Club race at Silverstone and since then has entered, year in year out, for all the most important vintage races staged in the British Isles.

THE MEN BEHIND THE MAN AT THE WHEEL

By 1905 the National Automobile Show at Madison Square Gardens displayed no fewer than 177 gasolene cars, some with the new 'square' hoods at the front, some with mechanical valves, honeycomb radiators, equal-size roadwheels, 'glass fronts', and enclosed passenger accommodation. Ford has been making cars for two years, Cadillac had established its name as 'The Standard of the World' with its Model A (remarkably similar to the Ford Model A), and Buick had set up business in Detroit. Packard too, now six years old, had moved from Warren, Ohio to 'motor city' in Michigan.

Other hopefuls had sprung into life all over the United States. By 1896 there were 300, reducing to about 150 in 1905, a year that saw 77,000 car registrations. America had buckled down to serious automobile manufacturing, with a few names already growing head-and-shoulders taller than the rest. The motor age had arrived, with the first sale of a car by hire-purchase, with the building of the first motel, the inauguration of the first Glidden Tours – an 870 miles run from New York to the White Mountains and back – with buses operating on the main streets of New York, and a new bill in Congress to regulate the use of automobiles on roads.

Automobile empires in the making

Behind this first upsurge in productivity and use were men whose talents lay in engineering or in promotion, individuals who at this stage had not been swallowed up by large organisations, and whose word in their business was, for the most part, still law. These men, some of whom gave their names to automotive products that we still use today, were both the foundation and backbone of the emergent motormakers and the hardcore of an American industry that – after some hard knocks in the last decade or two – flourishes still, and without whom Detroit might still be just a pleasant border town near the Great Lakes.

At the turn of the century it was just that. But there was one saloon in town in which motor vehicles were the main topic. Round a glass of beer Ransom Olds, Henry Ford, David Buick, Henry Leland and others would talk long about their plans to build automobile empires....

BUICK, David Dunbar (1855-1929). Scottish immigrant. Buick began as a plumber, saved his cash and founded the Buick Manufacturing Co. At the age of 48 he designed his first car, equipped with an overhead valve engine, setting the design principles for generations of Buicks. His brilliant engineering abilities did not save his infant company from disaster, however, and it was bought up by a wagon-making firm and moved to Flint in Michigan, where it continued to build cars under the Buick name. David Buick died destitute, but his claim to lasting fame is that his company formed the basis for the giant General Motors concern, formed by William Durant four years after he had purchased the Buick Company.

DURANT, William Crapo (1860-1947). William C. Durant was a millionaire wagon and carriage builder based in Flint. Early in 1904 he was asked by shareholders of the ailing Buick company (who had taken so long to produce their current car that money had run out) for financial help. He bought the firm, re-organised it and on 16 September 1908 formed his General Motors Company. In the next couple of years Billy Durant bought up Cadillac, Oakland (later Pontiac), Oldsmobile, Carter, Elmore, Ewing, and half-a-dozen other makers of cars or car parts. Money troubles forced him out of the organisation in 1910, but after a brilliant financial coup with Chevrolet he was back at the helm of GM, now a corporation, by 1915.

CHRYSLER, Walter P. (1875-1940). Even as a young apprentice in a railroad company he recognised the potential future of the automobile. Chrysler became works manager of American Locomotives, but by 1911 was in a similar position with the Buick Motor Co., and soon to be elevated to Vice President of General Motors. He took over the presidency of Willys in 1920, rescued it from oblivion, and in 1923 mounted a life-saving operation for Maxwell-Chalmers. With that company producing saleable cars again, he launched a new model under his own name in January 1924, the Chrysler '70'. The car was refused entry to the New York Auto Show that year – so Walter Chrysler displayed it in the foyer of a nearby hotel, and stole the show. The car had many advanced features –

a 6-cylinder high-compression engine, 7-bearing crank-shaft, air cleaner, hydraulic four-wheel brakes and re-placeable oil-filter. It set new standards for the American medium-priced automobile.

DODGE BROTHERS, John (1864-1920) and Horace (1868-1920). John and Horace had formed the Evans and Dodge Bicycle Co at Windsor, Ontario, after they had jointly designed a ball-bearing cycle. Both expert machinists, the brothers sold the company at the turn of the century, and moved across the river to Detroit to open a machine shop with an eye on the growing automotive business in the town. They made transmissions for the new Curved Dash Oldsmobile, the 'one-lunger' that was beginning to be seen on main street in a hundred Ameri-can cities; then Henry Ford, newly set up in a hopefully successful venture, asked them to make his engines if they would accept 50 shares each. They did, and became one-tenth owners of the Ford Motor Company. When Ford finally bought them out in 1919, they received $27 mil-lion for their original stake! Dodge cars had made their debut in 1914, soundly engineered and solidly built, 'Plain Jane' cars for rugged use. So popular were the first series that some 22,000 dealers all over the United States clamoured for agencies within a year of the debut.

KETTERING, Charles F. (1876-1958). Some say that Charles Kettering was the man behind the biggest change ever to take place in the progress of the automobile, a change that was to develop far beyond improved mechanics, and move into the realms of social evolution. Former National Cash Register specialist Kettering re-organised Delco, met Leland of Cadillac, and sold the company complete ignition systems. Leland told him one day that 'five of my men have broken their arms this week trying to start the cars', so Kettering developed an electric self-starter based on his work with cash registers, machines that needed a quick and powerful electric 'kick' to open the cash drawer. His starter, installed in Cadillacs by 1912 and throughout the rest of the world soon after-wards, introduced women drivers to motoring, changed the female fashion of the twenties from flowing garments to short dresses, and played no small part in raising the status of women to their present levels – in addition to saving much injury to arms and wrists.

CHEVROLET, Louis (1878-1941). A young Swiss with a walrus moustache, he came to America from his European homeland in 1900 to sell a wine pump he had developed. Second son of a watchmaker, he was a precision engineer of the first quality and had made the automotive industry his career, first with the French Mors company, then with De Dion Bouton, before emigrating. He took a job with De Dion in New York, later trying his skill with a racing Fiat. His prowess behind the wheel brought Louis Chevrolet to the notice of the GM president Billy Durant, who engaged him as a team driver for Buick. In 1910 Chevrolet persuaded GM to build one of his own designs, a light six in the European style which was marketed under his own name, the first commercially produced Chevro-let, and a high quality automobile. Durant wanted to cut down on the refinements and the cost, and market it as a cheap rival to Ford's Model T. Louis and Durant had a violent argument – and Chevrolet left the organisation. Two years later he formed his own company, Frontenac, building a precision-made car. Such a move was, sadly, too often a sure way to commercial non-viability, and the company lasted just two years, but Louis Chevrolet was a durable type and went on to more racing success before moving into the aircraft-engine designing business.

These pioneers, and so many others, were each part of the fabric of the industry, each meriting a niche in the halls of American automotive history. A panel of distin-guished motor historians once listed 26 such names, some of which will be known to the general public, others only to students of motoring history. Many of the great names here have been discussed in other parts of this book. . . .

Roy D. Chaplin	Norval Hawkins	Alfred Sloan
Walter Chrysler	Elwood Haynes	Charles Sorensen
James Couzens	William Knudsden	Harold Wills
Charles Duryea	Henry Leland	John Willys
Edsel Ford	Charles Nash	Alexander Winton
Henry Ford	Ransom Olds	Fred Zeder
	James Packard	

94

Previous page: 93. 1929 Mercedes-Benz. 94. 1929 Mercedes-Benz.

95

95. 1929 Mercedes-Benz.

96

96. 1929 Mercedes-Benz. Following pages: 97. 1935 Mercedes-Benz 500K.

98. 1908 Colibri.

99. 1930 Steyr.

100. 1938 Austro-Tatra

101. 1933 Maybach DS 8 'Zeppelin'. Following pages: 102. 1940 BMW.

103

103. 1922 Austro-Daimler.

104

104. 1922 Austro-Daimler.

105. 1938 Frazer-Nash/BMW. Following pages: 106. 1938 Horch.

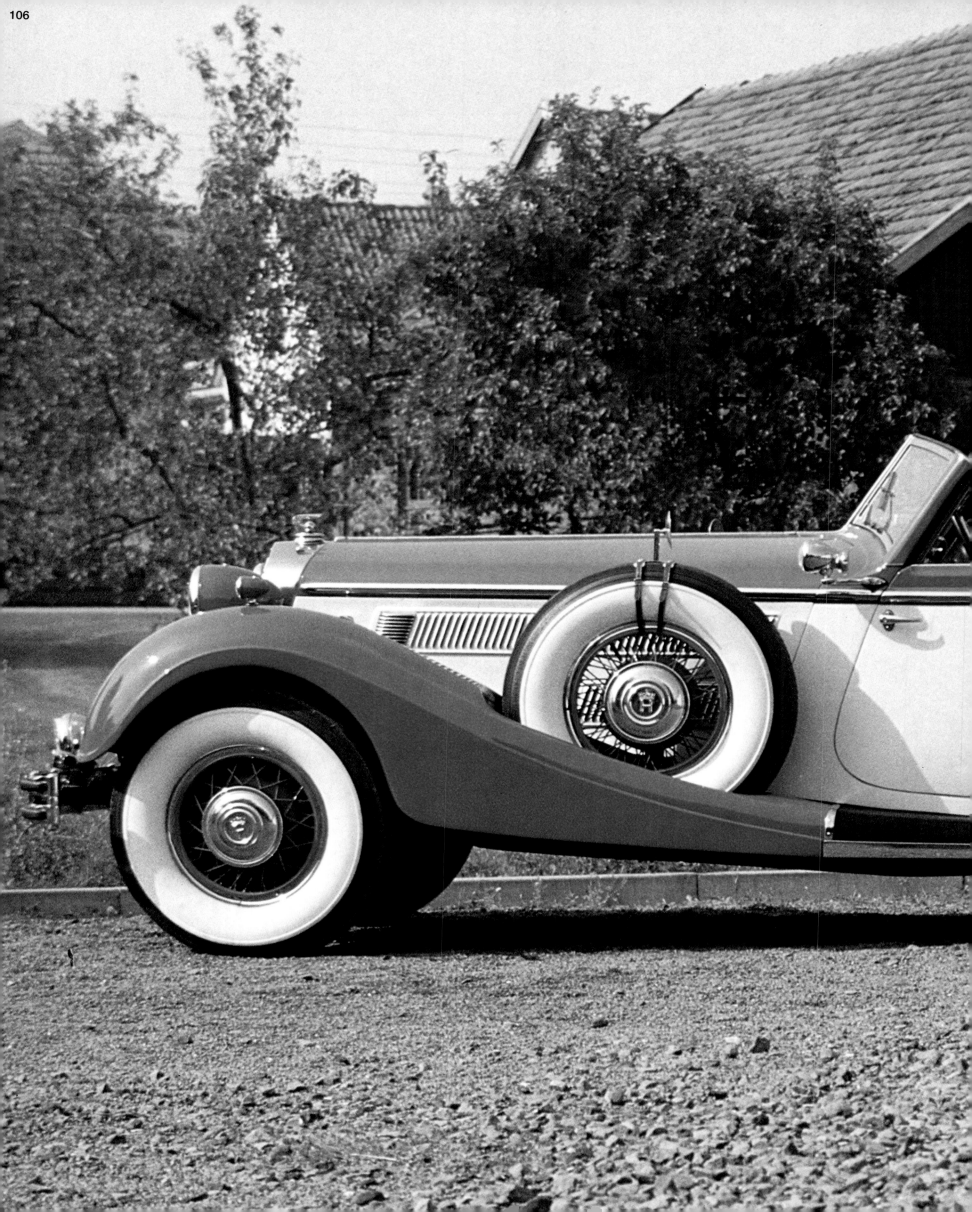

107. 1938 Horch.

108. 1937 Maybach SW 38.

109

09. 1939 Maybach SW 38.

110

10. 1936 Hansa. Following page: 111. 1929 Mercedes-Benz.

THE GIANTS

At the beginning of the 20th century, Daimler of Bad Cannstatt built the first Mercedes at the instigation of the company's South-of-France agent, Emil Jellinek, and laid down the guidelines for the basic design and mechanics of the automobile, much of it relatively unchanged to the present day. This was the time when so many significant innovations blossomed, the beginning of an age of technical progress when the world of science was like a Pandora's box of delights. The first escalator was seen at the Paris World Fair, the first Zeppelin chugged over Lake Constance, the Knorr Company introduced the first compressed air brake. Wireless communication was about to be born, movies were flickering into life, heavier-than-air flight was just around the corner, synthetic chemicals and medical miracles were making history. Against this background, the automobile represented only a small part of the emerging technical revolution.

THE BIGGER, THE BETTER

Despite all its drawbacks, the 'Age of Giants' was nevertheless an exciting phase in the history of the automobile. An unshakeable belief that there was no substitute for size of engine capacity was taken to excess. Even in the first genuine Grand Prix, the 1906 French race, there were no entries whose engine capacity was less than 12 litres, and the largest car, a Panhard, was powered by a huge 18.3 litre engine. The cars of the period produced about 10 hp per litre engine capacity, a puny power from bucket-sized pistons in an engine as heavy as a road-roller. No wonder they lurched and rumbled unsteadily and wore out their rear-wheel brakes and suffered a dozen flats a race. Their speeds, however, were impressive: a Renault won the 1906 French Grand Prix at over 62 mph – a terrifying velocity for one of these old iron skeletons.

In 1913 the Grand Prix organisers put a brake on this engine displacement madness, initially limiting fuel consumption, then the following year stipulating an engine size of not over 4.5 litres. However, in this chapter I want to limit myself to six of these 'monsters', all of which had an engine capacity of more than 20 litres.

The car with the exchangeable engine

If you were to take a holiday on the north coast of Norfolk in England, you might well be overtaken by a monstrosity of an old-timer, sprayed a deep brown colour, with polished, saucepan-sized Zeiss headlamps, a mammoth Maybach motor under the enormous hood, and enough top brass for a 5-star general. At the wheel is Douglas Fitzpatrick, out for a spin on his 1907 Belgian-made Metallurgique, a car in the same class as Rolls-Royce and Mercedes.

The Fitzpatrick Metallurgique already houses its second replacement engine, a Maybach 6-cylinder unit with 21 litre capacity, which produces 230 hp at a very modest 1300 revs. Some examples of this engine, built by Wilhelm Maybach's similarly talented son Karl, powered the Zeppelin airships in the First World War.

Automobile antiques like the Metallurgique are the subject of many fine stories, and this old giant is no exception. In April 1950 Douglas Fitzpatrick received a call from a farmer near Norwich. He had found the skeleton of an automobile, fit only for the scrap-heap, in a barn belonging to a farm he had recently acquired. Would he like to have a look at it? Fitzpatrick certainly would. His first impression was one of complete horror – a re-vamped body in the style of the 1920s, which distorted and disfigured the original Metallurgique design, and several other indignities. However, a look under the bonnet changed his attitude: 'Under the rust, corrosion and dust,

I discovered one of the biggest and most beautiful 6-cylinder engines that I had ever seen!' Douglas Fitzpatrick bought the wrecked titan, transported it to his home, Castle Shermingham, and started on research and restoration work that was to last for many years. The son of a former English Metallurgique importer was able to help in the identification: on the basis of the chassis number 577, it was the frame of a Metallurgique of 1907, which would originally have housed the manufacturer's 4-cylinder 10-litre engine and its shaft drive. The measurements showed that the chassis had been lengthened by about 18 inches in order to make space for the Maybach unit. The engine, with its six individual water-cooled cylinders, was 52 inches long. An enquiry at the Maybach Motorenbau in Friedrichshafen, accompanied by a photograph and the question, 'Is it one of yours?' elicited the prompt reply 'Yes'. Douglas Fitzpatrick then tried to track down the former owners. Such famous racing drivers as Ernest Eldridge popped up in its pedigree. Eldridge had built several special models for Brooklands races, and had himself driven in an Isotta-Fraschini that had housed the same engine as the Metallurgique. It would have been typical of Eldridge to squeeze a giant 6-cylinder engine into an originally small chassis like that of the Metallurgique. The Maybach engine (year of manufacture 1910) was probably installed in the Metallurgique in 1914; what is certain however is that Eldridge sold the Metallurgique-Maybach after the First World War.

From whom did Eldridge buy the car? Douglas Fitzpatrick is certain that he must have purchased it from the estate of the young American racing driver David Bruce-Brown, another name in the history of motors. At the age of only 18 he had become one of the best-known American racing drivers, in spite of the fact that his eccentric millionairess mother attempted, with all the means at her disposal, to prevent her son pursuing such a dangerous sport. When her 20 year old stripling entered a works Benz for the 1910 USA Grand Prix in Savannah, she chartered a special train in an attempt to arrive at the track in time to stop him racing. To the obvious delight of the press, she threatened to give her son a good whipping if he did not obey her orders. She was too late. The race had started. Son David was soon in the lead, however, and mother's mood changed to one of approval. She brandished her parasol at spectators who were not cheering on her boy loudly enough. When Bruce-Brown was first over the finishing line, his mother was with him before the racing team manager and the overjoyed mechanics.

The intrepid youth must have had the Metallurgique for only a short time, but an old greybeard of a mechanic from Marchienne-au-Pont, where the car was made, recognised it immediately as the 'Daveed-Bruce-Brown', when Douglas Fitzpatrick showed it to him in later years.

The Metallurgique is by no means just a museum piece; it is still active today in long-distance runs and competes in sprint trials. Douglas Fitzpatrick has driven the car from England to Greece and back without mishap, and on a German autobahn he can push the 24-valve 6-cylinder engine up to 100 mph. In the words of the proud owner: 'The driver can't keep that speed up as long as the engine, since there's no windscreen. You soon begin to feel like a motorbike rider without any clothes!'

At first sight the Metallurgique appears larger than it really is. The overall length is 15.5 feet and the overall height 5 feet. The petrol tank holds 41 US gallons, and the oil sump just under 9 gallons.

Count Zborowski's toy

Anyone who thought that, after the First World War, the 'Age of Giants' was a thing of the past was sadly mistaken. Business as usual was the order of the day at Brooklands and some of the pre-war giants, such as the Metallurgique and the Blitzen Benz, were reactivated, and there was still a sprinkling of rich amateur racing drivers who enjoyed driving the giants-on-wheels as their spare time pursuit. Racing enthusiasts like Count Louis Vorow Zborowski cultivated their eccentricities in unusual ways, and anyone who wanted to hold his own among such powerful cars at Brooklands during these early post-war years had to find a unit capable of matching the power of the multi-litre gang.

Although Count Zborowski considered himself an amateur, he had his own well-equipped workshop in his hometown of Higham near Canterbury in the south of England, where he installed a 1918 Maybach aircraft engine in the lengthened chassis of a 1913 Mercedes Tourer. It was a 6-cylinder inline unit, whose enormously large cylinders had a 165 mm bore and a 180 mm stroke, giving a total engine capacity of 23-plus litres, the largest automobile engine of its time. The power-pack was a mechanic's and technician's delight; four overhead valves per cylinder and 300 hp at 1500 revs per minute. The car had a primitive rigid axle and chain-drive and the hand brake and gearshift were located on the outside. Count Zborowski had four-seater bodywork installed since he thought that it might be pleasant to make some overland trips now and again in his colossus, or to go picnicking with some friends. . . .

Easter 1921 saw the car's first outing at Brooklands, cheered on by the many sports fans who had feared that the English track would never be the same as it had been before the war, and happier now that they could be entertained by drivers as crazy as the Count. He won the first race, a 100 mile handicap, at an average speed of 101 mph. In another race the car beat a 1914 Mercedes Grand Prix racer – and on one memorable occasion lapped the British circuit at an astonishing 113.45 mph.

Chitty-Chitty-Bang-Bang (that was the sound it made) produced an enormous air resistance due to its perpendicular architecture, and also had to be limited to relatively short races since the tyres were unable to withstand prolonged weight-speed stresses. In the next Brooklands meeting Chitty appeared with a two-seater bodywork, an elegant, almost endless, exhaust pipe, and an enclosed drive chain. Chitty proved itself in many handicap races at Brooklands, at the Southsea Speed Trials, and in private excursions, but in 1922 all this came to a temporary end when the car burst a tyre taking a steeply banked curve at high speed, mounting the slope, and smashing into a time-keeper's hut. Count Zborowski was only slightly injured, but it was the last time he climbed into the cockpit of Chitty I. Instead he set about building Chitty II and, subsequently, Chitty III, both with substantially smaller engines.

Chitty I passed eventually into the hands of the sons of Sir Arthur Conan Doyle, creator of Sherlock Holmes. They entered the car in several Brooklands speed trials in the early 1930s but soon lost interest in their toy. In 1934 Chitty-Chitty-Bang-Bang I appeared for the last time on the English racetrack, following which it was scrapped.

'Babs' Thomas Special – an engine on four wheels

The most down-to-earth of the giant-makers was undoubtedly the Welshman John Godfrey Parry Thomas. His brightly coloured Shetland pullover and his Alsatian dogs were a byword at Brooklands. He owned a bungalow on land inside the famous racetrack – and there was no driver better able to handle the idiosyncrasies of the circuit.

Parry Thomas had been chief engineer at Leyland for many years. He had designed the technically advanced Leyland Eight, intended to be an answer to the Rolls-Royce cars that dominated the luxury market.

When the Leyland Eight of 1920 was introduced to the connoisseurs it met with immediate and unqualified acceptance: a 7 litre straight-eight developing 145 hp, a combination of torsion and leaf spring suspension, vacuum servobrakes – a design and build that showed Thomas to be a gifted and inventive engineer. After internal disputes in his company concerning the policy for the future model range, he parted the best of friends and was even allowed to take with him a Leyland Eight as a keepsake. The canny Celt rebuilt it at Brooklands with an aerodynamic shape — and broke record after record with it. In 1924 and 1925 he broke the overall lap record with a speed of 129.36 mph, and by the end of the following year he had notched up some thirty-five world and class records.

Thomas used to wait patiently for it to rain before making a record attempt, as the tyres gripped better on a wet track. If there was no sign of rain, he would notify the Fire Brigade in Weybridge, who would obligingly pump water from the River Wey on to the track!

In addition to his record-breaking attempts, Parry Thomas ran a large tuning workshop at Brooklands, where sports cars and racing cars could be serviced, or their performance 'tweaked-up'. He not only tuned the famous Aston-Martin sports car 'Green Pea' in his workshop, but also built a number of 'flat irons', 1.5 litre supercharged straight-eight sports cars, which were called Thomas Specials.

Even Parry Thomas eventually succumbed to 'Gigantomania'. He purchased the Higham Special from Count Zborowski's estate, re-naming it 'Babs'. The ex-Zborowski car was driven by a 12-cylinder, 27 litre Liberty aero engine producing 300 hp, to which engine specialist Thomas managed to add another 100 hp. He built a streamlined body and, being a patriotic Welshman, chose to make his world record attempt on the firm beach at Pendine Sands in West Wales. On 27 April 1926 Thomas and Babs achieved their first 'trial' world record at 169.30 mph.

The following day he made another attempt, this time in front of official observers. Thomas had prepared a magic fuel for Babs, consisting of a mixture of 60 per cent aviation fuel and 40 per cent petrol. But his new Land Speed Record of 171.02 mph stood for only seven months. On 4 February 1927 Malcolm Campbell achieved a speed of 174.88 mph in his Napier-Campbell, again on the Welsh shore. Thomas had to respond. With Babs on her trailer, he arrived in Pendine on a rainy 1 March. After a few test runs the trials provisionally fixed for 1 and 2 March were called off because of the torrential rain.

Parry Thomas tried again on 3 March. It turned out to be his last drive. Babs began to slide and swerve wildly, and Thomas lost control of the car. The vehicle turned over three times. A rear wheel came off. Fire broke out. Thomas died immediately, his neck broken. Had he been struck by a drive chain that had come loose? The officials were inclined towards this view. It may be however that a dip in the sand caused the steering wheel to jerk violently.

Thomas was buried at Brooklands, and the shattered wreck of Babs was interred deep in the sand at Pendine. After a few years the wreck of the world-record car lay under some three metres of quicksand, where it remained

for 40 years. In 1967 Welsh schoolmaster Owen Wyn Owen decided to resurrect the car of his idol, and in 1969 the wreck was finally freed. After painstaking research, reconstruction and restoration work spread over six years Babs was in a running condition once more in the autumn of 1975. When Babs is paraded today at veteran meetings and is put through its paces, spectators study the engine and its twelve large-calibre exhaust tail-pieces with a mixture of pride and perhaps nostalgia for the old days when the giantmakers walked among them. . . .

The Triplex Special – based on a truck

The attempts on the world speed record for automobiles during the 1920s brought forth some strange and exotic blooms. It was primarily the sport of well-heeled gentlemen such as Kenelm Lee Guinness, Henry Segrave or Malcolm Campbell, as well as practical engineers like Parry Thomas. As speeds increased closed road circuits were no longer any use as world record venues – they were too limiting. Kenelm Lee Guinness had set the last record on a closed circuit (Brooklands) in 1922 in his 350 hp Sunbeam, reaching a speed of 133.75 mph. Ernest Eldridge tried his luck two years later, once more on a normal road, at Arpajon near Paris, in a 300 hp Fiat. He achieved an average speed of 146.01 mph.

New drivers turned increasingly to flat, broad beaches for their record-attempting runs. Some even had their cars shipped to the beach at Daytona in the USA, as did American-born British driver Henry Segrave in 1927, and at his first attempt in a 4-litre Sunbeam he achieved an average speed of 203.79 mph, faster even than most airplanes of those days. Malcolm Campbell, Britain's other speed king, wasn't going to be left out in the cold, and a year later reached a speed of 206.96 mph, also at Daytona Beach.

Americans were not at all pleased that the prestigious Land Speed Records should be set up by the English on their beaches. Two very different American record-attempting cars were built in a desperate attempt to beat the Campbell record time in 1928: a 16-cylinder, 3 litre supercharged Stutz, the 'Black Hawk', to be driven by 26-year-old Frank Lockhart, and the White-Triplex Special with an astonishing 81 litre capacity, Ray Keech at the wheel. Lockhart's first attempt in the Stutz ended when the car overturned. The driver and car were rescued, and Lockhart was fortunately only slightly injured.

Wire manufacturer J. M. White from Philadelphia hoped to redeem the 'national disgrace', as he called it, of the British world records and commissioned the construction of a truly monstrous vehicle, the Triplex Special. He took as a basis a large truck chassis, in which he packed three 12-cylinder 27 litre Liberty aircraft engines, a total of 81 litres capacity producing 1200 hp. Two of the power units were located behind the driver, and the third lived underneath the hood, in front of the driver. The power was transmitted via three separate drive shafts directly to the rear axle, without a differential. There was no gear box, clutch or reverse, with the result that, as a contemporary observer wrote, 'the speed of the car could only be controlled by the gas pedal and the rear wheel brakes'. Strictly speaking, the crude colossus did not satisfy the gearing regulations, but the cunning designer had a smart idea: he equipped his Triplex Special with an additional axle behind the operational one, which when necessary could be lowered to the ground by means of a lever and, through a worm gear driven by one of the engines, could move the car backwards at a speed of about 1 mph!

During the first record attempt by the four-ton giant a hose in the coolant system of the nose engine split, and boiling liquid caused severe burns on Ray Keech's thighs. However, Keech made a new attempt on 24 April 1928 in an improved Triplex Special. This time he burnt his arm, but with a speed of 207.55 mph he had beaten Campbell and set a new Land Speed Record.

On 27 April 1928 Frank Lockhart tried once more in his 3 litre supercharged Stutz. On the outward run he reached a speed of 203 mph, not fast enough to de-throne Keech. During the obligatory return run, a tyre burst when he was travelling at 218 mph. The white streamlined car went in a crazy spin, overturning three times, and Frank Lockhart was killed, a tragic end to the race between a David and Goliath.

The fight over fractions of a second continued. Henry Segrave reached a speed of 231 mph in his 'Golden Arrow'. The Triplex group naturally wanted to beat this time. Since Ray Keech could not be induced to climb back into the Triplex Special once more, Lee Bible undertook the task. Two days after Segrave's world record, the Triplex Special with the new driver rolled to the timing post. Lee Bible started despite the miserable weather and was involved in a fatal crash. Segrave returned to England as the new world record holder, and was granted a knighthood for his successes.

The Blitzen Benz – monster from Mannheim

The 1908 French Grand Prix, which took place on a road circuit near Dieppe in northern France, was a complete disaster for the host nation. German driver Lautenschlager won the race in a 12.8-litre Mercedes, leading two Benz cars, driven by Hémery and Henriot. The first French car past the post was a Clement-Bayard, in fourth

place. The race was run under highly unsatisfactory conditions. Chippings and gravel from the road flew past the drivers' ears, and the race marshalls considered it necessary to request the drivers to protect their faces. Racing goggles (with ordinary plate window glass!), scarves and face masks were worn, though they did not help much and scarcely a driver finished the race without some facial injury. Sharp stones cut the tyres, and Cissac, the Panhard driver, was fatally injured when a front wheel tyre punctured and the threads of the tyre became entangled in the drive chain.

These mishaps and the German wins, for this was an essentially French event, meant that there were no more Grand Prix races for three years.

The Mannheim firm of Benz decided to concentrate all its efforts on world speed records with the Blitzen (Lightning) Benz, a giant that had been developed from the 12 litre 4-cylinder Benz Grand Prix racing car of 1908, which could deliver 120 hp at 1500 rpm. In 1909 the chain-driven car was exhibited at the 'Brussels World Speed Championship Meeting', with the Frenchman Victor Hémery behind the wheel.

The connoisseurs were speechless: the Benz engineers under their manager Hans Nibel had conjured a sensational 200 hp (at a leisurely 1600 rpm) from four cylinders and an enlarged engine capacity of 21.5 litres. The front axle was a fork design, and the rear one a fixed axle. The track was 1.32 metres, the wheel-base 2.87 metres, and the car weighed 1.2 tonnes. Not much had been done for driver comfort: the seats were an ergonomic disaster: one sat rigidly upright with the small of the back painfully pressured, and the semi-elliptical suspension was teeth-rattlingly rigid and exhausting for the driver. The unprotected drive chain performed wild unchecked work, lashing about just a few inches below his right elbow.

In 1909 Victor Hémery set a new world mile record with the Blitzen Benz in Brussels; he drove a mile in 31.2 seconds, an average speed of 115.28 mph. The Frenchman shipped the car to Brooklands, where he continued to set new records over half a mile to one mile, from standing and flying starts. He also set a new Land Speed Record of 125.95 mph. Nobody could get anywhere near this speed at Brooklands until after the First World War.

In 1910 racing driver Barney Oldfield shipped a Blitzen Benz to the USA, where he raised the Land Speed Record to 131.72 mph. The following year American Bob Burman set up a new record of 141.73 mph on Daytona Beach. Unfortunately, this time was not officially recognised, although the 'German Giant' generally polished off records wherever it appeared.

L. G. Hornsted, who was Benz's English representative, already had a small fleet of Benz cars, including a

Blitzen Benz. With Hornsted at the wheel this car set an awesome total of twenty-seven world records, including the record over one kilometre from a standing start, in which a speed of 73.47 mph was established.

The Blitzen Benz somehow mysteriously survived the First World War and emerged again at Brooklands in 1922 and 1923.

According to documents in the Daimler-Benz Museum, various bodywork designs on the Benz chassis were tried out from 1909 onward. Contemporary photos of Daytona Beach dating from 1910 show the car with an alternative streamlined bodywork as well as with the traditional cladding. Joe Murcott, a passionate veteran and vintage collector in Birmingham, England, has an amazing model in his collection, a four-seater Blitzen Benz that is said to have been used as a service car by Field Marshal Von Hindenburg during the First World War, and which was confiscated as reparation material after the end of the war. This car can now be seen in the Birmingham Museum of Science and Industry, while the world-record-breaking Daimler Benz is at the Daimler-Benz Museum in Stuttgart, Germany.

Fiat S.76 – the problem child from Turin

As the early years of the 20th century passed, the Turin firm of Fiat was also affected by 'giant fever', having taken part since 1900 in automobile races of all types. In 1901, for instance, Felice Nazzaro, driving a modest 3.8-litre 4-cylinder car (which shared a lot in common with the Mercedes), won the Giro d'Italia. In 1907, Fiat's most successful sporting year, Italian driver Nazzaro won the Targa Florio, the Grand Prix and the Kaiserpreiz race in an 8-litre car. In 1908 Louis Wagner won the American Grand Prize in a Fiat, Vincenzo Lancia was second in the Targa Florio, and Felice Nazzaro brought the Fiat 'Mephistopheles', an 18.2-litre titan, to Brooklands to compete against Frank Newton's Napier, which he vanquished. . . .

At the beginning of the second decade of the century Land Speed Records represented the highest level of motor sport. The Blitzen Benz had set the pace and was the car that all the others tried to beat. Fiat believed it could shake the motor world to its foundations with the new 28.4 litre 4-cylinder long-stroke S76, built in 1911. The fact that a 6-cylinder supercharged Chadwick had already won the Vanderbilt Cup in 1908 and put up a creditable performance in the American Grand Prize did not disturb the Italian giant builders at all. They continued with their formula 'more capacity = more power'. Fiat felt up to the challenge, for after Felice Nazzaro's victory in 1908 in the 'Elephant Race' at Brooklands

against Newton's Napier, allegedly at a speed of 121 mph (according to the electric chronometer, a reading which is still doubted even today), the Turin company wanted to beat the world record over the flying kilometre.

Mephistopheles was now in private hands and no longer available to the Fiat works, so Nazzaro tested the Type S76 on Italian roads, and the Turin publicity department announced that this was the most powerful car that had ever driven on a road. Before the car was shipped to Brooklands, Nazzaro had decided to set up his own company, with the result that works driver Bordino had to take the wheel.

But it was one disaster after another. The S76 was embarrassingly unsuccessful, and nothing came of the world record attempt. Bordino shipped the S76 off to Saltburn, Yorkshire, where in 1911 it managed to set up an unofficial record on the beach, with a speed of 125 mph. But in Turin there were long faces, and the car was ordered back. The 21.5-litre Blitzen Benz from Mannheim remained unchallenged.

However, there was a second spring for the 300 hp giant Fiat. A Russian prince had seen the car in the Fiat showrooms. Expense was no problem for him and the S76 ended up, with the help of Russian finance, in the hands of the French driver Arthur Duray. In November 1913 he shipped the car to Ostend to make an attempt on the world record under the supervision of the Automobile Club of France. This time the electric chronometer functioned accurately and showed a speed of 132.37 mph, which would have been a world record but for the fact that it was not recognised as an official run, as record attempts over the flying kilometre must always be made in two opposite directions, and within 15 minutes of the outward run. Why did Duray not make the necessary return run? Unfortunately there was a blustery west wind, the roads were wet, and Duray considered it irresponsible to finish the record attempt according to the existing rules. Nevertheless, he was now, if unofficially, the fastest driver in the world.

The Russian noble soon lost interest in his toy from Turin. In fact, he had already realised the difficulties the Fiat S76 would have in negotiating the bad Russian roads, and he returned it to Fiat.

Time and science moved forward and in 1913 the auto world witnessed the twilight of the Giants. The French authorities declared that monsters like the Fiat were undesirable on French roads, and at Brooklands also it was questioned whether these 'track wreckers' should be tolerated any longer. By 1914, cars of 4.5 litres, infinitely more efficient and manoeuvrable and developing a significantly higher horsepower per litre, were being raced on European circuits.

DREAM TRACKS FOR MEN OBSESSED

Panem et circenses – 'Bread and circuses'. The ancient recipe of the Roman emperors for keeping the populace happy by providing them with food and entertainment is as effective today as it ever was. The Roman arenas where gladiators fought to the death have now made way for the racing tracks of the 20th century.

Death is as often a passenger today as it was two thousand years ago – and rescue vehicles have to be almost as fast as the highly sophisticated competition cars. The American journalist Jim Murray gave a macabre twist to the famous Indianapolis starting command: 'Gentlemen, start your coffins!' These men possessed – what is it that drives them on? Is it the thrill of speed? The longing for death? The need to know the limits of man and machine? The financial rewards? The gladiatorial fame?

BROOKLANDS

The new Brooklands Racing Course near Weybridge, to the south-west of London, presented a colourful spectacle on 17 June 1907, when Britain took a giant step forward into the motor sport era. Drivers of sports and racing cars who gathered at the starting-post were dressed like jockeys for easier identification and were flagged by Hugh Owen from the Jockey Club. The first meetings at the new track were very much in the tradition of the equestrian sporting world – just as Britain itself had adhered firmly to four-footed horsepower for some time after the rest of Europe had accepted the automobile. However, Brooklands was an important factor in pulling the sleepy British lion into the 20th century world of fast motor competition and road transport. . . .

Even today the name Brooklands has a special magic for English motor sport enthusiasts and has the same kind of national symbolism as Wembley, Cheshire cheese, the Tower of London and Ascot. In England Brooklands embodied the greatness of the Empire, sportsmanship, fairness, the pursuit of excellence, new speed records, ingenious improvisation, heroism behind the steering wheel, coupled with a happy-go-lucky feeling that cannot be recaptured. Brooklands was not just the first track in the world to be purpose-built for motor sport, it was also a sort of motor sport Disneyland which had been made possible by the pioneering spirit of the millionaire and architect H. F. Locke-King.

Moving Heaven and Earth

Hugh Locke-King was a very far-sighted man. In the course of his many trips on the continent he had been impressed by the enthusiasm shown by large numbers of spectators for long-distance races in France, Italy and Germany. He decided to build a 2¾-mile circuit which he intended to offer to the British automobile industry as a test track, where tens of thousands of spectators would be able to enjoy watching car racing. He had the necessary funds, and the extensive grounds required. Despite vociferous protests from the surrounding communities and environmental protectionists, despite many law-suits and injunctions, Locke-King began building in September 1906. Some 2000 workers arrived with a steam hoist, ten steam excavators, and a long procession of horse wagons, and began to transform the gentle, typically English park landscape around Weybridge into a noisy building site. A new river bed was dug out to re-route the Wey and the nearby railway was diverted. A couple of acres of forest-land was cleared and several farmers re-located. Locke-King, now obsessed, even had a hill removed. . . .

Although reports of the day dramatised the event somewhat, one can see what an enormous effort Locke-King put into creating the Brooklands Racing Course – and all in under ten months! Locke-King's pride and joy were the two banked bends. The Members' Banking was raised by about 7.5 m, the Byfleet about 6.5 m – these were the first steeply banked bends in the world designed to accommodate speed. A further constructional innovation was introduced at Brooklands: reinforced concrete. The track bridge over the River Wey was made of this new material and admired by engineers from all over the world. The track surface was made of cement 15 cm thick (200,000 tons of it) which was poured into prefabricated shuttering. Between the bends of the pear-shaped circuit were straight flat sections, some of which were occasionally also used for smaller races. And there were several repair shops where both racing cars and sports cars could be serviced or 'souped-up'.

Brooklands very quickly became popular with Londoners as a destination for weekend outings. Club members were provided with restaurants, a grand clubhouse, 2000 seats and standing room for 30,000, all under cover. There was ample room for a further 100,000 spectators round the track. Advice was given on conduct, and both public and drivers were asked to respect the local residents' need for peace and quiet on leaving the racetrack after a meeting.

Even before the track was officially opened S. F. Edge, the popular English driver, had already booked it for an attempt at the world record. In his 60 hp Napier he drove lap after lap for 24 hours (during the night the course was illuminated by an avenue of 300 lanterns) establishing an average speed of 65.9 mph.

In pursuit of new records

Brooklands immediately became the birthplace of countless long-distance and speed records. It would exceed the capacity of this book to go into them in detail, but we ought to mention that the Land Speed Record was broken at least twice at Brooklands. In November 1909 Victor Hémery recorded 125.95 mph in a Blitzen Benz (in that year only a single run was required), and in May 1922 Kenelm Lee Guinness managed to cover the kilometre in an 18.3 litre Sunbeam at a speed of 133.75 mph. In 1908 another attraction captured public interest; the aviation pioneer Alliott Verdun Roe, first Briton to get a powered plane into the air, achieved the feat at Brooklands. His 'do-it-yourself' plane had been made in an old garage at the edge of the Surrey race-track.

113

Previous page: 112. 1927 Bugatti 35B. 113. 1937 Bugatti 57C.

114

115

114. 1932 Bugatti 51.

115. 1927 Bugatti 37. Following pages: 116. 1929 Bugatti 43.

117

117. 1930 Bugatti 44.

118

118. 1929 Bugatti 35B.

119

9. 1930 Bugatti 35B.

120

o. 1926-1930 Bugatti 40. Following page: 121. 1921 Bugatti 23.

Other aviation pioneers soon followed Roe to Brooklands, and it rapidly became the proving-ground of the British aircraft industry with companies like Hawker, Sopwith and Martinsyde using the site for development projects. In 1909 a Monsieur Pegoud attempted the first aerial loop over British soil at Brooklands, and the Keith Prowse Company opened the first office for the sale of 'joyride' air tickets, at five shillings a flight.

Fast sports cars and faster racing cars on the track, flimsy flying machines in the air – Brooklands was 'it' as far as Londoners, tired of the big city, were concerned. Everybody with an interest in driving and flying met here, the office worker arriving by suburban train and the gentry discreetly chauffeured in the family Rolls-Royce Silver Ghost.

In the famous Brooklands Handicap Races, all classes of cars competed: Grand-Prix monsters against light-weight souped-up cars and touring types. The handicaps were gauged so that a skilled amateur in a small car might have a fair chance against a multi-litre racing entry. Ladies were also permitted to drive.

On weekdays proving runs were held at Brooklands. In the racing workshops cars were prepared for the week-end events; tyre firms tested their tyres, tuning shops breathed new life into lethargic cars, and over the freshly mown turf of the improvised aerodrome filigree planes rumbled to the starting line. Even the most sceptical spectators realised very swiftly that this sylvan Surrey corner was experiencing a new era of sport.

In 1921, during the 200 mile race of the Junior Car Club, course marshalls drove round on their motorbikes and fired flares as soon as an accident occurred. These shots led one young lady, familiar only with proceedings in horse-racing, into thinking that drivers who had been in an accident were being 'put down'. She was fascinated....

Brooklands had everything: an enormous leisure park for people in search of relaxation, a universal testground and open air laboratory for automobile, motorbike and aeroplane companies. Many great future racing careers were inspired by the magic of Brooklands; marques were made famous and the prestige of the British automobile industry was raised high at this circuit, and for several decades European and American automobile manufacturers considered it a national obligation to be present. Brooklands became the standard by which all motor sport events were measured and the model for many other similar race tracks such as Berlin's Avus, the autodrome at Monza in northern Italy, the Montlhèry circuit near Paris and possibly even the Indianapolis Motor Speedway.

What the pickaxe spared

The days of the Brooklands races ended with the Second World War. The track was adapted for use as a testing area for bomber and fighter planes and prototypes, and after the war the planemaking company Vickers took over Brooklands and most of the celebrated buildings and course sections, all rich in tradition, were demolished. The Brooklands Society, which is trying to save the last remains of this national monument, this acropolis of motor sport, is today fighting a running battle to recover and refurbish sections of the circuit. Occasionally vintage car races are held on the scanty remains of the cement track, events that always engender a great deal of current interest as well as many nostalgic memories....

INDIANAPOLIS

In the first decade of our century Americans looked on with envy at the various types of motor sport that flourished in the Old World, and at the solid publicity that they brought over the entire market spectrum. In fact they had little cause for envy – they had already made some spectacular pioneer advances. The Oldsmobile Curved Dash Runabout model for instance was the first large-scale production-car in the world, and was also built under licence in Germany under the name of Polymobil and Ultramobil. If the country that invented the car was attracted by it, the 'Merry Olds' *had* to be good!

And Americans learned quickly. After matching their Wintons and Duryeas against Panhards and Mercedes and usually falling ignominiously by the way-side, they had gone back to the drawing boards and examined very thoroughly indeed the details of the latest European machinery. By 1905 most US cars looked very like their European counterparts – but bigger, and often tougher. US engineers had thrown out their high-wheel, underfloor-engined buggy-type wagons and came up with some very fine products. Some 55,000 examples of 109 different marques could be seen on American roads five years into the 20th century.

Apart from the Vanderbilt Cup, which was held every year from 1904, and which was the USA's only major sport event, countless unrecorded 'country-fair' races of only local importance were held during the first decade of the century. They usually took place on bumpy farm tracks or dusty roads and looked more like rodeos than motor sport events. Ingenious salesmen were already putting together racing 'stables' and travelling from town to town with cars and drivers. Mention should be made here of the so-called 'Dirt-Track Races' which were run on temporary circuits about a mile in length. These were sand-and-ash tracks, and, depending on the weather, were either exceedingly dusty or deep in mud so that drivers were either half-blind from one or the other, and the cars suffered from breathing troubles or traction problems. These rugged competitions naturally played an important role in the technical development of the automobile in the United States.

The 'Board Track Races', which ran over wooden tracks of carefully cut planks laid together like parquet flooring, were somewhat more sophisticated. These board tracks were fashionable until the Thirties, and their attraction was twofold: generous prize money was paid and the layout was such that all spectators could see the entire race.

The first race catastrophe

US motor sport was given a tremendous boost when Carl G. Fisher, a businessman from Indianapolis, appeared on the racing scene. On his trips across Europe he had been fascinated by the large crowds of spectators attracted by racing events and the wily businessman deduced that it must be possible to make a substantial profit from the sport and its fans by putting motor racing on the American calendar. Together with three partners he bought a plot of land near Indianapolis and in 1909 he built an oval, 2½ mile racetrack, calling it the Indianapolis Motor Speedway. The track was 15 metres wide along the straight stretches and widened to 18 metres at the apex of the banked bends.

But in the very first race, on 19 August 1909, disaster struck: the track surface, composed of gravel and tarred ballast, began to disintegrate and peppered the drivers as they drove over it. The supervising AAA (American Automobile Association) stopped the race. Undaunted, Carl G. Fisher invested a further 155,000 dollars: the Speedway was re-surfaced with 3,200,000 paving bricks, and the barrier walls reinforced for the safety of the spectators. Official permission was given for the track to be used again on 18 December 1909, but now it proved to be unsuitable for winter use. So again progress was halted. During the following year races were held only in May, June and September. But there was little profit then, especially as the number of spectators was rapidly dropping. The organisers had to discover what was wrong with the Indianapolis Motor Speedway. Were there too many events? Drivers and representatives of the American automobile companies appealed for just one major

racing event per year to be held. This would be promoted with lots of advance publicity on both sides of the Atlantic.

And so the now-classic 'Indianapolis 500' was born. The race was run on 30 May 1911, Memorial Day. Fisher and his partners were sure that a contest over this distance would offer the spectators at least as much entertainment as several shorter races. The large sum of 25,000 dollars was offered as prize money and 40 cars were entered, most of them works teams. The race and the national entry was well publicised. Fisher's plan worked, and some 80,000 spectators flocked through the turnstiles – so many that they overflowed the circuit's five grandstands.

Former dirt-track racer Ray Harroun won the first Indianapolis 500 driving a six-cylinder Marmon Wasp (time: 6:42:8 hours: average speed 74.59 mph). Harroun and his relief driver Cyrus Patschke (who drove only for a few laps) went round the circuit without 'bouncing', a real hazard on this bumpy new brick track. Harroun had gathered experience in the races at this venue during the previous year and established how much the tyres could take from the brick surface. With this in mind he chose to ride alone – the only one to drive without a riding mechanic – so the car was lighter on its tyres. He and Patschke changed tyres only three times throughout the entire 500 miles; many other competitors were forced to make up to a dozen pit stops for new tyres. The major error made by these drivers was that they had reckoned on clocking lap speeds of about 80 mph, which naturally caused a great deal more wear to their tyres than those of the Marmon Wasp, which had been scheduled to lap at a more modest, but almost uninterrupted, 75 mph. Tactical planning triumphed over sheer speed mania. The winner received 14,000 dollars as first prize.

In 1912 the prize money was fixed at 50,000 dollars. That year too an American won the race; Joe Dawson, driving a 4-cylinder National. The number of entries had been limited to 33, and this still applies today. Only between 1931 and 1933 was the 500 run with a larger number.

European triumphs

In the four years following Dawson's success European cars dominated 'the fastest brick-yard in the world'; Jules Goux driving a Peugeot in 1913, Rene Thomas a Delage in 1914, Ralph de Palma in a Mercedes in 1915, and Dario Resta with another Peugeot in 1916.

In 1913, when English motoring journalist William Bradley, then resident in Paris, travelled through Europe as a 'driver buyer' for Indianapolis, telling European drivers about the '500', they, accustomed to relatively modest rewards, could not believe their ears. The prize money mentioned was a king's ransom. For them Indianapolis seemed rather like the Buffalo Bill Show: fairground hubbub and advertising tricks, primitive entertainment for the masses. They felt the individual prowess of the drivers was not going to be given its due recognition. There were other, even more negative reports about Indianapolis: you had to drive round in a circle for six or more consecutive hours on a bone-rattling track which shook your liver into your support corset . . . and at the end of the race you were black and blue. . . . But for 50,000 dollars prize money? Mon Dieu! They reached for their driving gloves. . . .

And so the 'Indy 500' became international. Italian-born US driver Ralph de Palma was fair-minded enough to brief the Europeans on their first trial run. But there were other American drivers too who constantly crowded the newcomers from Europe at practice to discourage them, and the AAA was forced to threaten to ban them. European scepticism was finally abandoned when Jules Goux returned to Europe in 1913 with a cheque for 14,000 dollars in his hand. And Goux told some pretty tales about the inducements: the cheque had already been on view in the pits before the start of the race, filled in apart from the name of the winner. After the tribute to the winner the drivers had been kissed by attractive girls, the public had generally seen much more fun than in Europe, and so on. Top drivers in Europe began to plan for the next 500 mile race at Indianapolis – and then came the First World War.

Wartime use as a runway

During the war years 1917-1918 the Speedway grounds were used by aircraft companies as a repair area and runway for overland flights, and in order to reduce running costs, fodder crops were grown in the centre of the racetrack.

In the first post-war year it was a European marque, a 4.5 litre Peugeot driven by Howdy Wilcox, that once again won the Indianapolis 500. But then things turned gloomy for the European automobile world. These were the Miller and Duesenberg years; from 1922 to 1936 the '500' was captured by one or other of these US-produced cars, both of which are today recognised as examples of the finest automotive engineering of the period. It was not until twenty years later, in 1939, that William Shaw was first across the finishing line in a Boyd Special; hidden behind this obscure name was a 3 litre Maserati 8CTF with an 8 litre in-line engine, making it a partly European win. Spring of 1937 saw the final days of the legendary brick track. First the bends were asphalted, then the straights. All that is left of the original brick track is a row 90 centimetres wide at the starting line, a nostalgic relic.

But unchanged throughout the years is the call to the drivers before they are given the 'off' for the 500 miles battle – the famous Indianapolis command: 'Gentlemen, start your engines!'

AVUS

In June of 1907 Kaiser Wilhelm II set off on a journey into the Taunus Mountains, near Frankfurt, to watch German racing drivers competing against foreign entries for the Kaiserpreiz, the 'Emperor's Prize'. The organisers of the race were counting heavily on the fact that many German firms would not only enter the race but would be among the winners. The course led through the delightful Taunus region from Saalburg via Usingen and Einhaus to Weilburg. From there it went on through Weilmunster, Winden, Riedelback to Esch and then via Glashutten, Konigstein, Oberursel and Homburg back to Saalburg. The course included part of the old Gordon-Bennett route, which had to be covered four times, a distance of just over 118 kilometres, in what were described as 'touring cars of less than 8 litres'.

At the start of the race, on 13 June, the Kaiser and his entourage were confident of a German victory. However when the race was finally won by a foreigner in a foreign car, namely Felice Nazzaro in a Fiat, there were gloomy faces. It was a 'national disgrace' that Wilhelm had to wait until the third car home to see a German vehicle. It was probably the best thing that could have happened, for as a result plans for a 'Motor Traffic and Practice Road' were laid. Heated debates about the location of this road followed; petitions and memoranda piled up on writing desks. Kaiser Wilhelm was told that his uncle, King Edward VII of England, occasionally amused himself at a place called Brooklands, a specially-built racing circuit. Not a bad idea! His Majesty suggested Luneburg Heath, the Eifel, or the Taunus regions as possible locations for a similar track, preferably as near Berlin as possible.

Bureaucracy rears its ugly head

In the elegant club rooms of the Kaiserlicher Automobil-Club at 16 Leipziger Platz in Berlin, interested parties had been negotiating for months. Unlike the comparatively straightforward Brooklands project, which was the result of the private initiative of one individual, in Berlin German bureaucracy intervened. Local authorities, town councils and the automobile industry wrangled over funding. Eventually the town council of Aachen raised the subject of the forest areas in the Eifel, which was at that time a sort of no-man's land, and meant little to anyone except perhaps a few walkers. Aachen was even prepared to finance the entire track. On 23 January 1909 however, the dice fell in favour of the royal preference, Berlin. A company called Automobil-Verkehrs-und-Übungs-Strasse GmbH ('Motor Traffic and Practice Road Ltd'), and therefore known as AVUS, was founded and endowed with a capital of half a million Reichsmarks.

Hugh Locke-King had taken ten months to build Brooklands. In Berlin it took four years before the clearing work, in the Grünewald near the capital, could even be started. The extensive invasion of Berlin's finest woodland area brought forth environmental protectionists who spoke of 'the murder of trees'. Compared with some of the violent reactions of modern times, however, the forest protectors were politely temperate in their protests and stood little chance against majesty and industry – and Wilhelm had given the plan his full backing. Then, just as construction was going apace, the First World War broke out. When the war started much of the track was almost complete, but it was of course abandoned for the duration of hostilities. Later, its location in the greenwoods of Berlin and the clever landscaping of the vicinity (all intersection roads, and the entrances to the local railway, were underground) helped to popularise it when it eventually opened in 1920.

Racing on the Autobahn

In his book *Rennen, Reifen und Rekorde* (Races, Tyres and Records), Richard Kitschigin writes: 'The fact that in those days ... public opinion was already against the testing of sporting performance on public roads was of advantage to the Avus organisation in its appeal to the motor industry, and the automobile clubs. The company itself made all the arrangements that were to turn the Avus not only into an *autobahn* between the west of Berlin and the suburbs to the south-west but also into a permanent race track. Both carriageways, with a height difference of only 15 metres between the highest and the lowest points of the 19.6 km track, were linked by a looping bend to the north with a radius of 244 metres and a tighter bend to the south between the Schlachtensee and the urban railway station Nikolassee. There was seating for approximately 7700 spectators in the eight stands erected in the areas near either bend. The entire track was fenced off and there were 65 booths where spectators could pay their entrance fee. Standing room cost between

10 and 25 marks, and in the stands it ranged from 50 to 200 marks....'

When the German Automobile Exhibition in Berlin was opened on 23 September 1921 a mood of euphoria, or renewed national self-importance, was awakening. This was further fanned by the first races on the Avus which took place during the Berlin Car Week. All the leaders of the German automobile industry were represented at the starting line: they included Brennabor, Fafnir, Falcon, Presto and Selve, plus of course Opel, Benz, Horch, NSU, Mercedes, and the Stinnes companies Aga and Dinos. The winner of this racing premiere was Fritz von Opel, piloting a car he had built himself, at an average speed of 79.8 mph.

The debut of a champion

From 1922 to 1925 the racing at the Avus was sporadic. Raging inflation, political instability, lack of confidence in the German automobile industry, discord among the organisers – all these factors impaired its further upswing. Finally, in 1926, efforts to revive it made by the ONS, the Supreme National Sports Council, paid off and the first German Grand Prix, held on 11 July 1926, was an event in motor racing history. Over 23,000 spectators besieged the Grünewald track and witnessed the birth of a new racing champion: the 25 year old Rudolf Caracciola. He and his racing companion Adolf Rosenberger each drove a 2 litre supercharged Mercedes K-type, both cars re-worked by Ferdinand Porsche. Designed in 1924, they had been improved and used in several races with various degrees of success. The twin-camshaft engine with its four valves per cylinder produced around 170 hp at 7000 rpm, but the cars were notorious for their appalling roadholding. This further enhanced the achievement of 'Caratsch', who dominated the 1926 German Grand Prix, driving at an average speed of 84.9 mph so supremely, despite the rainy weather, that he earned the title of *Regenmeister*, the Rainmaster.

The newly formed Daimler-Benz company had been literally forced into this racing success. As far as the company from Stuttgart was concerned the European Grand Prix in San Sebastian was far more attractive for 'export publicity' than the Berlin event. When Caracciola found out about this decision he drove to Stuttgart to convince the directors that participation in the German Grand Prix at the Avus was more important than an appearance in the Spanish race and, if the company could enter only one of them, then it should be the Avus event. He won the argument, and was allowed to compete at the German circuit, winning the race – and considerable prestige for his country.

NÜRBURGRING

The legendary Juan Manuel Fangio once referred to the 22-kilometre racing circuit through the Eifel forests west of the Rhine in Germany as 'a beautiful green hell'. But the Nürburgring is – even in its recently altered conformation – more than just simply the 'most dangerous, most difficult and most beautiful racing track in the world'. The Eifel region was originally chosen not only for its fascinating and unspoilt scenery but also because it was a depressed area: prosperity was to be restored by the construction of a race-track. The project had been raised by the Rhineland region of the ADAC, the national motor club, and the automobile industry, who were keen to organise grand-scale motor sporting events and try out new types of cars on the course. The idea was encouraged by the chief officer of what was then the Prussian rural district of Adenau, Dr Otto Creutz.

Dr Creutz must have been endowed with unusual powers of persuasion. On 15 April 1925 conversations took place in the Prussian Ministry of Welfare and in the Transport Ministry with the aim of declaring the construction of the course through the Eifel an emergency measure. Everything went smoothly and according to plan. It took barely six months from the day when the surveying commenced on 30 April to the laying of the foundation stone on 27 September. And the vast road-construction project gave work to many who were suffering acute hardship after the runaway inflation that crushed Germany's economy in the early twenties.

Sensitively blended with the landscape

Building work was carried out at the same speed. It took just 21 months of tough dedicated labour to complete the entire track – 17.55 miles of it, with a large loop at the northern end, another at the southern end, plus start and finishing loops – all blending in perfectly with the dark green landscape.

The undulating circuit had its differences in altitude and 88 left- and 85 right-hand bends to thank for its character; a unique and difficult circuit that took a large number of practice laps before one could learn the sequence of bends, some of which ran through thick woods and were totally blind and others which came immediately after a hump – a little characteristic that sometimes meant that a driver should be lining up his car for the next bend while still in mid-air! The start and finish were at a height of 616 metres above sea-level – the highest point of the race-track; the lowest point was Breitscheid at 310 metres. The day after the inauguration of the 'Ring' on 18 June 1927, a starting grid of competi-

tion engines revved up in noisy concert at the foot of old Schloss Nürburg, the ruined castle that dominates the area.

No-one who breathed the air at the 'Ring' on race days – that exciting mixture of smells combining racing fuel, sausages and camp-fires – could ever forget it. The first great races did not just 'take place' – they were celebrated like national festivals, which in fact they were. German racing fans could soon recite the names of the famous sections of the track – names like Hatzenbach (a swerving downhill run), Quiddelbacher Hohe, Metzgesfeld, Wehrseifen, Ex-Muhle, the whirlpool of the banked Karussell, the Höhe Acht, Brunnchen, Schwalbenschwanz and Antoniusbuche. Knowledgeable spectators would crowd into the best viewing places for the race and the even more experienced would camp overnight on their favourite spot, discussing the coming race with almost as much expertise as the drivers. Press coverage from the 'Ring' often read like war reports. One heard of 'fireballs' racing 'like missiles' from the Dottinger Höhe to the Antoniusbuche, of the 'heroism' of Rudolph Caracciola as he grappled with an overheated steering wheel, his hands covered with blood from abrasions and burns. For in those days, the halcyon years of the later thirties, the Nürburgring was indeed a battlefield, the victorious drivers the heroes of the day. Here in the Eifel Mountains the fight for supremacy and prestige in the automotive world was fought.

The inaugural races on 18 and 19 June 1927, watched by 84,200 spectators, were dominated by that same Rudolph Caracciola who was on the way to becoming a racing idol, following his triumph in Germany's first Grand Prix at the Avus a year earlier. He won the race in the up-to-8 litres engine capacity class, in a Mercedes-Benz Type S, a six-cylinder with a 6.8 litre supercharged powerpack of 180 hp (distance: 340.80 kilometres, time: 3:33:21 hours, average speed: 96.5 km/hour). Four weeks later, at the German Grand Prix, the winner was Otto Merz, also driving a Mercedes-Benz S sports car, which at the time was an almost invincible successor to the older hard-to-handle K-type.

The triumphs of the Silver Arrows

Throughout the years of world economic depression the Grand Prix did not take place and it was only in 1934, when the 'Silver Arrows' made by Mercedes-Benz and Auto-Union came on to the scene, that international Grand Prix racing returned to the track. Again the German cars took control of the 'Ring' and Hanz Stuck won the race in an Auto-Union rear-wheel drive car that had been created on the ubiquitous Dr Ferdinand Porsche's drawing board (race distance: 570.25 kms, time: 4:38:19.1 with an average speed 122.93 km/hour). The 'Silver Arrow' series of triumphs was only broken once – a year later, when Tazio Nuvolari won in an Alfa Romeo....

The fact that today the Nürburgring, the 'fastest one-way-street in the world', has been almost completely re-designed is, of course, another story....

HOW THEY STARTED IN THE 1914 FRENCH GRAND PRIX

1	Szisz (Alda)	8:00.0	21	(Caesar)	Non-starter
2	Jörns (Opel)	8:00.0	22	Porporato (Nazzaro)	8:05.00
3	Elskamp (Nagant)	8:00.30	23	Guyot (Delage)	8:05.30
4	Hancock (Vauxhall)	8:00.30	24	Resta (Sunbeam)	8:05.03
5	Boillot (Peugeot)	8:01.0	25	Clarke (Piccard-Pictet)	8:06.00
6	Champoiseau (Schneider)	8:01.00	26	Costantini (Aquila-Italiana)	8:06.00
7	(Caesar)	Non-starter	27	Fagnano (Fiat)	8:06.30
8	Nazzaro (Nazzaro)	8:01.30	28	Lautenschlager (Mercedes)	8:06.30
9	Bablot (Delage)	8:02.00	29	Tabuteau (Alda)	8:07.00
10	Chassagne (Sunbeam)	8:02.00	30	Breckheimer (Opel)	8:07.00
11	Tournier (Piccard-Pictet)	8:02.30	31	Watson (Vauxhall)	8:07.30
12	Beria d'Argentina (Aquila-Italiana)	Non-starter	32	Rigal (Peugeot)	8:07.30
13	Cagno (Fiat)	8:03.00	33	Juvanon (Schneider)	8:08.00
14	Sailer (Mercedes)	8:03.00	34	De Moraes (Nazzaro)	8:08.00
15	Pietro (Alda)	8:03.30	35	Duray (Delage)	8:08.30
16	Erndtmann (Opel)	8:03.30	36	Lee Guinness (Sunbeam)	8:08.30
17	Esser (Nagant)	8:04.00	37	(Aquila Italiana)	Non-starter
18	De Palma (Vauxhall)	8:04.00	38	Scales (Fiat)	8:09.00
19	Goux (Peugeot)	8:04.30	39	Salzer (Mercedes)	8:09.30
20	Gabriel (Schneider)	8:04.30	40	Wagner (Mercedes)	8:09.30
			41	Pilette (Mercedes)	8:10.00

LAUREL WREATHS AND SECONDS

In 1908, while the Coppa Florio race was making north Italian roads temporarily unsafe for normal traffic, a German man of letters, Otto Bierbaum, who was used to singing the praises of life and beauty, was journeying quietly in a 8 hp Adler from Frankfurt to Naples. Following this he wrote the first literary work on driving, and gave it the title *A Sentimental Journey*. According to Bierbaum, this tour was not meant to have anything to do with sport – or it would not have been a sentimental journey: 'For he who is a real lover of the automobile knows nothing of sentimentality . . . only when automobilism ceases to be exclusively a sport will it reveal in the art of travelling what its true destiny is'. He meant, of course, that he thought *all* motoring was an adjunct of sport – and he was right in those early days of the 20th century, when advice given to motorists often ran thus: '. . . the motor is left on the road at the spot nearest the stream, and should you decide to change the rod for the gun, or rejoin your wife, you may drive back to your garden, or possibly to bridge or ping-pong.' And the automobile was described as 'a vehicle rushing at great speed aimlessly across the countryside.'

THE HERKOMER AND PRINCE HENRY EVENTS – THE FIRST RALLIES

The sporting event that American publisher James Gordon-Bennett, owner of the *New York Herald*, devised while sipping an aperitif in Paris in 1899 was intended to end the fierce dispute among racing drivers about which nation built the best and fastest automobiles. Bennett, who had an innate sense of the spectacular, decided to settle this dispute in a proper sportsmanlike manner – and one that might do his newspaper no harm. He announced a competition in which national teams, each with three cars, would compete. Thus were the legendary Gordon-Bennett Races (1900 to 1905) born. The publisher wanted to bring some order into the chaotic competitive events and ambitions of auto-sportsmen and constructors, and he deliberately emphasised the national element. No restrictions were placed on the technology of the cars, so that the automobile manufacturers were able to indulge their wildest fancies in this respect.

Apart from the excitement and the popularity of the Gordon-Bennett Races, they contributed little to the development of the everyday automobiles. Something in the nature of a sporting event for cars that could be seen and bought by the public was needed, both to present an understandable aspect of the new sport and to 'improve the breed' by the severe testing of road vehicles over long distances and under hard driving conditions. It was, of all people, an illustrious figure from the world of fine arts, a painter, who gave his name to the first-ever rally organised on these lines: Sir Hubert von Herkomer. One of the most famous portrait painters of his time, he was a wealthy man, showered with honours; holder of the 'Blue Max', a Chevalier of the French Legion of Honour, and knighted by Queen Victoria. He was particularly fascinated by the shapes and forms of the new materials and by the artistic possibilities of the automotive world – he regarded the automobile as an aesthetic as well as a mechanical phenomenon.

The Herkomer Trials

As a member of the Bavarian Automobile Club, von Herkomer developed, in conjunction with the club's President, Professor Pohlmann, a plan for a 'reliability run' for touring cars. The Herkomer Trials were the first serious competitions in which designers and constructors were invited to enter touring cars suitable for everyday use. The first event was to take place in 1905, and it was intended to organise two further events in the two following years.

The invitation stated, among other things: 'All types of motor vehicles are permitted as long as they are for touring purposes. Every car must have at least four comfortable seats with backrests, an engine bonnet, mudguards for both front and rear wheels, as well as three lanterns, one of which must be mounted at the rear. Each competing car must also have at least two braking devices, a reverse drive mechanism, a safety device for motoring on hills and mountains, a horn, and an exhaust silencer. The external facilities of the car should correspond to the requirements of touring, for which purpose all shapes of cars (both open and closed) are permissible. No restrictions are placed on the weight or the horsepower.' The Herkomer event, forerunner of all rallies, was clearly designed to encourage drivers to take their road conduct seriously. The first meeting was to prove an excellent way to popularise the automobile and to present it as a developed and practicable means of transportation to the broad mass of the moneyed public. The trial was run through the length and breadth of the Kaiser's kingdom, bringing the automobile to the citizen, so that he could easily become accustomed at first hand to the new apparition.

A portrait in oils for the winner

Munich was chosen as the start and finish of the first Herkomer event. The organisers had sub-divided the reliability rally into three parts. On the first day there was an 'exhibition and evaluation of comfort, elegance and beauty'; speed trials took place on the second day – the first a hill-climb over 7 km to the Kesselberg, and then a 6000 metre flat race in the Forstenrieder Park. The third part, a 582-mile touring run, led in three stages from Munich, via Baden-Baden and Nuremberg, back to the starting point. Every car carried an umpire from the Automobile Club, whose task it was to ensure that the regulations were observed.

There were 102 entrants for this first-ever rally, including many foreign entries. Prince Heinrich of Prussia took the wheel of a 40 hp Benz and the entry was a mix of private and works' competitors. Makers used this stiff, practical competition to test their tourers, and they also hoped to obtain considerable publicity, particularly if they obtained a high placing in the overall classification. Sixtynine vehicles arrived in Munich at the end of the threeday run, twenty-six of which had not collected any penalty points, the winner being one Edgar Ladenburg, driving a 40 hp Mercedes. The organisers showered a cornucopia of prizes on the victor, and Herkomer painted a portrait of the winner in oils.

For the second Herkomer event in June 1906, the already strict conditions were further tightened. The event was held in seven stages over a total distance of 1023 miles, starting in Frankfurt. One hundred and fifty-five cars completed the journey via Munich, Linz, Vienna, Klagenfurt and Innsbruck back to the Bavarian capital, where the event ended. The hill trials took place on the Semmering, the speed competition was held in the Forstenrieder Park, and in the last stage the notoriously high and steep Zirler Berg between Innsbruck and Munich had to be conquered. The second Herkomer event was won by a 20 hp Horch.

The entry list for the Herkomer events illustrates the pioneering aspect of the times; several manufacturers – not their employed drivers – drove their own cars: G. Schulz, Paul Beckmann, August Horch, Fritz, Wilhelm and Heinrich Opel, Bernhard Stoewer, Henri Jeannin (Argus), Dr Alfred Sternberg (Protos), and Percy P. Pierce from the USA.

In the third Herkomer Trial in 1907, over a hundred and sixty vehicles started from Dresden, with a 700-mile run in front of them. The overall classification was won for the second time by Edgar Ladenburg since his driver, Fritz Erle in a Benz, led the points table at the end. The so-called Trial itself was something of a fiasco, with a number of accidents and, as one newspaper said of the original intention that the event should be for touring cars: '. . . "Tour" appears to be something of a misnomer. It seems to have resolved itself in a race of the most deadly order.' It was the last of the Herkomer Trials.

Prince Heinrich takes a bow

However, the three Herkomer events had set international standards governing the manner in which practical reliability trials should be held, and Prince Heinrich of Prussia continued the tradition of the Herkomer events with a 'tour' of his own name. Prince Heinrich (Henry) was the brother of the German Kaiser; and with the progressive development of the automobile he became one of the first representatives of the European ruling houses who became actively interested in the new means of transportation. He had acquired his first automobile in 1902 (an American steam car) and when he changed to gasolene-driven vehicles, he had decided from the beginning on the Benz marque, to which he remained true.

The rules of the Prince Henry Tours were similar to those of the Herkomer Trials. The first paragraph stated unequivocally; 'The Prince Heinrich event is an international reliability trial and not a race'. The engine bore and stroke were restricted although four and six-cylinder engines were now permitted. The regulations specified four-seater tourers. One hundred and forty-four drivers entered for the event for whom His Highness had prepared a 1368-mile route which had to be covered in various sections through central and northern Germany. An additional speed trial was held at Itzehoe, and a hill trial at Bacharach, on the banks of the Rhine. Fritz Erle, an old hand, who had already won the third Herkomer event, won in a Benz.

The critics reply

Not everyone was happy at the outcome of this first Prince Henry Tour. Already critical voices were raised, complaining that the competition had not allowed the same conditions for all entrants: in the opinion of a specialist journal: 'This first event . . . produced a certain disquiet among some participants due to the fact that the first places were won by cars whose victory was considered virtually inevitable beforehand. These were cars that did not infringe the conditions, but whose designers and constructors had utilised the latitude of the regulations with great skill so that in fact "special" cars, instead of the normal (showroom) tourers were entered. Since these were also generally in the hands of drivers experienced in other automobile events, the majority of the remaining drivers felt disadvantaged'.

The following year an attempt was made to meet these objections by awarding three bonus points to less-experienced drivers. The route led through national frontiers, through the High Tatra to Budapest, Bratislava, Vienna, Linz and Innsbruck. This time the winner was Wilhelm Opel at the wheel of a car of his own marque.

The third Prince Henry event, held in 1910, was a triumph for the Austro-Daimler marque and its designer the ubiquitous Dr Ferdinand Porsche, who drove the car to first place in the overall classification. He had designed a tourer specifically for this competition, a sleek vehicle whose 5.7 litre, 4-cylinder overhead camshaft engine produced 86 hp. This last competition sponsored by the Prussian prince was a tough 1200 miles held in three stages from Berlin via Braunschweig, Kassel, Nuremberg, Strasbourg, and Metz to Bad Homburg. Of 119 cars that started, 86 managed to reach the finishing flag.

The 1911 rally had more the character of a non-competitive promenade. It was an 'amicable social run on the occasion of the coronation of King George V of Great Britain', said the reports. From Bremerhaven the cars were shipped to Southampton and reached London after a round-trip through England and Scotland, a run that was virtually ignored by the populace and press. However, Sir Hubert Herkomer's and Prince Heinrich's reliability trials made automotive history. Not only were they the sponsors of the first properly organised rallies in the world, but with remarkable farsightedness they also drew up regulations which inspired designers and constructors of the old world to produce a new, practical touring vehicle, namely the 'Prince Henry Type' automobile, whose structural features were later adopted by many international automobile manufacturers. This new shape, with its cowl, smooth sides and lower profile, was imitated throughout the world, eventually to become the first true sports car design.

Prince Heinrich's objective, of encouraging automobile constructors to adopt and follow certain logical principles, had hit the nail on the head. The Kaiser's brother was undoubtedly one of the most important influences in the history of the automobile by laying the foundation of the framework and guidelines for his reliability trials.

Opportunity for self-expression

Manufacturers quickly realised that a golden opportunity had been presented to them by His Prussian Highness. Some of the products that had been entered under the description 'tourers' by the firms in the competition were wolves in sheep's clothing – in reality thinly-disguised racing cars. Their engines had been specially designed for the speed-trial sections of the events, since this was where the decisive points could be picked up. A reporter who had observed the acceptance and scrutineering of the cars in the 1909 Tour recorded his impressions thus: 'Normal tourers were present in very small number, and racers predominated'. In that year, for example, Fritz Poge's Mercedes had been disqualified because the exhaust mounted in the engine hood was unallowable. This was altered under protest. The Horch cars, too, were criticised, because their suspension had been lowered.

After the disputes and arguments of 1909, the manufacturers resolved to put their house in order and observe the entry regulations strictly. In the meantime, they discovered that it was beneficial to design vehicles with some sort of an aerodynamic shape (although the word was not yet in the dictionary) and they had also given a great deal of thought to developing a design pleasing to the eye, which led a commentator to write in 1910: 'One saw a number of extremely interesting and pleasant bodywork designs and – what deserves to be particularly emphasised – in many cases also extremely elegant designs. Typical of these are the Mercedes cars, with their large, wedge-shaped radiator surfaces, the conically shaped engine cowlings that transformed smoothly and continuously into the bodywork ... one of the most interesting shapes was Brenabor, which generated quite a stir and a certain amount of puzzlement. The boat-shaped bodywork tapers, so that the main parts offer practically no air resistance. The Dixi vehicle was the complete opposite, whose somewhat concaved sides were emphasised as a special feature'.

European automobile manufacturers had learnt several significant lessons from the Prince Heinrich events, and were determined to strike out in new directions.

THE AMAZING PEKING TO PARIS RACE 1907

Although it is true to say that the automobile was invented on the right bank of the Rhine (i.e. Germany), the cradle of automobile racing must be sought on its left bank, in France. French newspapers in particular were among the proponents of this form of sport. Newspaper proprietors were always looking for something new, and *Le Matin* was no exception. Searching for a publicity-generating enterprise, the editor hit on the bold idea of an automobile race from Peking to Paris. *Le Matin* announced it for 1907. More a long-distance all-in rally than a race in the strict sense of the word, said *Le Matin*: 'there are no formalities that have to be observed, or regulations that could act as a hindrance. All that is involved is driving from Peking in an automobile and arriving in Paris'. First if possible, of course. However, the newspaper recommended the participants to travel together in convoy in order to provide mutual assistance should any danger arise.

Knowledge of the road conditions (if any) in China and Russia in those days was nil, and none of the participants knew what hazards to expect. Who were the men who risked taking part in such a race? First, there was the well-known racing driver, Auguste Pons, who had chosen a vehicle that would have been better suited to emptying letter boxes in Paris than attempting a journey of over 9000 miles: a Contal three-wheeled carriage which was, in effect, a motorcycle with a box arranged over the two front wheels. The De Dion-Bouton company of France optimistically thought its products, too, stood a good chance, and a couple of its 2-cylinder 10 hp cars were despatched to China with works drivers Cormier and Collignon. A Spyker from the Netherlands, driven by the Frenchman Godard, was also considered to be in with a chance. Italian Count Scipione Borghese took his Itala; he not only had accumulated a great deal of earlier experience as an expedition leader, but happily was rich enough to establish staging posts along the route.

A further twenty applications were in fact received, but in the period between application and the start of the race many entrants clearly lost their nerve – or did not have the required entry fee of 2000 Francs. The competing cars were shipped to the Chinese coast and were then transported by train to Peking. The Chinese did not appear to be at all enthusiastic about the affair. In the end, it was more the desire to be rid of these modern 'fiery carriages', which would undoubtedly have aroused the anger of the spirits if they had been allowed to stay, that induced oriental officialdom to prepare the necessary paperwork for the outward journey. In Peking itself the cars were only allowed to be moved harnessed to teams of mules.

Trails and Trials

After completion of the formalities, nothing more than the terrain and the weather stood in the way of the start, and the five vehicles set off on the morning of 10 June 1907 on their journey into the unknown. Even after the first stage to Nankau – a distance of only 60 km – the cars were no longer in visual contact. Borghese in his Itala reached the place without too much difficulty; the Contal three-wheeler also arrived, but by train! Pons, predictably, was forced to retire shortly after leaving Peking; he returned to the city and had his car sent back to the start-line. The Frenchman however insisted on continuing the race from Nankau, where the other three competitors were still struggling somewhere in the countryside. One week after the start the competitors were reunited for the first time at the town of Kalgan, the gateway to Mongolia. How the intrepid Pons had made it in his three-wheeler remains a mystery. . . .

We are indebted to Italian journalist Luigi Barzini, who was travelling in Count Borghese's car, for the most detailed report of the journey. From him we learn that the Count had hired a team of coolies who accompanied the car as far as Kalgan. Superfluous bits of bodywork had been dismantled in Peking and sent, together with all the baggage that was not absolutely necessary, to Kalgan by train. The reason for this strange decision was that the coolies could not carry the Itala *plus* its bodywork! In fact human muscle-power played a far greater role than one would normally expect in a more rational automobile

race. Barzini reports on one of the first days of the race:

'We had covered 65 km, *20 of them with the engine*, since early morning', he writes blandly, as if this were the most natural way of touring abroad. The book subsequently published by Barzini has numerous photographs that clearly demonstrate how without human and animal haulage assistance the Itala would certainly not have reached Kalgan. Here, the bodywork was once more reunited with the chassis.

After a short journey the cars reached the Mongolian border and entered a wide desolate plain, where the drivers hoped that they could make quicker progress. The following night the competitors were once more together, before they set off at 3 am the following morning on the onward journey, led by the Contal three-wheeler. A 120-mile stretch had been set as the target for the day, a telegraph line through the steppe serving as a pathfinder. The Itala, which set off at 5 am, soon caught up with the other cars and waited for them in the evening in the agreed place. They later heard that Pons' car had been irreparably damaged, forcing him to return once again to Peking by train, this time to withdraw from the competition.

Soon the competitors decided that they should no longer travel together. Count Borghese in his Itala was way out in front, and naturally wished to consolidate his lead, while the French teams considered it better policy to stick together. Godard and his companion du Taillis found themselves stranded in their Dutch Spyker without gas in the Gobi Desert, and nearly died of thirst before help came. Their run of bad luck continued when their magneto ignition failed, and they were forced to transport their car by the Trans-Siberian Railway to Tomsk, where they had it repaired by the obliging local Polytechnic Institute technicians. They returned 500 miles with their car on a train to rejoin the route, and took up the race again where they had been forced to interrupt it. After determined day and night driving they finally caught up with the two De Dion teams in Kazan on 8 August, a journey of some 3000 miles, and some 14 days after starting on a section that had taken the De Dions 32 days to cover.

Through Siberia on railway ties

Once the difficulties in China had been overcome, the Prince was able to make the most of the greater engine power of his 50 hp car in the run through Mongolia and Russia. Sometimes he took to the Trans-Siberian Railway, where the teeth-rattling journey over the wooden ties at a steady 10 mph said much for the endurance of the travellers. On 20 July 1907 the Itala and crew crossed from Asia into Europe, having covered a distance of around

4000 miles. The Prince reached Moscow via Kazan and Nizhny-Novgorod (now Gorki), and was enthusiastically received by a large band of 'automobilistes' in their vehicles at the city boundary. Here he decided to drive directly on to St Petersburg (Leningrad), a further 440 miles on the route.

The Borghese Itala finally crossed over into German territory in Eastern Prussia. Berlin fêted the team in the appropriate manner, though they were anxious to push on to Paris, and the stop-over was restricted to just one night. Borghese reached the French capital on 10 August 1907, exactly two months after setting off from Peking.

The surviving three cars arrived in Paris on 30 August and they too were royally fêted. There was no official winner in this race; to reach the finish was sufficient. The incredibly gruelling Peking-Paris journey, one that has scarcely been rivalled by any comparable event in more recent times, is now a part of the colourful tapestry of automobile history.

In 1982 an event in memory of the Peking-Paris race was proposed, and although one can confidently assume that road conditions have improved a little during the interval, politics have not and a journey over some sections was not approved. How did Barzini describe the situation in his book? 'In the event, the Russian authorities behaved with unforgettable politeness, graciousness and readiness to help'. But then, he was writing in 1907, of course.

AROUND THE WORLD – ALMOST – IN 24 WEEKS

Early in the morning of 12 February 1908 Leutnant Hans Koeppen, with his co-drivers Hans Knape and Ernst Maass, drove in his Protos up to the front of the *New York Times* building to enter officially for the start of the New York-Paris long-distance race. Once again this event was the brainchild of the French newspaper *Le Matin*, which had organised what can only be described as the masochistic long-distance race from Peking to Paris the year before. This time the *New York Times* co-sponsored the trans-world safari.

A crowd of 250,000 packed Times Square. Melting snow made deep slippery ruts in the road and the air was fogged with condensation from both human and motor-exhaust sources. The cars, loaded with shovels, ropes, chains, furs, emergency kits and pickaxes, warmed-up in the starting enclosure.

The contestants included, in addition to the German car, an Italian Zust, a Thomas Flyer from the USA, and a De-Dion-Bouton, a Motobloc, as well as a 15 hp single-cylinder Sizaire-Naudin from France. Koeppen's Protos had a 4.5 litre, 4-cylinder engine which delivered 30 hp.

Have a nice day!

At 11.15 a.m. the President of the American Automobile Club, Colgate Heyte, sent the competitors off on their journey with his gold-plated pistol. Koeppen noted in his diary: 'The starting shot sounded, the engines fired, burst into life, and a fantastic cheer broke loose, wishing us well'. The competitors chugged up Broadway in line and out on to the Old Albany Post Road.

The crowd's good wishes were soon dashed for, as little as twenty miles outside New York, winter and mud struck mercilessly. It soon turned out that none of the drivers had even the faintest idea of the actual road conditions in the USA as one by one they got stuck in snow drifts. The little Sizaire-Naudin was out of the race with a broken axle within two hours. The German crew did not let themselves be put out by the adverse conditions. Their expedition equipment had attracted attention even at the start, and experienced members of the New York Automobile Club reckoned they stood a good chance of winning. 'You can see how thorough the Germans have been', they observed, 'they've got hatchets and saws, as well as sleeping bags and tents. And look how everything's packed so neat and tidy'. The trio from Germany was in fact prepared for almost any difficulty. The Berlin-built Protos had to haul nearly 7000 lbs from the east to the west coast of the United States. On board, the car contained, among other things, a built-in vice, army-issue tunics, eskimo suits, rifles, the German flag, six extra petrol tanks and – to provide inspiration – a framed portrait of the Kaiser!

Shortly before Buffalo, the engine of the Protos began to splutter. Knape discovered that the petrol line was frozen – unusual even in winter Germany, they thought, but an examination showed that the fuel contained 25 per cent water. The local gas-vendors had really pulled a fast one on them, and to prevent future breakdowns of this type the petrol was filtered through a suede cloth. Was this sabotage? Did someone want to obtain an advantage for the Thomas Flyer and the home team? This thought must have crossed the minds of the Germans later, when some American farmers demanded outrageous prices for work and labour when the Protos became bogged down far from any town in the mud of the Mid-West.

Near Chicago there were difficulties with the steering, so Koeppen obtained spare parts from the railhead town, and a village blacksmith helped willingly when the steering was damaged once more. Cold and physical exhaustion caused irritations and trivial arguments broke out in the team. Knape and Maass quarrelled with Leutnant Koeppen because he – according to their statements – had wanted all the publicity for himself, whereas in fact it had been they who had done most of the work. . . . So Koeppen hired an American co-driver by the name of O. W. Snyder, whom he described as a 'really competent fellow'.

The first meeting with indigenous Indians was a great disappointment. The redskins did not correspond at all to Koeppen's picture of the brave and proud warriors of his infancy.

The stock of spare tyres was exhausted more quickly than planned. The depot quickly despatched new sets of tyres, but the vagaries of the American customs system delayed delivery. Technical faults and breakdowns of the Protos increased in the Rocky Mountains but emergency repairs were always effected with fine words and not a few dollars in local workshops, although they took up valuable time.

Won – and then lost

The organisers spared the competitors the rigours of Alaska by changing the rules, although the Thomas Flyer was shipped there before the amended rules reached the crew, and had to return to Seattle. The three cars still in the race were now shipped from Seattle to Vladivostok, and there continued their journey to Paris. The American specialist magazine *Motor* sarcastically wrote: 'When one sees how easy the organisers have now made things, you may well ask why these vehicles were not shipped straight from New York to Le Havre'. The writer was a poor forecaster.

Conditions were cruel for the cars in the desolate Siberian countryside. The teams suffered, like Prince Borghese the previous year, on the spring-breaking sleepers of the Trans-Siberian Railway, and not once did they manage to cover more that 12 miles a day. Koeppen had left his co-drivers in America and had welcomed a new team in Vladivostok, chauffeurs Kaspar Neuberger and Robert Fuchs, both of whom had been seconded from the Protos works. The team continued their journey on 22 May 1908. Incidents and breakdowns were a constant problem. A wooden bridge that they had just crossed collapsed behind them. The bearings of the water pump disintegrated. Neuberger contracted malaria in the Siberian town of Omsk and his colleague Fuchs had a severe attack of gastritis. On one occasion the Protos sank axle-deep in heavy mud and was extracted only by the efforts of the Thomas Flyer's crew who hauled it out. The 31-year-old Koeppen provided champagne in thanks for 'a gallant and comradely act', before the Thomas splashed off into the distance.

However, there was little question of throwing in the sponge, for the Thomas Flyer was now in front of them. While the sick drivers struggled on towards Ekaterinenburg, 600 miles away, Koeppen had gone ahead by train to the town to order a desperately-needed new rear axle from Moscow, now within striking distance. At Moscow the car could be inspected and checked by the Protos representative there, as well as providing good food, clean sheets . . . civilisation. During the drive to the Russian capital the Germans came upon the Thomas Flyer in Kazan, out of commission for two days while a broken transmission was being repaired in a workshop. This was Koeppen's big chance. Four days later the Protos reached Moscow; the necessary repairs were carried out overnight, and they set off again towards St Petersburg. The last stretch from the ancient city to Paris was like a Sunday cruise.

From the German border onwards the route of the Protos became a triumphal procession. In Berlin the publishers Ullstein, who had sponsored the Protos, spurred Koeppen and his team to make one last effort to win the laurels for the Fatherland. The whole of Paris was on the streets when the Leutnant arrived at the Seine-Metropole Hotel on 26 July 1908. He had covered more than 13,000 miles in 167 days. Koeppen formally announced his arrival and claimed victory – in the event, mistakenly. The jury awarded first place to the Thomas Flyer, and its crew took the trophy, a giant global representation of the world.

Points and penalties

What had happened? The Protos, damaged beyond local repair, had been shipped from Utah to Seattle, collecting some penalty points – and the Thomas had gained 15 credit points for its side-trip to Alaska before the route had been changed by the organisers.

The Zust reached Paris about six weeks later to a rather muted reception, despite the fact that its crew had triumphed over a series of disasters that would fill another book.

Today modern highways run over the trans-American mud roads pioneered by the 1908 race, but we can still hope that there are many more 'impossible' safaris to be run before the earth we live in is totally encased in six-lane concrete. . . .

THE 1914 FRENCH GRAND PRIX –
A MASTERPIECE OF TEAMWORK

One of the unhappiest men in Lyon on the evening of 4 July 1914 was Monsieur Herriot, Mayor of the famous city at the confluence of the rivers Rhone and Sâone. The Grand Prix de l'Automobile Club de France (ACF) had proved an overwhelming success. The organization had been excellent, and the race, more than seven hours long, had been marred by no fatal accidents. Even the dispersal of the 300,000 spectators had gone smoothly. But the race had been won by the old enemy, Germany....

It was the first time a French Grand Prix had been held this far south. Since the first Grand Prix in 1907, the Automobile Club had always preferred the more northerly venues of Le Mans, Amiens, Dieppe, until a popular movement of motor sports enthusiasts in the Rhône Valley energetically clamoured for a race to be held in that area.

Nominations come in slowly

Lyon was able to offer the organizers an ideal triangular course, 12 kilometres to the south of the city. The start was to be at Les Sept Chemins, where today the D 42 meets the N 86. The route then ran clockwise, past Givors, in a south-westerly direction. At Chateauneuf, the route turned back towards the north, with a fast section some 10 kilometres in length, on which French racing ace Georges Boillot announced that he would be reaching speeds of 170 km/hour (106 mph). The length of the circuit was 23.38 miles, and the race involved 20 laps – a total distance of 467.68 miles.

Closing date for entries was 31 December 1913, but oddly enough many companies were rather slow in nominating their drivers and cars. The only punctual entries were from Opel, Sunbeam, Alda and Nazzaro. Why the delay? Observers suspected that some of the works teams were keen to wait and see what their rivals had come up with in terms of technical innovation, or that manufacturers had not yet completed the development work on their racing cars. There were rumours that Mercedes would be entering five cars, and that Fiat would have a strong presence once again, following their absence of the previous year. It was said that Delage had lost a great deal of time in moving into their new factory, but the famous French marque could still be expected to compete. With nominations coming in only very slowly, organising officials at the ACF became somewhat nervous, the mood changing to euphoric when, on 31 March 1914, the final list of entries comprised 41 cars, including many from the works of leading European manufacturers.

Official practice sessions were scheduled to run on 15 and 17 June, between 2.30 and 5.00 in the afternoon. This information went out at extremely short notice, causing a certain amount of panic, particularly among foreign competitors. The management justified their decision by saying that it would be impossible to close the public roads that formed the course for more than three hours on each practice day. This restriction placed those drivers who had just returned from racing at Indianapolis at a disadvantage – they had to dash from Paris to Lyon if they were to get any practice in at all. Those affected included, for example, *pilotes* Boillot, Goux, Guyot and Duray. Most teams did in fact take part in the official training, but the Vauxhall and Nazzaro teams were among those missing: their drivers had to familiarize themselves with the course on the day of the race itself.

The surface was mainly roadstone; only the bends had been asphalted. A giant car park for 3000 cars had been built at the rear of the 4000-seat grandstand. Pits were provided not only for racing cars themselves, but also for companies Bosch and Whitworth, and tyre manufacturers Dunlop, Continental, Pirelli, Englebert, Fourchet, and other ancilliary manufacturers.

Battle between brakes and acceleration

The safety measures customary for the time were taken: the organizers erected 17 miles of fencing; first-aid stations, equipped with telephones, were erected at intervals along the course; pedestrian bridges were provided over the track at various points, enabling spectators to cross in safety from one side to the other; tons of calcium chloride were strewn on the course to help keep down the dust; and 2500 soldiers and gendarmes were in attendance as race marshalls.

Knowledgeable observers were curious to learn whether the 1914 Grand Prix would witness the 'high-speed crankshaft breakthrough' that journalist H. Massac-Buist was writing about at the time in the British journal *Autocar*. The Isle of Man race that year had seen a Peugeot/Sunbeam 'shamelessly assembled' by constructors Louis Coatalen, from Peugeot and Sunbeam components, its crankshaft capable of 3000 rpm, a veritable sensation at the time. So the high-speed crankshaft was the latest thing at the 1914 Lyon Grand Prix. How could anyone hope, without it, to get the necessary performance from the stipulated 4.5 litre cylinder capacity?

In an eve-of-race report, Massac-Buist wrote of another technical innovation. Under the heading 'Battle between brakes and acceleration', he informed his readers that four companies would be sending racing cars with brakes on all four wheels to the starting line – Peugeot, Delage, Piccard-Pictet and Fiat. This, he declared was the most sensational event of the race. The Mercedes team cars were still conventionally equipped with rear-wheel brakes only. Massac-Buist calculated that the Peugeot's four-wheel brakes would shave a minute a lap off Boillot's times, giving him a decided advantage over competitors without the benefit of front anchors, as the French cars would be able to brake considerably later on each bend. In practice, however, the advantage proved to be two-edged. Boillot reported that yes, he certainly was able to put his foot on the brake between 50 and 60 yards later than Lautenschlager in the Mercedes, but the car's speed was sharply restrained and it accelerated out of the bend more slowly than the fastest of the field, the Mercedes and the Sunbeam. 'If the Sunbeam had been fitted with four wheel brakes too, the outlook for Peugeot and Mercedes would not have been good,' said Boillot, the French favourite.

'General Staff' preparations at Mercedes

Massac-Buist not only recorded technical innovations accurately but also commented impassively on the tactical and strategic exercises of the various racing stables during the preparatory phase. He considered the Mercedes team's plans in particular: 'Enjoying the same disadvantages as the British and other foreigners, getting to work on their drawings later, and noting the rules touching practice and so forth; nevertheless, did the Germans do some grumbling and leave the business to chance at the last moment like the Britishers? Not a bit of it. They said, "We will take a leaf out of the French book and beat them at their own game." The fact that it was equally open to any other manufacturer in any other part of the world to do exactly the same thing did not disturb the Teutonic equanimity in the least degree. They knew that in the game of patience and thoroughness they are the masters of the world. Essentially your Germans are not by any means high among nations as regards brilliancy; but they are right on top in the matter of taking pains to do everything thoroughly, with the most infinite expenditure of patience.

'Some three months before the race, there arrived on the course seven hefty-engined cars, nominally of the touring type and capable of something like 140 km/hour (87 mph), together with seven drivers and as many mechanics. At five o'clock each morning a whistle was blown. The drivers leapt from their beds and came down to find the cars ready, their mechanics being practically at the salute. From that hour until eleven o'clock they hunted round the course on those cars. There followed an interval for lunch and rest until two o'clock, at which hour the road was again taken until seven o'clock, then dinner and to bed at an early hour. This went on for a fortnight. I will leave you to calculate the thousands of miles each of those seven German drivers did at racing speed over the 23⅓ miles course.'

Massac-Buist concludes: 'Then the team went back to the Fatherland, where the race cars were ready awaiting them. There were embodied in them all manner of points, the desirability of which had been learned in the course of practice. Therefore, after an interval they came back to France with the racers, and found them a thought too long for the corners. So they went back and rebuilt them with shorter wheelbases and other features, for these people meant winning, and the work they put in deserved to be crowned with success.

'Like Peugeot, they worked up to the last moment. The German cars were being constantly driven across the frontier in the days immediately preceding the race, and a little point altered here and there. The drivers knew the course so well that, far from clamouring for more than four official days to practise it, they scarcely needed to use it on those occasions.'

Racing cars aren't horses

Just as the 'German Generalship' had impressed this reporter, so it irritated him that the French should celebrate their Bastille Day Grand Prix with such gay abandon: 'Some of the French peasants, the worse for the hot weather and the wine of the country, proved particularly objectionable when they saw foreign cars practising, and insisted on standing in the middle of the road. The fact that the Britishers always pulled up in these circumstances, at no matter what cost to tyres or brakes, seemed to have spoiled them. But they were soon disillusioned on trying the same trick on one of the Italians. Far from slowing down, the mechanic merely extended his arm so that his hand came in contact with the head of a gesticulating French peasant, who "looped the loop" twice, landing up in a field to collect his senses. The operation was far less dangerous than doing the same manoeuvre in the air in an aeroplane; but the effect of it was to the full as impressive.... Living in Lyon and experiencing the heat, you would doubtless have shared with us a joyous relief at the downpours of rain on the eve of the race, especially as that is always well for reducing to the minimum the element of luck in the matter of tyres.... The experience was quite new to the citizens of this perhaps most provincial of all the large French cities, who in consequence turned out and paraded their native streets with eyes as wide open as though they had never seen them (cars) before. Certainly they were tickled at the unusual spectacle of touring cars from all parts of the Continent with bodies seemingly designed with the sole aim of being inconvenient to their occupants, and all the engines with open exhausts. The vast majority of visitors by road arrive about dinner time, bespattered with mud and dust, spend hours till one or two o'clock at night at the cafes, then drive out to take up their predetermined stations round the course, the idea of sleep being scorned, with the incidental result that while the race was in progress on the morrow I saw hundreds sound asleep as the cars sped by them.'

Chauvinism aroused

Massac-Buist was not easily caught up by Grand Prix fever. England had not as yet played host in this prestigious racing circus invented by the French, and the British were at a loss to understand the partisan aspect of these competitions. For France, having created the Grand Prix, it was almost a national festival. Since the first Grand Prix in Le Mans in 1906, France had realised that a spectacle such as this not only allowed her to publicize her own automobile industry, it was also a relatively harmless way of releasing pent-up national emotions and resentments – and in any case Grand Prix motor racing was a wonderful gladiatorial form of popular entertainment.

The competing cars were inspected on Friday 3 July, at times in weather that looked as though it had a personal grudge against motor sport, although this in fact was beneficial rather than harmful to the conditions of the circuit. Throughout the night, special trains had brought hordes of spectators into Lyon from all parts of France and abroad. From buses to ox-carts, all available means of transport were used to cope with the enormous influx. The number of cars gathered together in Lyon for the Grand Prix was estimated at well over 25,000. At least 10,000 foreigners had come to this great city on the Rhône; some had to spend the night in the streets, as all hotels and guest houses, even the smallest private homes with a bed to spare, were brimming with people. In the surrounding area, even the simplest room cost the daunting sum of between 50 and 100 Francs ($10-$20) and in Lyon itself, food prices had shot up alarmingly, much to the annoyance of local consumers.

Scrutineering proceeded quickly and without incident; it was limited to a weight re-check, all other tests having been performed earlier. The limits of a maximum of 1100 kilograms weight, and 4.5 litre cylinder capacity, were a move in the right direction, after the impractical fuel consumption limit (of 14.2 mpg) of the previous year.

It was questionable until shortly before the race whether the three Nazzaro cars would in fact start, as their pistons had seized-up in practice. In the circumstances, it might have been better if the Turin team had stayed away: none of their cars lasted through the race.

An imposing field of starters

On the morning of 4 July a deep blue sky, typical of the south of France, heralded race-day, and a bright bronze sun rose to beat down on the spectators who streamed out towards every accessible point on the circuit. Every tree, every bank, every hill and house with a view, however distant, of part of the racing circuit, was teeming with people. Some enterprising Americans had even bought themselves places on a temporary stand erected on a three-storey house on a sharp bend in Sept Chemins, offering a unique bird's eye view of one of the most hazardous points. At 8 a.m. the first two competitors were punctually sent out onto the track. The flag-start, using a new system of sending off two participants at a time at intervals of 30 seconds, was completed in ten minutes.

A glance through the starters (page 158) reveals a number of marques that disappeared decades ago. Alda cars, for example, were built by French racing driver Fernand Charron, a motor sport pioneer. In 1897, he switched from racing cycles to cars, driving a Panhard. Four years later, he joined French drivers Giradot and Voigt to found C.G.V., then left to form his own company, building Alda cars; the last was produced in 1922.

In starting positions 3 and 17 were two Nagants, made by a Belgian company that built some extremely robust cars between 1900 and 1928, some of which, even before the First World War, used twin overhead camshafts. In places 6, 20 and 33 we find the name Schneider. Between 1910 and 1931, Theophile Schneider, after leaving the company Rochet Schneider, built light sports cars and solid touring models. The last was sold in 1931. Switzerland was represented by two Piccard-Pictets, whilst the Aquila Italianas, numbers 12 and 26, were designed by Italian engineer G. C. Cappa (later of Fiat and Itala); these were all cars of extremely advanced design for the day, using a great deal of aluminium in their manufacture, and already having frictionless crankshafts.

To quote the report in *Automobil-Welt/Flug-Welt* of 12 July 1914: 'Hardly had the last competitors left the start and disappeared from view than spectator race-fever took over. The first cars could be expected past the pits in about 20 minutes, and all eyes and all fieldglasses were trained on the heights down which the track descended in a series of hairpin bends in full view of the grandstands. This

123

Previous page: 122. 1907 Rolls-Royce Silver Ghost 123. 1928-1935 Rolls-Royce Phantom II.

124

124. 1934 Rolls-Royce Phantom II.

25. 1935 Rolls-Royce 20/25. Following pages: 126. 1935 Delage.

127. 1925-1929 Rolls-Royce Phantom I.

128. 1931 Rolls-Royce Phantom II.

129

129. 1933 Rolls-Royce 20/25

130

130. 1910 and 1914 Rolls-Royce Silver Ghosts. Following pages: 131. 1907 Métallurgique.

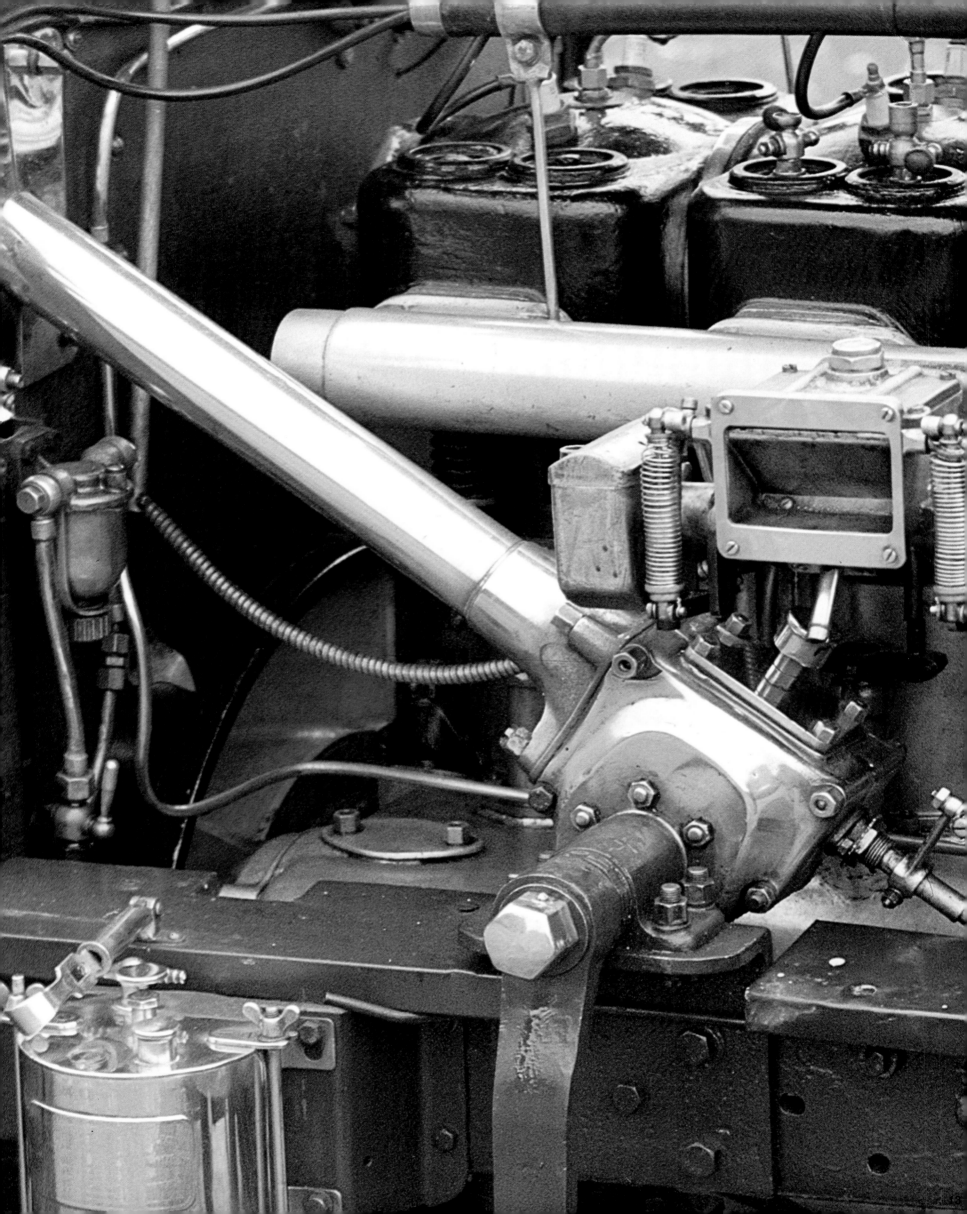

132. 1929 Riley Brooklands 9.

133. 1934 Ford Roadster.

134. 1913 Sunbeam.

135. 1936 Lagonda. Following pages: 136. 1930 Bentley Speed Six.

137. 1914 Humber.

138. 1923 Bentley 'Blue Label'.

39. 1930 M.G.

140. 1929 Bentley 4.5 litre. Following page: 141. 1929 Birkin-Bentley.

excellent visibility greatly increased the tension at the stands, adding to the excitement of the event itself. Hungarian driver Szisz was the first to lap the circuit in his Alda: but the best time was made by Sailer, in a Mercedes. When the German managed to maintain this best time over the next four laps, there was no doubt about it: not only were Mercedes cars extremely steady, which none of their opponents had ever seriously doubted, they were also fast – very fast. Already, at this early stage, the marque eventually to prove victorious had distinguished itself from the rest of the field, in brilliant fashion.'

The placing after the fifth lap – with 116.9 miles covered – gives us the respective positions of the German drivers and of the French favourite, Georges Boillot. 1, Sailer (Mercedes) 1 hr: 43 min: 16 secs. 2, Boillot (Peugeot) 1:46:00. 4, Lautenschlager (Mercedes) 1:46:57. 8, Wagner (Mercedes) 1:50:24. 11, Salzer (Mercedes) 1:51:43. 19, Breckheimer (Opel) 2:01:52. 25, Erndtmann (Opel) 2:14:03. 26, Jörns (Opel) 2:17:34. The chaff then gradually began to be separated from the wheat, a situation described as follows by our reporter at the time: 'In five laps, Sailer had taken 1:43:16 to cover 188.155 kilometres, the Frenchman Boillot in the Peugeot, the next fastest driver, had taken 1:46:00. The French broke into loud rejoicing when, after the fifth lap, Sailer skidded into a field and was forced to retire. To the frenetic applause of his compatriots, Boillot thus took the lead in the thundering, clattering, smoking mass of racing titans flashing past the stands – but still being pursued by rivals hot on his heels who refused to be shaken off. Where the other Mercedes in the race had previously held back cautiously, first Lautenschlager abandoned his reserve, and pulled his car ever closer to the Frenchman, whose lead had increased to 52 seconds in the eighth lap. The second Peugeot favourite, Goux, lay 1 minute 44 seconds behind, with the Mercedes drivers Wagner and Salzer.

The duel begins

'Soon, the exciting spectacle of the cars pulling into the pits area in front of the stands to change their tyres, to fill up with fuel and water, or to make minor repairs, began. Spectators' nerves grew taut at the sight of these perspiring drivers and mechanics being forced to stop when being pursued in a race in which seconds could mean victory or defeat. Assisted only by their riding mechanics, drivers had to carry out every operation with the utmost care since their lives could hang on a screw, a split pin or a hub, and the slightest negligence could mean disaster. A driver's time at the pits was measured by a stop watch; Boillot, for example, changed two pneumatic tyres in a phenomenal 54 seconds, whilst Lautenschlager took 1 minute 4 seconds for the same job. Where the French team was fast, the German team was the more disciplined. The Mercedes changed their tyres once only, and then merely as a precautionary measure. . . .'

After the tenth lap, it was clear that the battle for victory would now be fought out between Peugeot and Mercedes. There were only 23 cars left in the race, speeding around the track at an average of 60-plus. On laps 12, 13 and 14 Boillot managed to retain his lead, and even in the 15th lap the race looked very promising for Peugeot. In the 16th lap, the curtain to the final act was raised. 'The battle of the giants, between Boillot and Lautenschlager, was becoming increasingly exciting, increasingly heated; the impression was that each of the two champions was progressively giving of his very best, his ultimate. What the German gained on the circuit, he lost once again in the pits. The public became ever more impassioned – waving their hats, cheering, roaring, on the crowded stands and bends, exhorting the drivers to superhuman effort. It was clear just how much the French would have liked to see their compatriot win. The way Boillot managed to hold off his rivals, the dazzling driving skill that he demonstrated for such a long period of time, assured him of the fullest and most unreserved recognition from every authority. In every nerve of his being he showed himself to be absolutely first rate. In the 17th lap, he had a 17 second advantage. Eventually it was the 18th lap that cost him the lead in the race that he had defended so long, and until then quite brilliantly held.' So ran the breathless report in *Automobile World*. . . .

The French spectators were unable to conceal their desperate disappointment when Lautenschlager took the lead at a truly fiendish speed, but they conducted themselves with composure, even when the final lap put Boillot completely out of action as his rear axle disintegrated. The two Mercedes drivers Wagner and Salzer moved in front of Goux, leaving him in fourth place. The three victorious Mercedes sped past the stands in the final lap in a 1-2-3 victory, followed some distance behind by the blue Peugeot driven by Goux. The final classification after twenty laps (752.62 km):

1	Lautenschlager (Mercedes)	7:08:18
2	Wagner (Mercedes)	7:09:54
3	Salzer (Mercedes)	7:13:15
4	Goux (Peugeot)	7:14:47
5	Resta (Sunbeam)	7:29:17
6	Esser (Nagant)	7:40:28
7	Rigal (Peugeot)	7:44:28
8	Duray (Delage)	7:15:32
9	Champoiseau (Schneider)	8:06:51
10	Jörns (Opel)	8:17:09

And so the Grand Prix victory went to Mercedes, with a team win that has been repeated very few times in the sport – perhaps the most noteworthy parallel being the 1955 British Grand Prix result, when a later generation of Mercedes Grand Prix cars performed precisely the same miracle, with Moss, Fangio and Kling as victors.

The Daimler company issued a commemorative brochure on the occasion of the 1914 Grand Prix; the writer solemnly and proudly addresses himself to the subject: 'It was a magnificent victory – but not an easy one. The various manufacturers had summoned up all their strength, and had built racing cars that were quite literally "the last word in engineering". The course had a number of steep hill climbs and descents, and many sharp bends (M. Saulin, General Commissioner of the Grand Prix, had dubbed it "the course of the hundred bends", while others described it as like a children's playground slide). The management of the Mercedes works realized that in view of the importance of the Grand Prix, attention had to be paid not only to technical matters, but also to organizational aspects.... It was in fact possible to build five competitive racing cars without great disturbance to the company's other production activities . . . the racing cars all had 4.5 litre 4-cylinder engines with a 93 mm bore and a 165 mm stroke, four valves per cylinder, a cooling water pump, a honeycomb radiator, a Mercedes carburettor, forced lubrication, four speeds, a Cardan shaft and Bosch magneto ignition, plus Rudge wheels, with smooth tyres. Their unladen weight was 900 kilograms (1818 lbs), optimum engine power was at 2800 rpm . . . The Mercedes people were working to a well-conceived plan. Engineer Sailer had assumed the somewhat thankless but all the more important role of bringing the competition to their knees. He immediately set a pace that the field was barely capable of following. He drove the fastest lap of all (69.76 mph) and the others, whether or not they wanted to, were forced to follow suit, even to the extent of taking the risk of running themselves out. It was as if a fever had taken hold of them all. The race stormed onwards. After the end of the fifteenth lap, the Frenchman was still in the number one position, pursued by Lautenschlager, Wagner, Goux and Salzer. The pace seemed to hot up even further. Excitement seemed to open up the throttle. In the twentieth lap, Boillot met his fate: near Givors, he was forced to drop out of the race and leave the field to the others – the Germans, the enemy.'

Did France lose its composure in the face of this 'national disgrace'? Not at all, as *Automobil-Welt/Flug-Welt* reported on 12 July 1914: 'The French press have expressed the utmost admiration for the impressive discipline demonstrated by the winning German team: it is largely to this strict sense of discipline that they attribute its success.

'Mercedes' entire organization both before and during the Grand Prix is said to have been exemplary, right down to the tiniest detail. The drivers knew the course intimately, and even those who built the cars' engines were said to have studied the requirements of the road in brilliant fashion, taking these requirements into account in their design. The same recognition has been given to the tactics, and the single-minded, united approach, adopted by the Mercedes team. And following this line of thought, the French press has rebuked its own industry for having incorrectly estimated the strength of numbers, never having entered five cars from the same manufacturer.'

Another weakness of the French cars was undoubtedly their tyre quality, again criticised by the French press. *Automobile World* comments: 'The French were very impressed by the Mercedes team having changed their tyres without being forced to do so by actual defects, but simply because it was a customary precaution to do so in hard drives such as this. For a hot-blooded Frenchman, it is difficult to imagine such extreme self-discipline. The French are too fond of trusting to luck, to chance, in sports as in other fields. Boillot had two anti-skid tyres fitted at the start of the race because he feared rain: repeated (enforced) tyre changes cost him several vital minutes. Mercedes used smooth tyres from the outset. The clean German victory is acknowledged unreservedly by all.' The French journal *Aero* wrote: 'We have to express our fullest recognition of this success. It was, after all, the sheer superiority of the drivers and cars that won the race. This was where all our fears were directed and those fears have now been realized. But this success, however hard it may be for our *amour propre*, cannot be lessened in any way: the race was won by the best.'

A tragic sequel

On 3 August 1914, Germany declared war on her sporting neighbour. The sad conclusion to this historic motor race, a sporting event that marked the end of an era, is illustrated in the British automotive journal *Autocar* in a later review of the 1914 Grand Prix: 'Boillot had run his last race, and lost it. Four weeks later the drivers of the three Peugeots (Boillot, Goux and Rigal) were in uniform . . . and a little more than a year later Georges Boillot, now an airman, went off to patrol in the east of France and met three German hunters. Prudence suggested retreat, but Boillot was never prudent when his life was in danger. He accepted the unequal battle, and with a bullet in his heart fell into the French lines.'

LE PATRON

Alsace, the region in eastern France that has been buffeted back and forth between Germany and France throughout history, is an Eldorado of epicurean delights, with its famous choucroute braised in white wine and prepared with meat and sausage or pheasant, its warm onion tarts, its rich pâtés, and such delicacies as pike with dumplings, its soft fermented cheeses . . . accompanied by a Chasselas or a Sylvaner wine, fresh and sparkling. . . . It is easy to see why a connoisseur like Ettore Bugatti – even if he had not been drawn there when the Alsace branch of the De Dietrich company bought the design rights of his first car – kept his own later carmaking company in this comparatively outback region of France. Molsheim was Ettore Bugatti's Shangri-La. . . .

ETTORE BUGATTI – CARS FOR THE ELITE

On 1 September 1907 a tall, well-dressed young man entered the works at Gasmotorenfabrik Deutz in Cologne, Germany. 'Whom should I announce?' asked the door-man. 'My name is Bugatti, and I'm the new chief engineer'. Ettore Bugatti, born in Milan on 15 September 1881, was to lead Deutz, pioneer engine designer Nicolaus Otto's old company, to new horizons.

At the age of 17, from an unfinished car at Prinette & Stucchi (the company with whom he was serving an apprenticeship), Bugatti built himself a light competition vehicle in which he competed in the Paris-Bordeaux race on 24 May 1899. Six months later, with a De Dion tricycle, he won the 60-mile Nice-Castellane race. Further wins on three and four wheelers were to follow. In 1901, at the International Motor Show in Milan, he won the French Automobile Club Grand Prix with the first complete car of his own construction. It had a 4-cylinder engine (bore 90 mm, stroke 120 mm) with chain drive, four forward gears and reverse. Series production was thwarted by the death of one of his sponsors. Bugatti bought the design rights and sold them to Baron de Dietrich, owner of the De Dietrich company in Alsace. But once again his good fortune was short-lived; in 1904, the company closed down its works in Alsace.

A brilliant wandering designer

The nomadic Ettore, now 23, was already doing a healthy trade in licences, and built the Hermes racing car for Emil Mathis of Graffenstaden near Strasbourg, then in Germany. Bugatti and Mathis soon split – allegedly after a quarrel – and Ettore founded his own company in Illkirch, only two kilometres away from Graffenstaden. In 1907, a prototype was ready for production. The 4-cylinder car had a power output of about 50 brake horsepower, a bore of 150 mm and stroke of 150 mm, an overhead camshaft, chain drive and four gears. It was with plans of this model in his suitcase that he began his job at Deutz.

The ties between brilliant, eccentric Bugatti and engine construction giant Deutz were short-lived, however, and held out just long enough for two Deutz models to be built. The two parties' understandings of car manufacture were worlds apart – Bugatti wanted to build cars solely for their own sake, while Deutz thought in commercial terms. The basis for co-operation had at first been exceptionally good. The Cologne company, Utermohle, took over construction of the bodywork, new representatives were engaged, a Deutz director travelled to East Prussia and Russia to show the car there, and to bring in orders. The engine and chassis of the Deutz-Bugatti

proved highly successful, and German car enthusiasts were happy to see another German factory capable of reducing the avalanche of cars from the French.

But manufacturers Deutz were not happy. It is clear from a memorandum that the Deutz-Bugatti car made a profit for the salesman but a loss for the works. As Deutz engineer Dr Goldbeck recalls: 'The vertical shaft drive was expensive and difficult to produce, and considerable difficulties were experienced with the transmission – eventually resolved only by buying-in a different transmission system.' This was bound to cause technicians and salesmen to squabble. Bugatti undoubtedly failed to recognise that he and his methods would have to adapt to the production methods of a company experienced in manufacturing. He appears not to have been prepared to do this – as indeed is clear from the records of Gasmotorenfabrik Deutz. Dr Goldbeck wrote: 'In spite of the strongest influence, Bugatti proved neither able nor willing to implement changes to his design to adapt to manufacturing, hence to a necessary reduction in costs. Since he also lacks a feel for business discipline and logic, he is putting both our internal and external business at risk'.

Difficult words to swallow for a young man eager to turn the automotive world inside out. There can be no doubt that this unhappy phase with Deutz in Ettore Bugatti's career became the turning point of his life. Deutz were not ungenerous; they paid the young designer $10,000 compensation for the broken contract, which should have run to 31 August 1912. In 1912, Deutz discontinued car manufacture: they had by then produced just 50 examples.

The car in the cellar

Bugatti's many biographers barely mention their idol's failure at Deutz. Yet in fact here on the Rhine Ettore had pulled off a particularly bold trick. To compensate for his frustration at the difficulties he was experiencing with Deutz cars, in his free time he was building (in the cellar of his house on the works property) the first genuine unadulterated Bugatti car, 'Le Pur Sang' (Thoroughbred), as it was known to its intimates, the first car to bear the Bugatti name. It housed a 4-cylinder, 1.3 litre eight-valve unit (bore 62 mm, stroke 100 mm), a prototype that formed the basis of the later Bugatti 13. Thus the first of the legendary Bugatti racing and sports cars was born, underground and in semi-secrecy.

When Bugatti's old friend, mechanic Ernest Friderich, came home from military service, they dismantled the car in the cellar, dragged the parts into the yard, and there rebuilt it. The little Bugatti 'bath tub' soon became a familiar sight on the streets of Cologne. After his successful crossing of the English Channel in 1909, French aviation pioneer Louis Bleriot visited his friend Bugatti and charged him to start his own company with the prototype as his first stock-in-trade. One thing had become clear to young Bugatti; he would only succeed in running a business that was tailormade for him. At the end of 1909, Ettore Bugatti drove his 'bath tub' to the door of the Strasbourg branch of the Darmstadter Bank, and invited the Manager, de Vizcaya, to take a look at it. The motor-enthusiast banker was impressed. He provided credit and good advice, and found a factory site in Molsheim, 13 miles west of the city.

By the end of January 1910, Bugatti had a full complement of staff and equipment, and production could begin. Le Patron (the boss), as Bugatti soon became known to everybody in the small Alsatian town, avoided, in this early venture, any showy technical innovation. He was still very conscious of the traumatic experiences at Deutz.

Bugatti ignores the competition

How did the market look at the time? Oldsmobile was producing its enormously popular 'Limited', a 6-cylinder 60 hp winner. Spyker from the Netherlands had offered some years back the first car with four wheel drive and a 6-cylinder engine, and were now well established, with a new T-head engine. In 1907, Rolls-Royce's Silver Ghost had arrived on the market, and Chadwick in the USA had built the first supercharged car. In 1908, Henry Ford had launched his Model T, of which he had sold 19,000 in 1909, the same year as Wilhelm Maybach and Count Zeppelin founded the Maybach Company, Isotta Fraschini fitted his cars with four-wheel brakes, and the Blitzen Benz appeared, the most powerful machine to date with a 22 litre engine.

Bugatti historians question whether the genius at Molsheim was in fact aware of what was going on around him in the motoring world. At the 1910 motor show in Paris, Bugatti sold five Type 13s – the entire year's production. His philosophy was not directed towards achieving maximum numbers, nor was he a man to build cars simply to get from A to B as quickly as possible. For Ettore Bugatti, car manufacture was a matter of aesthetics, an art form. In his sphere he ranked himself with his contemporaries, the sculptors Auguste Rodin and Aristide Maillol. In this respect, Ettore was every inch the son of his father, Carlo Bugatti, an eccentric designer and cabinetmaker of high standing and renown, whose principles influenced his son throughout his life, and a fitting brother to Rembrandt Bugatti the sculptor.

The Bugatti legend – car manufacture as an art — at the beginning of the twenties was promoted not least by his tendency to give his engines a classically beautiful, angular, squared-up shape. The followers of cubism regarded Bugatti's engines with fascination. They invited him to Paris – and Ettore needed little persuasion to go. He was lavishly wined and dined, and when asked to speak did not mince words. Le Patron read them a lecture and told them he regarded them as nothing more than mediocre artists. . . .

Any attempt to find an intellectual aspect to Bugatti's allegedly cubist design and to value it in terms of art history must founder when we remember the way in which it was conceived. Bugatti made a virtue out of necessity. His engine design was developed according to Ruskin's principles, demanding from the craftsman only that form of skill which he personally was able to master. He recruited unskilled workers from small farmers and vine growers in the area around Molsheim, and gave them the basic concepts of automotive engineering and construction, then they had to 'get on with it'. It was by this means that the simple, uncomplicated form of the rectangular engine block was born, its smooth straight surfaces being easier to work.

It seems an amazing stroke of luck to most of us that this curious rule led to a design that even today is unsurpassed in its beauty. The second reason for this system of working is to be found in considerations of cost. Bugatti was furious if time or material was wasted: he had given his workers the simplest forms to reproduce, smooth, with no awkward corners, recesses or edges. He couldn't make it easier for them, cladding cast-iron parts with bright polished smooth aluminium.

There are some intriguing stories concerning Bugatti's worker relations. He regularly held consultation sessions with his employees in his office, and after retirement he voluntarily continued paying them a quarter of their final wage – in a time when such benevolence was rare. All this was because he wanted to live and work in an atmosphere where everything was in accord. So it hurt him all the more when in 1936 – incited by the 'Front Populaire' – his workers went on strike, like millions of other Frenchmen. He had believed that it couldn't happen to him, to the universally respected Patron. 'But you are all my family!' He was wrong. Work stopped, red flags were waved, and a sit-down strike crippled production. Ettore was upset, and left Molsheim. He passed over the running of the operation to his 25 year old son Jean, lived for most of the time in Paris, and only occasionally reappeared in the little town in Alsace.

Bugatti created an impressive environment for himself in Molsheim. He kept eight horses and between 30 and 40 pedigree terriers that he had imported from York-shire and for whom a specialist in dog-care was engaged. At the works there was a brass-cleaner whose job it was from morning to night to polish the bright fittings on the heavy oak doors to the workshops, and gangs of sweepers were always to be seen at work with their giant brooms. Bugatti himself was always decked out like a dandy: he dressed in fine fabrics and wore a jaunty brown derby on his patrician head. His shoes were fashioned like gloves, each toe having its own section.

'Molsheim Flair'

We have Bugatti's daughter L'Ebé to thank for an affectionate description of 'Molsheim Flair'. In her book, *The Bugatti Story*, she mentions her father's quirkiness when it came to cleaning-cloths. Ettore, while indulging his mania for cleanliness, meticulously ensured that the quantity of rags was always checked by his bookkeeper, Pracht. Even the authorities had no easy job dealing with him. When one day the electricity bill seemed excessively high – being accompanied, furthermore, by a curt letter from the electricity authority – he announced to the works manager of the power station: 'Come back in a year. Then I'll be able to show you something very interesting'. What was it? Ettore Bugatti had designed himself a small electric generating station to power his plant.

The ministering angel at the Bugatti home in Molsheim was his wife, Barbara, nee Bolzoni. She came from a prominent Milan family, and was on exactly the right mental wavelength to receive and implement the creativity that radiated from Ettore. In the little bar in the house was a cocktail recipe book so that every guest could express his own special wishes. Expensive Persian carpets deadened footfalls on the marble floor. Comfortable chairs were scattered around the lounge. The cellar of the house had been converted to a cinema in which luxuriantly upholstered seats invited one to while away the time and relax. Next to the projection room were seats for the workers who – albeit separated from the Bugatti family by a glass wall – could nonetheless share in the boss's enjoyment of the cinema.

Ettore also tried his hand as an hotelier, offering customers who had visited his works a taste of the Bugatti ambiance in their overnight stay; the number of beds available, however, only became sufficient when Ettore had some henhouses converted into extra bedrooms. They had been built earlier when he conceived the idea of becoming self-sufficient in eggs. They were, of course, designed to the car manufacturer's elitist standards, fully insulated against the heat of summer and the cold of winter. When he later abandoned the egg project and the

henhouses became hotel rooms, they were popular with his guests in view of their exemplary insulation!

Ettore Bugatti's liking for fashion fads left a great impression in America when in 1914 he accompanied his racing-chassis'd Garros (named after aviator Roland Garros, a friend and distinguished prospective purchaser of the car) to the race in Indianapolis. The *Los Angeles Times* wrote in its edition of 10 May that year: 'Bugatti is known throughout the world for his fashion ideas . . . and surprised the whole of New York with the five-centimetre cuffs on his morning coat'. His wealth of ideas is also reflected in the number of patents that he registered: Bugatti historians have come up with approximately one thousand inventions (most of them highly improbable) which include a safety razor, an operating theatre with sterile ventilation, an automatic sailing boat, a machine for taking dogs for walks, a device for setting broken bones. . . .

Although Bugatti had never studied mathematics or engineering, the hurried sketches that he drew on small pieces of notepaper were the outlines for the fascinating touring, sports and racing cars that came out of Molsheim. He had a sixth sense for the 'inner functions' of an engine, and could diagnose faults in a car by placing his hands on its engine. He could almost 'see through' materials and was able in a matter of seconds to visualise technical faults. This gift worked in similar fashion with people. When he first met motor mechanic Ernest Friderich in 1914, he instantly recognized his all-round knowledge as a technician, test and racing driver – and as a loyal companion, through good times and bad. Bugatti without Friderich was almost unimaginable.

Le Patron lived in Molsheim as if in an ivory tower. He showed little interest in what his competitors were doing. In many technical fields Bugatti was conservative: at the beginning of the thirties he was still using outdated cable brakes, and he came relatively late to the supercharger. It was not until the 1100 cc Type 35, the racing car built specially for the 1926 Alsatian Grand Prix, appeared that he used a blown unit. His car bodies became more sophisticated from 1927 onwards, when his son Jean began to handle the cladding design, notably the gigantic Royale and the Type 51.

Change of front

The outbreak of the First World War placed the Italian-born Ettore, who earned his money in Alsace, at that time a territory of the German Reich, in danger. On the day of mobilization, 2 August 1914, he closed his factory and left Molsheim. Daughter L'Ebé reports in her memoirs that the family left behind all its possessions. Madame Bugatti quickly gathered up her savings, around 50,000 marks (about $13,000) and a few items of jewellery. The Bugattis were unable to draw on their bank accounts, which had been frozen. They went first to Milan: Ettore was in such a hurry to catch the last train that his children had no alternative but to put their coats over their nightclothes.

On the move again

In November the Bugattis were off on their travels once more, this time to Paris; and when Italy entered the war, in May 1915, Ettore was called to the aviation department in the French capital. During his Paris years he demonstrated how quickly he was able to adapt to new situations and unfamiliar technical requirements: on instructions from the French Government, he developed an 8-cylinder aero-engine and a 16-cylinder 500 hp unit with a 37 mm gun firing through the propeller. The Americans, too, were interested in the larger of Bugatti's aircraft engines and and took one across the Atlantic for testing in the United States.

The First World War had put a stop to the further development of the range based on the Type 23, itself a version of the Type 13. The *pièce de résistance* of this range was the Bugatti 19, his only car with chain drive, also known, as already mentioned, by the name of 'Garros', in deference to the French air-ace Roland Garros who bought the car in 1912. As Ettore Bugatti's closest friend, he merits a further mention. Garros won the first Grand Prix organized by the French Aeroclub, flown on a triangular course over central France in stormy weather on 17 June 1912. He was also the first pilot who dared to fly across the Mediterranean; on 13 September 1913 he flew from St. Raphael to Bizerta, North Africa, in a Morane Monoplane, unquestionably as daring a venture as Lindbergh's flight over the Atlantic 14 years later. Bugatti sought advice from Roland Garros when he wanted to develop a gun capable of synchronous firing through the propeller of a fighter plane, not having heard that Marc Birkigt had already patented this system. Haunted by a premonition of his death, Garros, back in 1915, had put his house in order and appointed his friend Ettore as his heir. L'Ebé Bugatti recalls how it happened; Garros reportedly said: 'I have 200,000 Francs in the bank. You are helping to win the war in your way, as I am in mine. And I know what difficulties you have. You have a wife and three children, while I am a bachelor, likely to die at the front. Here is my cheque book. All the cheques are already signed. If I should die, withdraw the money'. In October 1918, Garros was killed in action over the Western Front.

For the Indianapolis Grand Prix on 30 May 1914, Ettore built an 'American' version of the 5 litre Type 19. The stroke was lengthened from 160 to 180 mm, and in place of chain-drive shaft transmission was used. The car, driven by Ernest Friderich, developed a fault in the differential and was forced to retire when lying in third position. An example of the rare Type 19 belongs today to Nigel Arnold-Forster, a British enthusiast. He has traced back the history of his showpiece and is convinced that the engine was built in Cologne by Ettore Bugatti back in 1908, having undergone its trial runs in a Deutz chassis. Bugatti, according to Mr Arnold-Forster, had this engine in his baggage when he left Cologne and Deutz in 1909 in the direction of Strasbourg.

The Bugatti 35 – a great design

Bugatti financed his fresh start after World War I primarily by granting licences to companies such as Diatto in Italy, Rabag in Germany and Crossley in England. These were the 'golden twenties' for Bugatti in the truest sense of the term, the years of the Bugatti 35 series. With the supercharged Bugatti 35 B (2.3 litre, 8-cylinder in-line engine, 135 brake horsepower at 5000 rpm) he laid one of the most important milestones in the history of motor car design.

When Ettore delivered the first Type 35s in 1924 (followed by the various model variants), owner-drivers queued up at Molsheim with their cheque books, which was of course Bugatti's intention. He vetted his buyers. Wild test drives on the twisting hill roads of the Vosges served to ascertain whether the aspiring 35 owner had the celebrated 'Bugatti seat', that inefinable feeling for the car – the ability to drive by the seat-of-the-pants. The passion for a Bugatti 35 B undoubtedly had an erotic side to it too; Sigmund Freud would have been delighted to study owners of the car.

The sports successes achieved with cars from the 35 series are almost too numerous to recall. The record stands at 1851 race-wins between 1924 and 1927, but the list may be incomplete. In 1926 alone, his cars won twelve major international races, including the Targo Florio and the Grand Prix de Monaco. With the Type 35s, Le Patron entered the Pantheon of the Automobile Age, not only as the designer of some deliciously sensuous racing cars, but also as one of the most significant trendsetters in the history of automotive design. The 7500 or so cars that Le Patron produced in his life were strictly 'art-for-art's sake' – even when the market for the 12.5 litre Royale (designed as 'the car of kings') failed, he diverted his attentions to railcars designed and manufactured for French Railways, each of which was driven by four Royale engines!

Bugatti's success began to take a downward curve before the Second World War. With the appearance of the 'Silver Arrows' from Mercedes Benz and Auto Union on the racing circuits, his now outdated racing cars became less and less competitive. His son Jean died on 11 August 1939 during a test drive near Molsheim and 57 year old Ettore never recovered from this stroke of fate. From the beginning of the thirties his eldest son had become indispensable as works manager at Molsheim and he had also acquired many of his father's creative powers. Although Jean was unable to overcome the dominating personality of his father and doubtless suffered as a result, in the design field he was a congenial partner. He helped with the twin camshaft 225 hp model 50 – its engine developed from that of the 46 S – then with the blown 2.3 litre 190 hp Type 51, which many consider to be the climax of Bugatti racing design. This model differed from the legendary 35 B only in the angled position of the valves in the cylinder block, and the two overhead camshafts.

Jean's death is surrounded – to the distress of Bugatti admirers – by a number of secret rumours. His death on this test drive is said in reality to have been suicide, the high insurance payable on Jean's demise having served to restore the financially ailing works to health.... But among many Bugatti chroniclers there seems to be a tacit agreement to go no further into these matters.

During the Second World War, Ettore moved his company to Bordeaux, at his own cost, and in Molsheim the Germans built amphibious military trucks. After the end of the war, Bugatti was tried for alleged collaboration with the Nazis. He fought every stage through the courts, and eventually won in 1947. He died in the same year, on 21 August.

The Bugatti cult lives on, producing some fascinating blooms. Activities are centred on two main centres: Prescott Hill Climb venue near Cheltenham, England, and Molsheim, now in France again. Prescott Hill belongs to the Bugatti Owners' Club; nestling in gentle green meadows, between apple trees and broom, this hill course is unquestionably the most idyllic motor sport venue in the world. Here, the members of the club chase up the winding track as if seeking to bring back the Roaring Twenties. And roaring it is, in the truest sense of the word; anyone who hears and experiences the screeching, tearing sound of a Bugatti supercharged car for the first time as a 35 B changes down into second gear at Pardon hairpin bend will remember that cacophony for the rest of his life. No wonder that many Bugatti fans in Prescott Hill stand at the racing track eyes closed recording the inimitable Bugatti noise in stereo on cassette recorders. Said one: 'For me, music has just two great B's – Bach and Bugatti...!'

The Supercharger Te Deum

Once a year, many Bugatti drivers take a rest from their expensive hobby and visit Molsheim. Then the old former mechanics travel in from the surrounding villages of the Vosges, proudly sporting their Bugatti pins in their lapels. Great-grandfathers explain to their grandsons and great-grandsons the overhead camshafts, the suspension or the gear shifting gate of the Bugatti 35. The Bugatti drivers never fail on these occasions to adorn Ettore's grave in nearby Dorlisheim. A giant wreath is lashed to the roof of a car, and some of the Bugatti drivers dress in the fashion of the year in which their cars were built. When the cavalcade, with roaring, brightly polished exhausts, has passed through the little Alsatian villages, after a few minutes' meditation at the grave of the great master, a supercharger 'Te Deum' is played for an immortal car manufacturer.

143

Previous page: 142. Métallurgique 1907. 143. 1929 Sunbeam.

144

144. 1929 De Soto.

145

45. 1930 Invicta.

146

46. 1929 Delage. Following pages: 147. 1929 Duesenberg J Type.

148. 1932 Alvis.

149. 1931 Alfa Romeo 8C 'Monza'.

150

150. 1930 Lagonda.

151

151. 1934 Alfa Romeo 8C 'Monza'. Following pages: 152. 1926 Sunbeam.

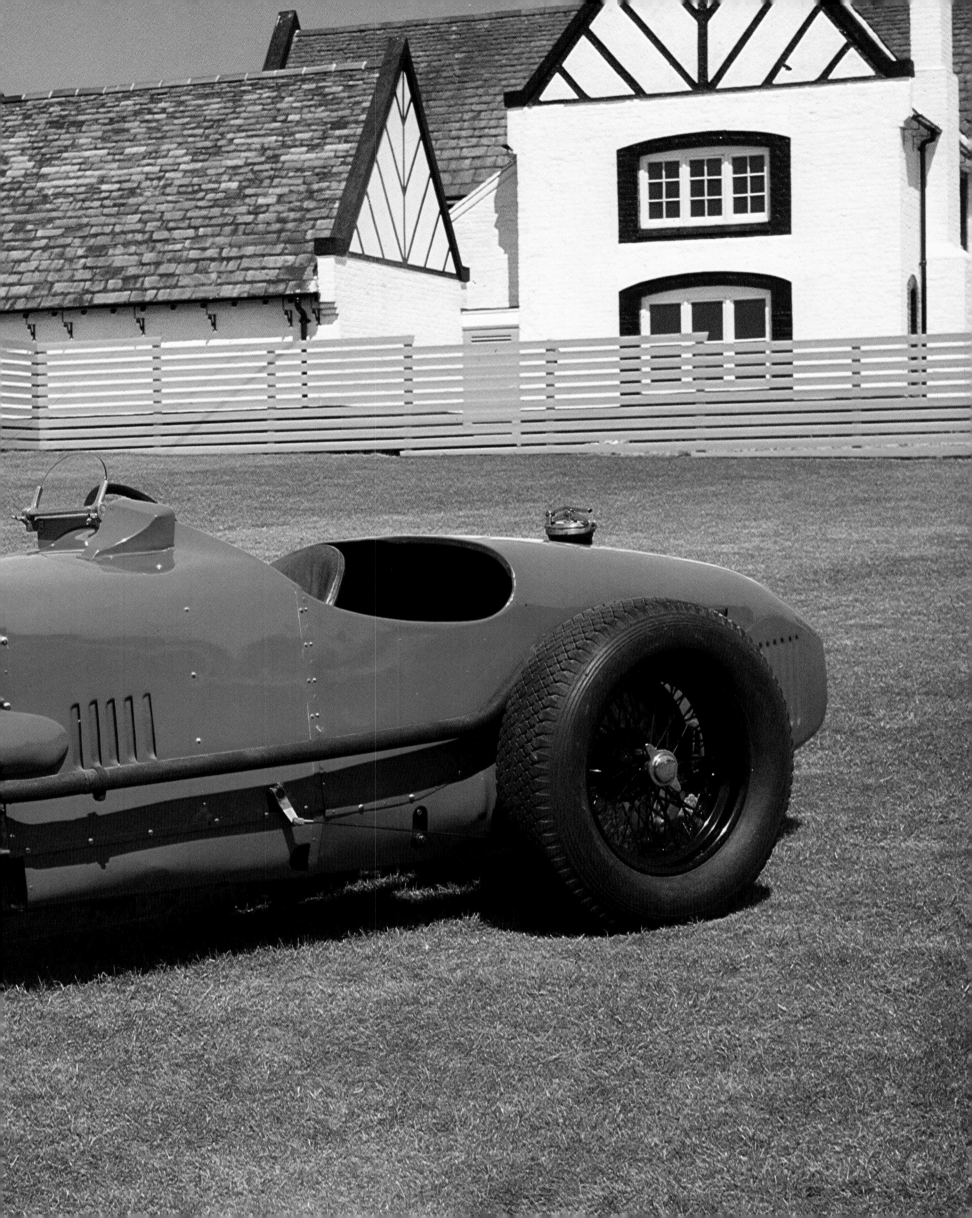

153

153. 1932 Hotchkiss.

154

154. 1919 Hispano Suiza.

55. 1904 C.G.V. Following pages: 156. 1907 Rolls-Royce Silver Ghost.

157. 1910 Grégoire.

158. 1910 Renault.

159. 1911 Panhard-Levassor.

160

160. 1911 Turicum. Following page: 161. 1914 Opel.

FROM AUTOMOTIVE INFANCY TO ADULTHOOD

In 1901, the Mercedes was born. What was going on, in the first year of the new century, to capture men's imagination? Tsar Nicholas II attended the German fleet manoeuvres, Max Planck gave the world his laws of radiation, Wilhelm Röntgen was awarded the Nobel prize for physics, Marconi sent the first messages from Cornwall to Newfoundland by wireless telegraphy, the Lindauer brothers brought a garment called the brassiere onto the market, the vacuum cleaner was invented by an American janitor, and the Montagne Pelée volcano erupted on Martinique with a death toll of 26,000. And the engineers of the Daimler works at Cannstatt in Germany took their latest product to Nice for the gala sports week held there every year. . . .

THE AUTOMOBILE GROWS UP

The automobile grew up remarkably quickly, from being a mere infant in 1885 to what might be described as an 'advanced adolescent' in 1901. The leading adolescent of 1901 was the new 35 hp Mercedes, and it is instructive to compare this car with what went before and what came after, up to, and including, the cars of the nineteen-twenties, which were not dissimilar to the Mercedes, but very different from the cars of the 19th century.

The first car to be built, the invention of Karl Benz of Mannheim in 1885, had only three wheels, designed to avoid the steering problems posed by a front axle, and consequently the obvious place for the engine was at the rear. Strangely enough this first car had one or two 'advanced' features which were not to be in general use until some years later, notably electric ignition and a mechanically-operated inlet valve, this actually being a slide valve designed on steam-engine principles. Later production Benz cars, which had four wheels, reverted to the then-popular though less efficient 'automatic' inlet valve, held closed by a weak spring and opened by the suction from the downgoing piston on the inlet stroke, although Benz cars continued to have electric ignition when many of their rivals had archaic 'hot tube' ignition, whereby a high melting-point tube, usually of platinum, was inserted in the valve chest and heated at its other end by a blowlamp, so that it ignited the mixture on the compression stroke.

To modern eyes the bicycle-inspired tubular chassis and wire wheels of the first Benz car look more advanced than the first car built by the Wurttemberger Gottlieb Daimler at Cannstatt in 1886, for Daimler had simply bought a horse-drawn carriage, removed the shafts, and adapted it to take an engine. But Daimler was very much an 'engine man', and it was he who had developed hot tube ignition.

Both the Benz and the Daimler cars had a differential, traditionally first fitted to a steam carriage by Pecqueur in 1828, but where Benz's used gears, Daimler's was a cruder affair of leather discs which were designed to slip when one rear wheel turned faster than the other on a corner.

Benz's engine was a horizontal single-cylinder unit with the cylinder-head facing forwards under the seat. It was of large capacity, 1691 cc, but at ¾ hp did not have enough power to get the car away from rest, when some human encouragement in the form of a push was required. Transmission was by a single belt to a countershaft (incorporating the differential) and then to each rear wheel by chain, so there was only a single speed, and the use of a belt obviated the need for a clutch. Later four-wheel production Benz cars had two belts and two speeds.

To come to our 1901 car, which had close links with earlier Daimler cars but not with Benz, who was not nearly so progressive and had improved little on his original design over the years. The Mercedes, named after the daughter of Emil Jellinek, the man who financed it, was produced by the Daimler company and designed by Wilhelm Maybach, who took over the running of the firm on Gottlieb's death in 1900. Several features on the Mercedes had been pioneered by Paul Daimler, Gottlieb's son, on a car he designed in 1899, but the overall conception of the car, which was longer, lighter, lower and more powerful than Paul Daimler's design, was Maybach's. All future cars produced by the German Daimler factory were called Mercedes, although their commercial vehicles were still called Daimlers.

Forefather of the modern car

Certain of the features of the car had been born in France, such as the position of the engine at the front of the chassis. Emile Levassor had experimented by placing a Daimler engine in the rear, centre and front of a Panhard-Levassor chassis, and in 1891 had settled on the latter position, thus anticipating the chassis layout which was to be followed even up to the present day by the majority of manufacturers. Behind the engine were exposed sliding change-speed gears (not enclosed until the 1895 Panhard appeared), of a type which had first been seen on a rear-engined Daimler of 1889. Panhards had a cone clutch between the V-twin engine and gearbox, and the drive was carried by a shaft from the 3-speed gearbox to a countershaft fitted with a differential, and then by side chains to the rear wheels.

The first advanced feature of the Mercedes was its 'honeycomb' radiator at the front, which had been pioneered by Paul Daimler. Apart from its good looks, it also cooled the water efficiently. Previous water-cooled cars had either had no radiator, like the Benz, which consequently used gallons of water, or a long tube bent backwards and forwards into a stack and fitted with fins situated at the front of the car. Below the radiator was a starting handle, rather a difference from the early Benz cars, which had been started by grasping the rim of the flywheel of the rear engine and pulling.

The chassis of the Mercedes was made of pressed steel rather than of armoured wood as featured on earlier cars. The 'artillery' wheels had wooden spokes, but were shod with pneumatic tyres. In the past decade most cars had used iron-shod wheels or solid rubber tyres, although as far back as 1895 Michelin had entered a Peugeot car in the

Paris-Bordeaux race fitted with pneumatics. From the turn of the century pneumatic tyres were in general use, but they were expensive and punctures were frequent; on a fast car air-filled tyres were essential, and the Mercedes *was* fast, capable of over 50 mph.

Problems with punctures

Wheels were non-detachable, so the tyres had to be removed and punctures repaired with the wheel still on the car. A detachable rim was then invented, one which could be bolted on to the fixed wheel with a new inflated tyre and tube attached to it, and this assisted Szisz's win in the Renault in the 1906 French GP. In fact, in the days of fixed road wheels, light cars often beat heavy faster cars in early town-to-town races, as they had less tyre troubles and thus fewer delays.

The suspension of the Mercedes consisted of semi-elliptic leaf springs all round, although most other early cars had three-quarter elliptic springs. There were no dampers although Mors had pioneered these in 1899 with a friction-type shock absorber. The most famous friction shock absorber, the British Hartford, dates from 1906, and the pioneering French hydraulic, the Houdaille, from 1908, though Mors fitted a dash-pot type in 1902 and Renault invented a hydraulic lever arm type in 1905. Semi-elliptic springing all-round became standard on most cars until independent front suspension began to be fitted in the nineteen-thirties, though leaf springs could also be fitted transversely and could be fully elliptic, three quarter or quarter elliptic or, in rarer cases, cantilever.

Independent front suspension by sliding pillars and a transverse leaf spring first appeared on a French Decauville voiturette in 1899, and Adler (with Edmund Rumpler as their designer) and Sizaire-Naudin were in the field with a similar system a few years later. The latter firm raced successfully in light car events, commencing with the 1906 Coupe des Voiturettes race at Fambouillet when Georges Sizaire himself was the winning driver in a 1357 cc single-cylinder car at 58 kph over 4 hours. Lancia, in Italy, were the first large production manufacturers using i.f.s. with sliding pillars and coil springs in their Lambda model from 1921, although Morgan, in England, used a similar system on their 3-wheelers from 1910.

Front-wheel-drive

Independent front suspension most usually went with front-wheel-drive and the Latil company of Marseilles seem to have been first in the field with f.w.d. at the turn of the century. Walter Christie in the USA built several front-drive cars between 1904 and 1910, with a transverse engine and sliding pillar i.f.s., including a 7.7 litre Grand Prix car in 1906 and an even bigger car of about 19.5 litres which he drove in the 1907 French GP at Dieppe. Similar i.f.s. was used on J. A. Gregoire's French Tracta cars from 1926. Production British f.w.d. Alvis cars from 1928 to 1930 used transverse quarter elliptic springs for their front independent suspension, and they also had full independent suspension at the rear, although independent rear suspension was unusual on f.w.d. cars and rarer on rear wheel drive cars in the years before 1931. The German Edmund Rumpler used swing axles at the rear on his small production rear-engined streamlined 'Tropfenwagen' (Teardrop car) in the early twenties, having patented his idea in 1915. Later he built a front wheel drive swing axle Rumpler.

The 1901 Mercedes brakes, conventional enough for the period, were controlled by a hand lever on the rear wheel sprockets, and on the transmission by pedal – in fact there were two transmission brakes operated by separate pedals.

Braking, changing and breathing

Experiments were made at this time by Mercedes with pneumatically operated front wheel brakes, but front wheel brakes did not come into general use until the twenties, when transmission brakes were gradually phased out. Metal-to-metal brakes with steel shoes lined with cast iron were still in use in the early twenties before asbestos compound linings became universal, and front brakes on steered wheels were mistrusted, as is evidenced by the fact that on the Austin Seven introduced in 1922 the pedal worked the rear brakes and the handbrake the front ones, though we know now that the front brakes are the most effective if balanced by action on the back ones.... Hydraulically-operated brakes did not start to be fitted to popular cars until the twenties, initially in the USA where they were pioneered by Duesenberg and Chrysler.

Following the precedent set by horse-drawn carriages, 19th century cars had smaller wheels at the front than the back, but front and rear wheels on the Mercedes were virtually the same size, although larger tyres were fitted at the back. A less advanced feature on the Mercedes was the chain final drive, which did not survive the 1914-18 war on the majority of cars, bevel or worm drive to the rear axle through a universally jointed shaft being generally adopted, this having been pioneered by Louis Renault in 1898, together with direct drive in top gear. On the other hand the gate-change gear shift on the Mercedes was a big advance on the earlier quadrant design, which had resembled a modern motor cycle transmission in that it was necessary to go through all the gears when changing up or down.

The first 4-cylinder car engines were developed jointly by Daimler and Levassor from 1890, and the Mercedes was a 'four', 116×140 mm, 5918 cc. At the Nice Speed Trials in March 1901, Wilhelm Warner on a 35 hp Mercedes covered a flying kilometre in 41 seconds, equal to 53.51 mph, and put up the fastest time by a gasolene driven car, though a Serpollet steam car averaged 62.45 mph. Yet over the 15.5 kilometres of the La Turbie Hill Climb the following day the Mercedes took 18 min 6.5 secs and the Serpollet 24 min 11.6 secs, illustrating the main reason why steam cars proved unpopular – the drivers needed much more skill to get the best out of them than the drivers of gasolene cars.

Mainly due to low-efficiency carburettors, which could not automatically vary the fuel/air ratio at different engine speeds, early car engines were designed to run at a constant speed, like contemporary stationary engines. With electric ignition, the driver had some measurable control over engine speed by advancing and retarding the spark, but with hot tube ignition he could only alter it slightly by a lever controlling the air supply. Automatic inlet valves also militated against big variations in engine revolutions, and to prevent the revs increasing too much under certain conditions a governor cut in and closed the exhaust valve or valves.

A question of ignition

The Mercedes, which employed side valves operated by two camshafts in the crankcase, had mechanically operated inlet valves, a proper throttle, so that engine revolutions could be controlled by the driver over a wide range (although on the 1901 35 hp engine speed was limited by a variable lift device on the valve gear), and low tension ignition. Benz's electric ignition used a trembler coil in which a vibrator, working on the electric bell principle, induced a constant high voltage current to the plug, which was made to fire at the right moment of the four-stroke cycle by means of an engine-operated switch or interrupter gear. Trembler coils were unreliable, although until the mid-twenties they were used, one for each cylinder, on Model T Fords, in which primary current was supplied by 16 permanent magnets on the flywheel facing 16 field coils on a stationary plate – a form of flywheel generator. At least the trembler coils on the early cars made a reassuring buzzing noise when they were working! Low tension ignition, as fitted to the Mercedes, was introduced by Robert Bosch in 1896, and by this system low tension current from an engine-driven generator was used to produce an arc between the contacts actually inside the

cylinder, and this worked well for fairly low speed, low compression engines. In 1903 Bosch introduced his engine-driven high tension magneto, and this held sway throughout the twenties, even though the Americans had introduced battery-and-coil ignition on Cadillacs back in 1912. Charles F. Kettering was the man responsible for that advance, and he is also credited with introducing the electric self-starter on 1911 Cadillacs. Many American, and some European, cars used coil ignition in the twenties, but most European sports cars stuck to magnetos, an exception being the Italian Alfa Romeo (from 1926 onwards) designed by Vittorio Jano.

The power increases

The Mercedes engine was considered smooth and quiet for its time, but these criteria were improved upon by Montague Napier in England with his distinguished 6-cylinder car, introduced towards the end of 1903, and subsequently by Henry Royce's 6-cylinder Rolls-Royce Silver Ghost from 1906. Back in 1904 the Dufaux brothers in Switzerland had produced a straight eight cylinder racing car, but it was not until 1910 that V8-engined cars were produced as a commercial proposition by De Dion in France, even though French V8 Ader cars had run in the 1903 Paris-Madrid race, using two V4 engines coupled together. Cadillac in the USA built successful V8 cars from 1915, in which year Packard produced a V12.

From 1903 to 1912 racing cars were made more powerful by having their engine capacities increased, and their engines could have side valves, inlet over exhaust valves, or overhead valves operated by pushrods or an overhead camshaft. Then, in 1912, the Swiss Ernest Henry produced a twin overhead camshaft engine for Peugeot, a revolution in design which has dominated racing and high performance engines right up to the present. A 1913 3 litre Peugeot with 4 valves per cylinder was capable of over 93 mph, only 5 mph slower than a 7.5 litre Grand Prix car of 1912.

Pistons were cast iron or steel up to the First World War and, although Aquila Italiana of Italy had fitted aluminium pistons as early as 1906 in cars designed by Giulio Cappa, it was the influence of aero-engine design during the war that led to their general adoption in car engines. First World War aero engines probably influenced car engines more in the matter of improvements in metallurgy and production methods than in actual design. Some war surplus large-capacity aero engines were fitted to prewar chain-drive chassis for track racing at Brooklands in England in the years following the armistice, often with dramatic results....

USA in the supercharger lead

It is said that a supercharger was first fitted to a car by Lee Chadwick in the USA in 1907 as a desperate measure to improve the performance of a 6-cylinder engine with poor porting and manifolding, although Mercedes were the first firm to race supercharged cars after the war in the 1922 Targa Florio race, and Fiat introduced them to Grand Prix racing in 1923 to augment the power of their small high-revving 2 litre engines, which were made possible due to improvements in metals and fuels. From then onwards superchargers were virtually universal in Grand Prix racing in the 1920s and 1930s. They never became popular on touring cars, although low-pressure centrifugal superchargers were fitted to some American cars, whilst in Europe superchargers became most popular on some sports cars towards the end of the twenties in either Roots or vane type form.

Sleeve valve engines, famed for their quietness though notorious for their high oil consumption, also reached the peak of their popularity in the nineteen-twenties, and then faded away. Expensive makes in Europe like Daimler, Panhard, Peugeot and Voisin fitted them, but in America they featured successfully in more modestly-priced cars such as the Willys-Knight.

Synchromesh gearboxes first appeared on Cadillacs in 1929, the design of Earl A. Thompson, while the less successful epicyclic pre-selector box dates from 1928. Epicyclic gears, demanding no skill from the driver in changing ratios, had appeared in the 15 million-plus Model T Fords manufactured between 1908 and 1927.

For night driving, very early cars had candle lamps, followed by paraffin lighting, and acetylene lamps from 1896 (they were made in large quantities by the firm headed by Louis Bleriot of cross-Channel flight fame) and electric lamps from about 1910.

Windscreen wipers were not in general use until the nineteen-twenties, when there were certainly no windscreen washers or direction indicators on the vast majority of cars – and as for seat belts, these were strictly for aviators until another thirty years had passed.

PETER HULL

ART AND ARCHITECTURE OF THE CAR

The earliest cars looked like light carriages, bath-chairs, or fugitives from a bicycle-shed; they were very short in the wheelbase as their engines gave little power. 'The improvement in looks' wrote Hugh Weguelin, an English pioneer in 1902, 'dates from the Paris-Amsterdam race of 1898. For the first time motor cars lost their hideous "horseless carriage" appearance and became what they should aim at being – road engines. The winning 8 hp Panhard had its engine at the front, a gearbox in the middle and rear-wheel drive – the famous *systéme Panhard* which almost everyone was to follow for the next 35 years. This was not the first car built on that principle but it was incomparably the best-looking car to date, and we know who was responsible for its lines: his name was Leon Auscher, of Rheims & Auscher, coach-builders.'

Leon Auscher was the first true architect of the car and the most influential. He had first shown his genius for compactness and equilibrium in 1894 when he designed the carriage and 'steam horse' tractor with which De Dion made best performance in the Paris-Rouen Trial. That 'steam horse' looked like a sports car in its own right, and perhaps Camille Jenatzy had it in mind when he briefed Auscher to design that electric torpedo of his, the *Jamais Contente* of 1899, the first car to exceed 100 km/hour (62.1 mph). Auscher was responsible too for the stream-lined Paris-Madrid Dauphin Mors; but first we should examine how touring cars developed (once engines be-came powerful enough to cope with four people), becoming longer and more civilised.

From two-seater to family tourer

The problem of fitting four-seater bodywork to a short chain-drive chassis was solved by Hugh Weguelin on his own Paris-Amsterdam Panhard. 'From a coachbuilder's catalogue I took the front half of a phaeton and the rear half of a wagonette and sent the drawing to Leon Auscher' (whose firm was now called Rothschild et Fils). Everyone faced forward and there was a central door at the back. Amateur and professional between them had invented the tonneau, a style that remained popular until longer wheel-bases and shaft drive allowed room for doors at the side. Then, instead of the tonneau, the Double Phaeton was introduced, with its two-row body with tipping or swivel-ling front seats. By 1901 there was even a Triple Phaeton (Rothschilds again) with 20 hp engine and 10 ft wheel-base, which Baron de Zuylen drove in the 'tourer' category of the Paris-Berlin race. Kaiser Wilhelm II became a convert and used triple phaeton Mercedes cars for touring and ceremonial occasions at least until 1908. Another royal motorist was King Leopold of the Belgians. One day this monarch remarked to his lady friend Mme Cleo de Merode that car seats were somehow never as comfortable as the chairs at her home. 'Why not have mine copied?', she replied. Rothschild's man (Fernand Charles this time) was sent for and the result, ready in April 1901, was a body with four form-fitting Louis Seize *bergères* (armchair-type seats) upholstered over the arms and back. 'Roi des Belges' luxury bodies with this style of seating sold well for the next ten years.

Rear-seat passengers played a significant part in the evolution of open cars, much more so than those in the front who, whether amateur 'whip' or paid coachman, had always lived an outdoor life, and were dressed accordingly. For years keen drivers would not have windscreens and doors for their bespoke-bodied vehicles, although their passengers clamoured for protective screens, side doors and some sort of weatherproof top. Soon phaeton (open touring) bodies had a 'Cape cart' canvas hood, or a canopy and sidescreens. A detachable canopy in conjunction with panelled or glazed rear quarters was known as a 'ballon' or 'limousine'.

By 1904, when powerful engines made longer wheelbases practical, most cars were of the side-entrance type, and were fitted with running-boards (known as 'the platform step'). The coachbuilding trade, having been bitterly hostile at first, now offered cars open and closed in every equine variety: landau, victoria, berline, landaulet, even hansom cab; they had noticed that cars were renewed more frequently than carriages had ever been! Traditional coachbuilders' bodies were often old-fashioned and overweight, but soon private owners took an interest in closed cars. In 1905 racing driver and salesman Charles Jarrott reported 'this is the year of the big closed-in car'. The owner-driver sedan (saloon) had arrived: heavy, cumbersome and high to accommodate tall hats and plumes, but practical for town and country use.

Open cars meanwhile grew less *al fresco*, even in front. Daimler of Coventry began panelling the top and sides of the dashboard in 1902, to keep out some of the rain; but this 'hollow dash' was only a start. The following year, for the Paris-Madrid race, Leon Auscher designed the Dauphin Mors, prototype of all front-engined racing and sports bodies. The bonnet, like an upturned boat, merged with a scuttle giving full protection to driver and *mecanicien* (riding mechanic) and this cowling continued smoothly past the cockpit to blend with a rounded tail. The clean lines of the Dauphin may have helped Gabriel to average 65.3 mph from Paris to Bordeaux; the industry dismissed them as freakish, but artists immortalised the Dauphin both in porcelain and bronze.

Cars were beginning to achieve a sculptural form. They grew simpler, rear doors rose to elbow-height and doors, only ankle-height at first, also invaded the front area. Open models still looked like a flight of steps with a grandstand view from the rear seats, and their panelling, in plan, might overlap, as an admirer put it, 'like the petals of a rose', but some Tourist Trophy cars of 1905 and 1906 featured a straight 'elbow line' and flush sides. German designers, especially, were impressed, and when Prince Heinrich of Prussia, the Kaiser's enthusiast brother, announced a competition to replace the Herkomer Trophy Tours, they applied the latest lessons of aerodynamics. Their cars shocked the motoring diehards just as Matisse and Picasso scandalised the world of art. The 'Prince Henry' was not for 'touring cars driven by gentlemen', they moaned, 'but appears to have got into the hands of professional drivers with racing cars'. And very clean, purposeful and efficient those Mercedes, Benz, Opel and Austro-Daimler cars were: they even conquered the Paris Salon, where Auscher showed a Racing Phaeton that 'looked as though the bows had been cut from a modern torpedo-boat and a car bonnet put in its place'. Straight lines, flat flanks, mud-guards reduced to planks, they anticipated the functionalist architecture of the 1920s and 30s. Their beauty stemmed from their fitness for purpose, and their influence was immense: it is known that Gropius after leaving the Weimar Bauhaus (which he founded) in 1928, designed at least one car, a cabriolet for the Adler company. Here is one instance, one feels, in which motor engineering influenced technical design as a whole.

The car becomes high fashion

During the Prince Henry period (1908-1911) a number of prominent motorists were airmen as well, but the fashionable influence was boats. Perhaps René de Knyff had something to do with this. Having raced in the early days, the Chevalier was now chairman of Panhard et Levassor; he was also a rowing man. He asked Jean Henri Labourdette, the Paris coachbuilder, to build him a body like a skiff.

'Doors will weaken the structure.'
'Very well, no doors; I shall step over the side.'
'But Monsieur, the ladies. . . ?'
'They can climb in too, it's time they showed a bit of leg!'

By the following year, 1913, Paris was in sailor-suits and French cars had mahogany planking, motorboat sterns, ships' ventilators, rowlock door-handles. This 'regatta' continued until after the First World War. The tall new hood of the 1919 Hispano-Suiza married very well with a boat-decked body. *Concours d'elegance* were held in the Bois de Boulogne and suddenly smart people adopted the car. From being a minority interest, motoring became *chic*. During the run-up to the *Arts Decoratifs* exhibition of

1925 car interiors received as much attention as a film-star's apartment: new brightly patterned materials, lacquer cabinets by Jean Dunand, decorative glass from Lalique, rich veneers with bronze or silver stringing, 'companion sets' in silver, silver gilt, enamel and shagreen. Exteriors were as carefully chosen as a dress from Lanvin, Patou or Chanel. The painter Robert Delaunay designed a dress with Voisin car to match. Gabriel Voisin invented a tartan of his own. Sham caning (simulated wickerwork applied from a tube) was resurrected from pre-war days: ivory on green, black on beige, even gold on panels of crimson. From 1926-1928, when women wore lizard and snakeskin shoes and handbags, cars were furnished to match, snakeskin replacing veneers and furnishing fabric. Smart bodies were lithe and angular, like cabin aircraft. In Germany, Bauhaus ideas combined with bevel-edged concave or 'tulip' panelling inherited from Prince Henry designs.

Such magnificent follies came to an end with the Wall Street crash. When the world resurfaced, high fashion and flair gave way to flamboyance – the difference between the SS and a 540 K – or to the sober virtues of a Savile Row suit. Interiors lapsed into a lethargy of broadcloth, walnut and leather. Proportions changed, bodies grew wider, engines moved forward. However, some thought was given to aerodynamics, in France by Andreau, in Germany by Jaray; the latter's 1937 Adler *Rennlimousine* gave 80 mph from 40 bhp. Fiat 1100 cc Mille Miglia coupes did much the same. These contrasted sharply with Chrysler's 'Airflow' sedans, whose 'stream-lining', despite the recessed headlamps and spatted wheels, was salesmanship rather than science – although airflow influence was immense on packaging and presentation in many fields. The motto was 'Whether it moves or not, streamline it!'; so everything manufactured became bulbous – streamlined buses, milk-jugs, tooth-brushes – and with the bulbosity came applied ornament, chromium streaks and 'flashes' which spread from cars to the living-room.

Bulbosity and applied ornament have receded, to the relief of all, mainly because today's cars are not produced in separate 'bits' any more and there is a strong unity of design. About 1946 coachbuilders in Turin, having few grand chassis to clothe, turned their attention to popular models. There are limits to what can be done with steel unitary bodies, so they designed welded steel hulls of their own. Using Fiat or Lancia running-gear they showed – and still show – 'collections' like those of Dior: clean, slim new coupes and saloons, the product, like sculpture, of one man's taste. Dazed, manufacturers everywhere signed up the key men as consultants: Pininfarina, Bertone, Vignale, Michellotti, Zagato. . . . Crisp cars have brought crisp furniture, haphazard instrumentation and fancy dials have given way to well-planned fascias and neat switches which have influenced, for example, the TV and radio industries.

It is fascinating to watch the interplay of fashions in architecture, automobiles and clothes. Early closed cars had tall interiors and seats with deep backrests because people fancied large hats. In 1907 the fashon for cartwheel hats died because they were too wide for car doors and by 1914 low coupes cured Parisiennes of the later plumed headgear. In the 1920s it was open cars, not female emancipation, which caused women to crop their hair and go into cloche hats, and it is low cars which keep them in trousers today. Men too have been redesigned. After 1929 the car roof came down, ostensibly for looks but really to save weight and materials. So men gave up wearing hats; and now that all cars have heaters they have given up overcoats too. Accustomed to low-built cars we have accepted low ceilings at home, and we sprawl on low chairs and sofas that might have been made for a car.

A CHICKEN IN EVERY OVEN AND A CAR IN EVERY GARAGE

Sometimes it was an either-or choice, and many young men back from years in the trenches of France opted for transport of any sort and left the chicken until later in life. In 1919 when most of them were home again, the old order, in Europe and in America, had vanished for ever. No longer were street-cars the 'people's gondolas', as one unfortunate politician had said; now the ordinary man wanted his own wheels.

The first British and French offerings were scandalous. Mushroom 'cyclecar' companies cobbled up feather-weight contraptions of wood and fabric, driven by midget engines and steered by wire-and-bobbin arrangements. The gullible newcomers bought them in their thousands – and for some they doubled as coffins. One or two exceptions in Britain and France survived – the Morgan, Salmson and others that went on to grow up into real automobiles. By 1922 however, an event in England burst the cyclecar bubble. A small car with all the attributes of a full-size model was shown to the British public, and was soon to be built under licence in places as far apart as France, Germany, Japan and the US. It was called the Austin Seven. It sold, at the end of 1922, for £165.

Herbert Austin had been making cars in Birmingham, England, for 16 years – and in 1921 the company was in the sort of financial state that caused 'Pa' Austin to go for long cycle rides in the country rather than face the bank on paydays. Herbert suggested developing a new small car. The directors were unimpressed. Herbert persisted, employed a young draughtsman, and between them they designed – mostly on the billiard table at Austin's home – a small sturdy car for the thousands of returned war veterans. It was a four-seater, give or take an inch or so – the two in the back would be the small children that the young ex-soldiers would now have – and it had a proper 4-cylinder water-cooled engine, transmission and live axle.

'Buy one for each foot!' jibed the press, but Herbert Austin had built better than he knew; now the impecunious youngster who could previously afford only a motorcycle-and-sidecar had a genuine car within his grasp – and he liked it. For 17 years he continued to buy the little Seven, a baby that can still be seen proudly jogging along the byways of Britain in the hands of proud – but no longer impecunious – owners.

The US suffered like every other country from a shortage of materials in 1919 but was in a better position tham most of Europe, which had been blasted by war. To get production lines moving again an almost nation-wide 'scissors-and-paste' operation began. With the exception of the main mass-producing companies, manufacturers stopped making their own components. Some companies, many of them new, bought *everything* from outside sources, merely assembling the bits to produce a characterless product. However, the market was there, and they sold well during the post-war boom, when some 8 million cars were sold in the USA in a single year.

The first 'people's car'

Germany, in profound trouble in the early twenties with a runaway inflation that could ruin a solid citizen overnight, had little scope for enterprise. Some carmakers, Opel in particular, were even forced to pay their workers with money printed in their own factory, so unstable was the Reichsmark. However, Germany managed to produce the Hanomag 'Kommissbrot', a slabsided two-seater flimsy, built for the slimmer German. The little car was so narrow that it could turn corners without a differential, and was driven by a one-cylinder coffee-pot engine, but it was Germany's first real 'people's car' a generation before the Volkswagen Beetle. Opel's little 'Laubfrosch' (Tree Frog) of 1924 was another winner, as was the Dixi, the Austin Seven copy, which was in manufacture for some time after 1928.

One of the largest munitions factories in France was run by engineer André Citroën, who had made millions of shells for Allied guns during the war and who had turned to motor transport to keep his plant running and his men employed. Citroën firmly believed that Henry Ford's moving-belt production system was the only road to success, and adopted it wholesale along with a one-model policy.

The Citroën Model A could not be called elegant. Its 1.3 litre engine could work this tin torpedo up to around 45 mph and, as most users commented, it was easier to go than to stop. With a big, empty market waiting to be filled it was an undoubted success, however, and was soon improved to become a worthy rival to the other French giant, Renault, established in the Paris suburb of Billancourt, and now producing a small-car challenge to the Citroën, the 951 cc KJ-Type with 3-speed gearbox and advanced suspension. Citroën countered with a 855 cc 5CV, which, with its yellow ducktail body, was immediately dubbed the Citron Citroën.

Fiat announce their first baby

The fourth great European automotive power, Italy, was stirring again soon after the return of peace in 1918. Its people owned fewer cars per thousand than the other motoring countries, but now that a recovery programme had been inaugurated there was an eager public waiting for the chance of its first essay into the world of mechanised mobility.

Fiat of Turin was even then the biggest industry of any type in Italy. The first attempt at a car for the people had appeared just before the war – the Tipo Zero, a model that pioneered Fiat's flow-line production of reliable cheap cars. In 1919 the Italian giant spawned the 501, a 1½-litre with all the latest advances to be expected in a mid-market car, but turned back to smaller engines later with the tremendously popular 990 cc Tipo 509, a light and nippy car, usually found in open tourer form, which had many of the refinements of the larger Fiat vehicles. For nearly five years the 509 was a best-seller throughout Italy and neighbouring countries.

A dozen other manufacturers struck gold with their smaller cars in this postwar decade before the financial holocaust that changed everyone's life in 1929. The working man, the small professional, the aspiring young, all had a chance to spend a picnic day in the country or to visit relatives in the next town over a weekend, for the first time in history. Social habits changed rapidly, commuting to work from outer urban regions began, long-distance vacation travel opened up the country to the population. The open road beckoned....

163

Previous page: 162. 1925 Salmson. 163. 1922 Aston Martin.

164

164. 1935 Aston Martin.

65. 1928 Aston Martin. Following pages: 166. 1921 Calthorpe.

167

167. 1924 Alvis.

168

168. 1921 'Babs' Thomas Special.

169

69. 1925 Lancia Lambda.

170

70. 1934 Austin. Following pages: 171. 1934 E.R.A.

172. 1932-1937 Multi-Union.

173. 1910 Bédélia.

174. 1924 Chénard Walcker. Following pages: 175. 1922 Delage.

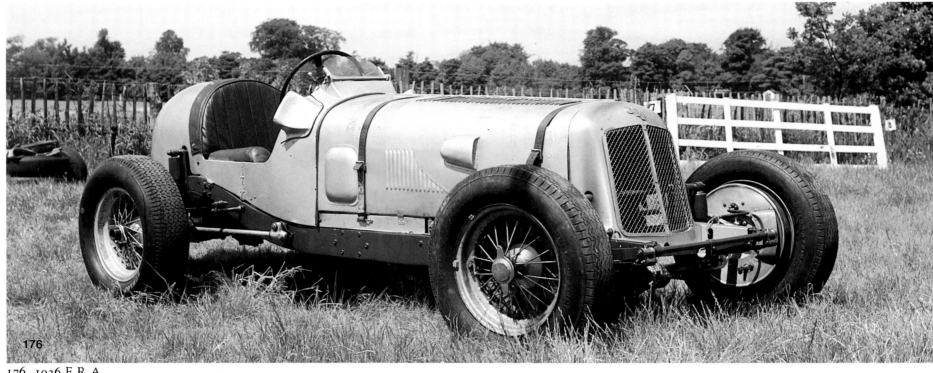

176

176. 1936 E.R.A.

177

177. 1926 Renault.

178

78. 1923 Amilcar.

179

79. 1930 A.C. Following page: 180. 1929 Bugatti 35B.

GENIUS IN THE SHADOWS

The work of most of the pioneers of the early days of the motor car would never have been possible without their alter egos. Many of the great designers and makers drew their strength from a partnership born out of loyalty. Often it was the 'number two' who gave the encouragement to carry on, who swept away the doubts, who led the thinkers and dreamers among the pioneers of the motor car into reality. Berta and Karl Benz, Clara and Henry Ford, Louise and Emile Levassor, Henry M. Leland and his son Wilfred, Gottlieb Daimler and Wilhelm Maybach – these couples have left their decisive marks on the history of the motor car. Ettore Bugatti's life's work would have been inconceivable without his friend Ernest Friderich. Le Patron set the tone at an early stage: when he and his later mechanic Friderich came together for the first time in 1904, Bugatti was already riding his high horse to work at Mathis, whilst Friderich went by tram – but without the faithful number two, Bugatti cars might not have become the jewels in the crown of the automotive world. . . .

CLAUDE JOHNSON –
THE MAN WHO PUT THE HYPHEN
BETWEEN ROLLS AND ROYCE

How did Rolls join Royce? The early history of the most prestigious make of car in the world has two basically different roots – one bourgeois and one aristocratic. Let us begin with the bourgeois origin. In 1884, 21 years old ex-railway apprentice and electrical engineer F. H. Royce founded an electrical company in Cooke Street, Manchester, England. Royce and his partner A. E. Claremont quickly achieved success with lamp holders and electric bells, and soon moved into manufacturing dynamos and electric cranes. Engineer Royce was deeply interested in the rapidly developing automobile and in 1903 bought himself a second-hand 10 hp Decauville. From the outset the small French car was unreliable, noisy, and far from elegant.

These various weaknesses annoyed the perfectionist Royce, who resolved to build a car himself. He retained the good points of the Decauville (electrics, carburettor, gear shift assembly) and worked on the rest. On 1 April 1904, the first Royce car started out on its maiden journey. Its 1800 cc 2-cylinder engine developed around 12 hp at 1000 rpm. The press were invited to take a trial ride in the new car and the newspaper reports the following day were loud in praise of the car 'that made all others sound like an avalanche of tea-trays' as one scribe wrote.

Royce built a further two prototypes for his partners A. E. Claremont and Henry Edmunds. Edmunds then became one of the most important matchmakers in the history of the motor car: not only was he already an experienced 'automobilist' in 1904, instantly recognizing the finer qualities of the Royce, but he was also friendly with the Hon. C. S. Rolls.

Who travelled to whom?

Charles Rolls, who was born in 1877, was the third son of Lord Llangattock. He was already importing cars from the continent, including Panhard & Levassor, Minerva, Whitlock, Astor and Mors cars, but was searching for a British product to promote. Business developed so well that he set out to look for a reliable partner with specialist knowledge. He found him in Claude Goodman Johnson, Secretary of the Automobile Club of Great Britain and Ireland. In 1904 Rolls and Johnson founded a trading company, and just one year later moved into elegant business premises in London's Conduit Street, where they are still to be found today.

Henry Edmunds and Claude Johnson managed to bring the two men, Rolls and Royce, so different in character, to a round-table discussion. It was no easy matter – since who was to travel to whom? Royce lacked the social graces and was born stubborn: he announced that in no circumstances would he travel to London. So the more outgoing Rolls travelled to Manchester. In May 1904, the two men met in the presence of Edmunds. After lunch, the Royce was put to the test. Rolls was delighted with the smooth, quiet running of the car. When Johnson, too, had taken a test drive, they quickly agreed on a commercial deal. On 23 December 1904, a contract was signed between C. S. Rolls & Co. and Royce Ltd.

Rolls took over the marketing of all cars produced by Royce, which took the name Rolls-Royce. Royce undertook to produce four models: a 10 bhp 2-cylinder (price £395), a 15 bhp 2-cylinder (£500) a 20 bhp 4-cylinder (£650) and a 30 bhp 6-cylinder (£890). Johnson and Rolls began to market the new marque with professional skill. They entered two 20 bhp cars for the Isle of Man Tourist Trophy in 1905. C. S. Rolls was forced to retire with transmission problems, but the other car, driven by Percy Northey, came second.

The famous name is registered

Johnson very soon advised that the company should be reorganized to cope with the necessary expansion. On 16 March 1906, it was registered under the name Rolls-Royce Ltd. with a capital of £60,000. Johnson and Rolls were now free to develop a market-orientated model policy.

From 1906 onwards, everything went like clockwork. Rolls demonstrated the qualities of the 20 bhp car in a number of races in the USA, the production works were moved from Manchester to Derby, and the company was floated on the stock exchange with a share capital of £200,000. All these activities were conceived and co-ordinated by Johnson. In this way, Rolls had plenty of time for selling, and Royce was left in peace to develop the new car. At that time the 'battle of the cylinders' was in full progress in the motor industry, and a number of companies had produced 6-cylinder cars with a fanfare of publicity. Both Rolls and Royce wanted to get in there, and in the fall of 1906 they launched the 40/50, which would in itself have secured the young company a lasting place of honour in the automotive manufacturers' Hall of Fame.

The Silver Ghost as a status symbol

This model, the immortal Silver Ghost, was launched, clad in a silvery aluminum body, at the London Motor Show. Its 6-cylinder engine initially developed 50 hp at 1200 rpm, and its silent mechanism and luxury coachwork were aimed, with Johnson's intuitive flair, at a particular target group – the aristocracy, the *nouveau riche*, Indian rulers, members of the landed gentry.... As well as a box for life at Ascot, a town house in Mayfair, a hunting lodge in Scotland, and a yacht on the Riviera, life for the rich now meant owning a Silver Ghost too. Johnson's timing was perfect, and testified to an unfailing flair for marketing. He also managed to gain acceptance of his model policy in the company's production plans; from 1907 to the beginning of the twenties Rolls-Royce built only a single model, the Silver Ghost, albeit with constant improvements. Thus in 1909 the cylinder capacity was increased from 7036 cc to 7428 cc, and from 1913 a four speed gearbox was installed to help the car's flexibility. Carlos Salamanca in a Silver Ghost promptly won the first Grand Prix in Spain. With its 40/50 model, Rolls-Royce had finally arrived in the international motor car industry – and soon began to dominate it at its upper levels.

However, commercial success was interrupted by tragedy and sickness. Charles Rolls, always restless and searching for new sensations, had turned to flying as a hobby, and in 1910, piloting a Wright biplane, he suffered a fatal crash at the seaside town of Bournemouth; in 1911 Henry Royce became so seriously ill that from then until the end of his life he needed medical care. In these difficult times Johnson surpassed himself. He was the one who found a feasible arrangement for Royce to be cared for without the company being forced to dispense with his technical ability. Johnson built him a house in Le Canadel on the French Riviera, with adjacent office space in which Royce and a number of engineers could work undisturbed. From that time forward an uninterrupted flow of notes, drawings, letters, memoranda and statements passed between Le Canadel and the works in Derby. During the First World War, Royce lived in a country house in Kent. Apart from the continuous further development of the Silver Ghost, Johnson pressed for aero-engines to be developed, the most successful of which was the V12 Eagle, which, constantly improved, developed 360 hp. The Silver Ghost was adapted to the requirements of war and saw duty as an armoured vehicle, particularly in the war in the desert.

Rolls-Royce-Johnson?

After the First World War, both Johnson and Royce realized that the era of the Silver Ghost was gradually drawing to a close. In 1922 Royce offered a smaller model, the Twenty, a 3.1 litre car which old-school Rolls-Royce owners sniffed at but which was built in the true Derby tradition.

In 1920 Rolls-Royce opened a factory in Springfield Mass. for the production of Silver Ghosts, then Phantoms. For a while they sold well, but Americans could not believe that the US-made car was built to 'Derby quality' and the plant closed down in 1931.

On 11 April 1926, Claude Johnson died. At this time the 20/25 type, a medium-range car, and the Phantom II were ready on the drawing board. Many Rolls-Royce historians are of the opinion that the company should really have been named Rolls-Royce-Johnson – so highly do they rate the significance of entrepreneur Johnson in the distinguished British company. Johnson was outlived by his old friend and partner, Sir Frederick Henry Royce, whose life he undoubtedly prolonged by clever work-sharing and organization, and who died in April 1933.

WILHELM MAYBACH – GOTTLIEB DAIMLER'S ALTER EGO

Without Wilhelm Maybach, there might never have been a Mercedes. The history of this prominent marque began shortly before the turn of the century, in the South of France, at the time when the seaside town of Nice was in its heyday. The town decked itself out ever more splendidly from one year to the next for its constant stream of wealthy visitors. The steam craft and sailing yachts of Europe's rich were to be seen bobbing up and down in the harbour, and already there were numerous cars clattering and hissing their way along the coastal roads to Cannes or Monte Carlo. A few of the more stout-hearted motorists were already braving the Col de Turini, high above the town, whilst others were chasing up the zig-zag hills to the mountain village of La Turbie, perched in the sky behind Monte Carlo.

One of the most enthusiastic motorists in Nice at the turn of the century was Emil Jellinek, a bright bird of paradise among the super-rich of the Cote d'Azur. Jellinek was Austrian Consul General, a leading businessman, and general agent for the Daimler Motor Company. He was also a sales genius with a sixth sense for the unspoken wishes of his clients, many of whom paid more attention to their cars than their wives. Jellinek already knew all about 'hidden persuasion'; 'A car should have a woman's name, to be loved and pampered,' and in Nice Week, at the town's gala automobile contest, he launched a promotional gamble.

A 'Mr Mercedes' appeared in the list of entrants for the various races. It was under this pseudonym that Jellinek entered the recently-completed Daimler 24 hp Phoenix. His young daughter Mercedes had allowed him to use her name and on 21 March 1899 the incognito Jellinek won the Nice touring competition in the Daimler. And so it was that the name Mercedes appeared for the first time in the motor sport pages of the Nice newspapers. Jellinek rubbed his hands contentedly: 'Mercedes' must be the new morque name for cars from Cannstatt. It sounded so much better than the German 'Daimler' at a time when memories of the Franco-Prussian war had not completely faded. It was an easy matter for Jellinek to persuade the two closest colleagues of the ailing Gottlieb Daimler, Wilhelm Maybach and Daimler's son Paul, of the attractiveness of the new name. He also took the opportunity to raise the question of a more powerful Daimler engine and a more stable construction, with a lower centre of gravity. Both men trusted Jellinek's sales psychology, and the triumphal progress of the Mercedes marque was set to begin.

A name makes motoring history

Shortly after Daimler's death in 1900, Maybach began work on the new Mercedes. The car had an entirely new shape: longer and lower, with a pressed steel frame, a 4-cylinder engine with a honeycomb radiator, multi-speed transmission with gate shift mounted behind the engine and clutch, and same-size front and rear wheels. Compared with the 1899 24 bhp Phoenix (with a total weight of 1800 kg and a maximum speed of approximately 38 mph) the 4-cylinder engine of the first Mercedes developed 35 bhp from 5.9 litres. The car weighed only 1000 kg and was capable of a peak speed of 56 mph. The motoring world was taken by surprise by the favourable power-to-weight ratio of the car, the new cooling system, the axle design, the transmission, and the braking system in which a pedal-actuated transmission brake acted on the layshaft whilst two brakes operated by a hand lever were coupled to the rear wheels. Wilhelm Maybach's Mercedes left all other manufacturers behind and was now regarded as the ultimate in automobile construction. Maybach's formula; 'Maximum power in the smallest space', had been excellently put into practice, and at the Paris Motor Show of 1902, the French dubbed Wilhelm Maybach 'King of the Designers'.

At the 1901 Speed Week in Nice Wilhelm Werner, with the brand-new Mercedes 35, beat all other competitors over the flying kilometre, and also won the Nice-Salon-Nice race, and the dangerous La Turbie hill-climb. Encouraged by their numerous sporting successes, Daimler increased the power of the car, first to 40 bhp with a cylinder capacity of 6.8 litres, calling it the Mercedes Simplex. Then in 1903 came the renowned 9.2 litre 60 hp machine. The next year, Maybach gave his successful model a further stimulus – 90 bhp from a cylinder capacity of almost 12 litres. Other car companies were now taking their inspiration from the Mercedes – Fiat, in Italy, for example, Rochet-Schneider in France, Star in England, and Locomobile in the United States all came to the market sooner or later with Mercedes look-alike models.

The old Campaigner

But even the 'old' Mercedes 60 still went on from success to success. Belgian driver Jenatzy won the 1904 Irish Gordon-Bennett Race in a 60; Vincenzo Florio came third in the 1904 Coppa Florio. Wilhelm Maybach could feel pleased with himself. He had taken the life's work of his now dead friend, partner and mentor to new heights. In Cannstatt, they now worked to the principle that 'today's racing car is tomorrow's touring car' as indeed the first Mercedes racing vehicles already were.

Gottlieb Daimler and Wilhelm Maybach had met in Reutlingen, Germany, in 1865. Daimler, then aged 31, was running the engineering works of the town's 'Bruderhaus', where the 19-year-old Maybach was a pupil and apprentice. In the Reutlingen Bruderhaus young people, many of them orphans, were brought up in the Christian faith and introduced by sympathetic instructors to the skills of the most widely varying range of crafts. When the successful engineer Daimler met the young Wilhelm Maybach, the latter was already a first-class technical draughtsman. Gottlieb Daimler was impressed by his obvious talent, and took Maybach with him when in 1869 he was appointed to the board of the Maschinenbau-Gesellschaft in Karlsruhe.

There a partnership was formed that left its mark on an entire technical age. A writer described the collaboration between the two men thus: 'What Daimler formulated mentally would take tangible, technical shape on the drawing board in Wilhelm Maybach's hands. It was a partnership born out of mutual loyalty, fairness, and human respect'.

A key experience for both was without a doubt the meeting with Nikolaus Otto and Eugen Langen in 1872 at the Deutz Company – a meeting of the Titans. The four most significant engine technicians of their time agreed to collaborate at Gasmotoren-Fabrik Deutz, and Nikolaus Otto's four-cycle stationary engine became the basis for Daimler's and Maybach's brilliant development work.

Daimler and Maybach were, in particular, concerned with ways in which the engine could be used for a wider application. The Otto (or gasolene) engine changed in the course of time from a stationary power machine to a vehicle-driving source – where there were virtually no limits to its use. Daimler's and Maybach's great service was to bring the gas engine to practicable industrial maturity in several fields of transportation.

In 1882 both men left Gasmotoren-Fabrik Deutz after interminable and depressing disputes (as indeed did Ettore Bugatti, some 30 years later). Thus the Cologne company became the involuntary launching ramp to fame for the headstrong Daimler, Maybach and Bugatti.

Wilhelm Maybach played his part as Gottlieb Daimler's alter ego with an admirable consistency. Over a period of 35 years, he served – in the most creative sense of this now unfashionable term – a great man, his ideas and his legacy. Leonard Setright, in his book *The Designers*, draws attention to a monument devoted to Sir Frederick Henry Royce in the English city of Derby, bearing the simple inscription 'Henry Royce, mechanic', and in Set-

right's view Wilhelm Maybach too was worthy of this honourable title. In 1893, William Maybach presented the automotive industry with the spray carburettor, essentially resolving the problem of the use of volatile substances as fuel. Virtually every carburettor today is still based on the atomization of fuel with the aid of a spray nozzle.

A ripe old age

The year 1907 brought Maybach to pastures new again. Following some disagreement with the management, he left the Daimler Company and took up Count Zeppelin's offer of collaboration. In Friedrichshafen, they founded Luftfahrzeug-Motorenbau and Maybach's son was appointed Managing Director. With their lightweight, powerful aero engines, the Maybachs caused a sensation in Zeppelin aviation – as Londoners found to their cost when Maybach-engined airships showered bombs on the city during the First World War. In the twenties and thirties Carl built expensive luxury cars, vehicles that became known as German Rolls-Royces. Until his death on 29 December 1929, aged 83, Wilhelm Maybach still took an active part in the soaring development of his company's motor car and engine manufacture.

VITTORIO JANO –
FERRARI'S GIFT TO ALFA ROMEO

In the 77 years of its history, the Italian car manufacturing company of Alfa Romeo has never really come in out of the cold. Its chequered life forms one of the most fascinating chapters in the history of the automobile. It has always been linked with the names of important automobile pioneers and designers, including that of French pioneer Alexandre Darracq, and when A.L.F.A. (Anonima Lombarda Fabbrica Automobili) began producing cars in 1910 in Portello, it was on his work that the company was able to build.

The horseless carriages of the French automobile designers were sold, at the turn of the century, to almost all Western European countries, in some cases under different marques, including Opel, but Darracq's Italian adventure had begun in February 1906 with a major blunder. He founded the company Societa Italiana Autombili Darracq (Siad) in Naples, found his lines of communication were too long, sold the works in the shadow of Mount Vesuvius and built a plant in the Milan suburb of Portello. But even here, Italo-Darracq failed to get going. The independently-minded Italians simply didn't take to it; the car just would not go up the local

Alpine mountain roads. In 1909, only 61 vehicles left the company site. Siad's workers knew that their jobs would be at risk if Darracq were to fold.

The birth of Alfa Romeo

In this precarious situation, Siad Director Ugo Stella decided that a new designer would have to be brought in. He managed to interest Giuseppe Merosi, former chief designer at the Bianchi motor works, who had designed a car of his own, and formed an alliance with the Milan Agricultural Bank. On 24 June 1910, A.L.F.A. was founded. Until the outbreak of the First World War, the company flourished. First produced was a healthy 4-cylinder monobloc car of 12 hp or 24 hp, tough enough to negotiate the hilly northern hinterland of Lombardy and sportive enough to be entered in the 1911 Targa Florio. A pointer to Merosi's interest was shown in the next model, a car developing 60 bhp from a 6 litre cylinder capacity which Count Ricotti took up to 130 mph on test drives in 1913, closely followed by a purpose-built Grand Prix car with a 4.5 litre twin-ohc 4-cylinder engine that sadly failed to perform (and which was put under wraps and kept totally secret for some fifty years before the company would admit to this ancient gaffe).

In 1915, the last shareholder with Darracq connections left the company, selling his shares to a banking organization. A.L.F.A.'s financial cover had now become so thin that a new backer had to be found. Industrialist Nicola Romeo was approached – a man always on the look-out for profitable investments for the fortune he had made in the mining industry. Romeo joined A.L.F.A. – and Alfa Romeo was born.

During the First World War, the company concentrated on railroad rolling-stock, tractors and aero engines. A full order book, but the continuing crisis in Portello could not be brought to an end. When post-war car production everywhere in Western Europe was increasingly adapting to market requirements, Alfa Romeo still believed in the possibility of improving their image primarily by success in motor sports. But when engineer Enzo Ferrari joined Alfa Romeo in 1920 a sharp, clean wind soon blew through the workshops.

Enzo Ferrari was a technician who also raced brilliantly, and was well-versed in the struggles that took place behind the scenes in racing car manufacture. It was already happening in those days; if a company had designed a new Grand Prix car, its competitors would move heaven and earth to get hold of the plans. And what was the best way of obtaining the information? Designers were enticed away by rival companies.

Vittorio Jano leaves Fiat

Nicola Romeo got wind of this game of musical chairs and asked: 'Why shouldn't we get in there, too?' He wanted a Grand Prix racing car that would be well ahead of other designs. His drivers Ascari, Ferrari and Campari strengthened his resolve. And so Enzo Ferrari was instructed to hire the man he had recommended, Vittorio Jano, then with Fiat.

The name Jano was known only to a few insiders in the trade. His family originally came from Hungary, where their name had been Janos. Father Jano was in charge of the largest weaponry arsenal in Turin, and he also had a great technical talent. Vittorio had inherited this talent from his father; he had been one of the best pupils at Turin's Istituto Professionale Operaio, before he joined Giovanni Ceirano in 1909 as a technical draughtsman building racing cars at his Rapid works. Two years later, 20-year-old Jano moved to Fiat where, in 1917, he became chief designer and, in 1923, racing team leader.

In the winter of 1923, the first discussions took place between Ferrari and the initially sceptical Jano. The latter insisted that Nicola Romeo should approach him in person. Romeo then sent his close friend, Giorgio Rimini, and a contract was signed.

It was not the higher salary that attracted Jano, but the possibility of building a Grand Prix racing car to his own design, and at the same time being able to lead the production team. Within a few days, the move was made. Jano, his wife Rosina and their two-year-old son Francesco moved into a flat on the first floor of 71, Corso Sempione, in Milan. Jano's move from Fiat to Alfa Romeo created quite a stir at the time. It was a blatant case of industrial espionage, or so it seemed to certain sectors of the Italian car industry.

The P2

Jano began his career at Alfa Romeo with the P2 racing car. It is now certain that the P2 – or more especially its predecessor the P1 – was 'developed' from the 2 litre Fiat Type 804-404, a twin camshaft 6-cylinder car, all of which is hardly surprising in view of Jano's past employment. The 804 was the most successful Grand Prix racing car of 1922; its design made excellent use of the possibilities offered by the 2 litre formula introduced that year, which also specified a minimum weight of 650 kg and a 120 kg load in the form of two occupants.

Jano had set himself a target of a successful 1924 season. In developing the Fiat-like P2 he used as his basis the Merosi-designed P1, withdrawn from the Grand Prix at Monza in 1923 due to a fatal accident when Alfa Romeo driver Ugo Sivocci came off the track of the fast Viallone bend. On 10 October 1923, development work on the P2 was completed 'after work executed with military precision', as Enzo Ferrari noted. At the end of May 1924, Jano finally released the car for racing after a number of successful tests. Compared with the P1, Jano's first car for Alfa Romeo had a shorter stroke and increased bore, designed to achieve a lower piston speed; a formula, combined with other advanced technics by Jano, that was designed to make the Alfa Romeo P2 one of motor sport's historic classics.

At the French Grand Prix, held in 1924 at Lyon, Giuseppe Campari took first place in a P2. He attributed his victory in part to the new balloon tyres from Firestone that had been fitted to the car. A further technical refinement was the hydraulic brake-booster system operated by transmission oil. The P2 demonstrated just how good Jano was at supercharged engines with a small cylinder capacity.

Alfa Romeo P2 type engines, in all their variations, were around until 1930, taking advantage above all of the Formula Libre of 1928-1933, a formula that imposed virtually no restrictions on engine size, although total weight was held to between 550 and 750 kg.

The Basic Type 6C

Jano's second stroke of genius at Alfa Romeo was the basic type 6C (6-cylinder) built from 1926 to 1933, with all its fascinating model variants. The 6C 1750 in particular, which he developed in 1929 from the 6C 1500, contributed greatly to his reputation. Not only did Jano have a flair for powerful racing cars in the style of the P2, he also knew that clients were looking for a sports car that they could use in normal road conditions. From 1929 to 1933, there were four different versions of the 1750. A total of 2579 cars were built, the 'hottest' version providing the wheels with a stark 108 bhp. The sports record of the 6C 1750 is impressive; the cars recorded more than 200 victories, including the Spa 24 hours in 1929 and 1930, and the Ulster Tourist Trophy in 1930.

Vittorio Jano enjoyed being able to play confidently on the keyboard of the many versions of the same model. The basis was established: all Alfa Romeos would have a twin camshaft engine and an excellent chassis as standard. So it was easy, in 1932, to follow the 6C 1500 and 6C 1750 types with the 8C 2300 sports car, in the short chassis, long chassis, Le Mans and Grand Prix Monza versions.

The Monza Type

The 'Monza', in particular, merits as prominent a place in the hall of fame of motor sport as the Bugatti 35. The Monza, at the time of the Formula Libre, was used as a Grand Prix car. It would be an over-simplification to regard the 8C 2300 as a straightforward 6C 1750 with two extra cylinders; the 8-cylinder engine consisted of two 4-cylinder light metal blocks with steel liners for the cylinders. The running gear, constructed in the conventional manner, had rigid axles on longitudinal leaf springs. Two relatively comfortable seats were built-in to the semi-streamlined body. The 2.336 litre supercharged engine developed 165 bhp at 5400 rpm in 1931 (170 bhp at the same engine speed by 1932), and had a maximum speed of 130 mph. As usual, Jano produced brilliant variations on the 8C 2300 theme: he was helped by Enzo Ferrari, who had left Alfa Romeo in 1929 to found the Scudari Ferrari, his own motor racing stable.

Famous racing drivers such as Nuvolari won many races with the Alfa Romeo Monza, including the 1931 Belgian Grand Prix, the 1932 Mille Miglia, the Targa Florio, the 1932 24 Hours of Le Mans, Spa, the Mille Miglia, the Tunis Grand Prix, the Targa Florio, the Tripoli Grand Prix, the Eifel race and again Le Mans and Spa in 1933. Rudolf Caracciola, too, drove a Monza in 1932 when he lost his contract with Mercedes Benz due to the economic situation. The 1931 Italian Grand Prix at Monza was the race that in fact gave the Alfa Romeo Monza its name and its first win.

The Type A

Vittorio Jano also experimented at Monza with his Type A, powered by two side-by-side supercharged 6-cylinder engines, with a total cylinder capacity of 3504 cc, developing 230 bhp at 5000 rpm. With its twin propellor shafts and two gearboxes, operated via a single gear lever, it was unique. The Type A was intended to make life difficult for Bugatti and Maserati, as their only serious rival, but it was to remain no more than an experiment – the competition was too fierce for the new car. In the period between 1926 and 1930, Ettore Bugatti's type 35 and 35C won many great sports car and Grand Prix races; in 1931, the motor car wizard from Molsheim launched his type 51, a 2.3 litre supercharged car, in which Louis Chiron won the Monaco Grand Prix. Maserati sparkled with its 'Sedici Cilindri', a 16-cylinder car, its engine having a displacement of 3958 cc and developing 300 hp.

At the very first training session for the 1931 Monza Grand Prix, the Italian Arcangeli suffered a fatal accident in a Type A, although Campari and Nuvolari took first and third place with the car in the 1931 Coppa Acerbo in Pescara.

The P3

However, the Type A rendered good service as a test car for the development of the legendary Alfa Romeo Grand Prix racing car Type B, or P3. The P3's engine had a capacity of 2654 cc and consisted of two 4-cylinder in-line blocks, each with a supercharger, developing a total of 215 bhp at 5600 rpm. The arrangement of the pedals and gear lever was somewhat curious. The gear-shift gate was located between the driver's legs, the gear lever, for reasons of comfort, was curved to the left, the clutch pedal was located to the left of the gear case, and the accelerator pedal was to the right of the brake pedal.

Jano modified the P3 several times. The capacity was increased to 2.9 litres, then 3.2, and finally to 3.8 litres, giving the remarkable power of 330 bhp. The rigid front axle was replaced by independent springing with torsion bars, greatly improving roadholding qualities. The 1932 season was a great year for the P3. Not only did it win the majority of the Grand Prix races, including the Italian and, with Rudolf Caracciola at the wheel, the German

Grand Prix at the Nürburgring: it also won many sports car races on the circuits of Europe.

However successful the 1932 season may have been for Alfa Romeo, the company still had some cash flow problems: the six P3's were withdrawn and passed over to Enzo Ferrari, who used them from 1933 on, racing them against the Maseratis and Bugattis of the day.

When the Silver Arrows from Mercedes and the supercharged V16 Auto Unions began their triumphal progress on Europe's Grand Prix circuits in 1934, the years of racing dominance by Alfa Romeo, Bugatti and Maserati were over. Yet Jano refused to be discouraged, and until 1938 continued to build more new racing and sports cars, like the 1936 12C, a Grand Prix car with a 4495 cc capacity provided by a V12 engine, in which Nuvolari won both the Spanish and the Hungarian Grand Prix that year, beating the full might of the German opposition, as well as scooping the Milan GP from Auto Union and taking his 12C to victory in the Vanderbilt Cup held at Long Island.

The Alfa Romeo 12C was the last successful car built by Jano for Alfa Romeo, and it is inseparably linked, in the minds and hearts of all enthusiasts of the sport of motor racing, with his name.

Previous pages: 181. 1929 Bugatti 43. 182. 1929 Birkin-Bentley. 183. 1934 Lagonda.

184. 1926 Bentley 'Blue Label'.

185

85. 1931 Bentley 4.5 litre.

186

86. 1930 Bentley Speed Six. Following pages: 187. 1935 Rolls-Royce 20/25. 188. Dufaux 1905.

FAST WOMEN AND CRAZY GUYS!

The car has been a male domain for almost eight decades. Whenever in the past courageous women have dared to become involved, they have been regarded as somewhat strange and exotic. How must Baron Campbell von Laurentz have felt as, at the beginning of this century, a passenger beside his car-crazy wife, he was bumped and shaken over the dusty roads of Europe, when he would desperately have preferred to travel by train to avoid the tortures of a car journey? And the Baron was by no means a softie. Indeed, he had been made a peer by the Duke of Saxe-Coburg-Gotha for his services in the Franco-Prussian war of 1870/71.... Nor did the residents of Washington find it totally acceptable when Alice Roosevelt, daughter of the American President Theodore Roosevelt (1901 to 1909) drove her silent White steam carriage around the capital of the USA. When she set out on her daily drive, shocked cab-drivers were obliged to curb their horses, who were also disturbed by this new mode of locomotion....

WOMEN, FOUR-STROKES AND
PLENTY OF SPEED

The first female racing driver in the history of motor sport is said to have been a Madame Laumaille. In 1898 she took fourth place in the two-day race from Marseilles to Nice in a De Dion three-wheeler. However, women in motor sport – even today – are a rarity. Certainly any woman who was brave enough to drive a car at the turn of the century, and in so doing invaded the male domain, had a rough time of it. Queen Victoria, the mistress of discipline of the age named after her, pronounced a curse on the motor car when she heard of the first English car driver to suffer a fatal accident. But to no avail – courageous women disregarded all middle class conventions and began to take an interest in cars, and the freedom that they represented. Suffragette leader Emmeline Pankhurst of England, who had founded her militant Women's Social and Political Union in 1903 and had been thrown into prison on several occasions, gave courage to many women in the cause of greater freedom for the female.

The New Woman appears

The real cause of interest in the motor car, however, lay more in feminine curiosity, and when, in 1901, Edward VII acceded to the British throne, the Victorian shackles were loosened. The new ruler became the model of fashion and sports – and the new king had nothing against the lady motorists' skirts flapping in the wind. It even became socially acceptable for women to be interested in technical matters. The first female drivers came from well-to-do circles – like British Baroness Campbell von Laurentz. By 1900 she had already covered thousands of miles, a nervous husband at her side, in Locomobile and Serpollet steam cars, before she decided to change over to a gasolene car, the first German Dixi from Eisenach. If she had any problems with the car, the Baroness was never at a loss to know what to do. When the tubes gave out after a number of punctures, she stuffed the tyres with hay – and on she went! When unable to continue climbing a steep hill in the Cotswolds in first gear, she turned the car round and went up hill in reverse.

The Baroness also had a gift for designing practical accessories. She developed a set of removable motoring suitcases tailored to take the wardrobe of a married couple with lady's maid and chauffeur, and leather travelling bags which she made herself, providing a place to stow away tools of all kinds that tended to rattle around the car. That last problem is a familiar one, even today!

Baroness Campbell bought herself a more powerful car in 1907, a 6-cylinder Belgian Minerva, more suited to her long-distance treks. On her return from a trip to the Mediterranean, she complained of the 'crowded Riviera, where there was really no more room for motoring....' With her later purchase, a Rolls-Royce Silver Ghost, she travelled some 1500 miles on North African soil in 1911 and wrote in minute detail of her experiences behind the steering wheel, and with her book *My Motor Milestones* became one of the very first motoring and travel writers.

Sweat and tears – the travels of Princess Borghese

Another English lady motoring pioneer, Dorothy Levitt, in her book *The Woman and the Car* gave her female car-driver colleagues some rather peculiar advice. She recommended taking a revolver – she preferred a Colt – whenever one went out for a drive, and thought that a mirror would be useful not only for one's make-up after a drive over dusty country roads, but also if one wanted to see what was happening in the road behind one! With this suggestion, Dorothy Levitt was well ahead of her time: the first fixed rear-view mirrors did not appear until 1914.

Driving instruction books for ladies appeared, usually beginning 'At the front of the car you will notice a handle....' and so on, and male automobilists would reluctantly offer such gems as 'Whatever the limitation of the average woman driver, an automobile is safer in her hands than those of a male companion who admires her and is anxious to know if the admiration is mutual....' One piece of advice made sense; 'Do remove your rings before taking the wheel as the road surface will loosen the stones until they drop out....'

However, these well-meaning counsels would have been of little help to the Italian Princess Anna-Maria Borghese, even if she had known of them; where she indulged in her passion for cars there was nothing but blood, sweat and breakdowns. Already, at the turn of the century, the Borgheses had ventured on some madcap drives through Asia Minor. In 1907, she had helped her husband, Prince Scipio Borghese, in the preparations for the epic long-distance race from Peking to Paris.

The tender oil-smeared hands of the Princess Anna-Maria Borghese and the ease with which the motorists' language fell from her lips at parties given by Italy's nobility impressed others of her sex. This combination of female charm, diamond necklaces and sable, mixed with the penetrating smell of *benzina*, unquestionably had its attractions.

The young Baronessa Maria d'Avanzo must have felt the same way at the beginning of the twenties. She was a trump card in the Alfa Romeo racing team, in which she drove a ES 20. In the Brescia Speed Week in 1921 she came third in the general classification at a number of trials, chasing Count Masetti, driving a 1914 Mercedes GP, and Count Caselli in another ES 20. At Brescia a race was held with a name that was an affront to the daring Italian ladies: the Gran Premio Gentlemen, a competition involving 25 laps of the 17.6 kilometre course. Maria Antoinetta d'Avanzo was unperturbed by the organizers' tactlessness, and entered her name in the list of participants, using her initials only; in her Alfa Romeo she took third place behind Masetti's Mercedes and a Ceirano. The blue-blooded lady motorist encouraged many of her female sporting colleagues to take the wheel and not to be dissuaded by male chauvinists – which, it must be said, in those days meant every male, in or out of the sport!

The female sports pioneers of the twenties were mainly English lady drivers, all amateurs of the first order, mixing cheekily with the male starters on the grid. The racing women felt particularly at home at Brooklands, with its own charming country-club atmosphere. The atmosphere suited them: no exacting timetable, time for small-talk and high tea, a level of racing that allowed the ladies to make virtually no concessions to the environment, even in their clothing. A leather cap, goggles, leather gloves, perhaps, but a scarf from Chanel around their necks, and after the race a mink jacket placed on their shoulders by a considerate companion.

Fast women and World Records

The Ladies Outer Circuit at Brooklands was specially named for female racing drivers, Mrs E. M. Thomas in 1928 having reached a speed of 121 mph there in a Bugatti. But seven years later, after Gwenda Stewart drove a Derby-Miller supercharged model at 135.95 mph, and little Kay Petre had driven a huge 10.5 litre Delage over the cement in a record attempt, this bumpy dangerous 'ladies' stretch was no longer allowed to be used for such ventures.

Another Eldorado for lady amateur racing drivers was Montlhèry near Paris. There in 1929, a number of speed record holders gained distinction, among them Gwenda Stewart, Mrs Victor Bruce and Violet Cordery. At the beginning of 1929, Mrs Bruce had set a remarkable record. At the wheel of a 4.5 litre Bentley, she drove for 24 hours non-stop, covering 2149.7 miles (average speed 89.57 mph). Record attempts in these days still had a human side; the lady racing driver's pit-stops, necessary

for technical reasons, were also designed so as 'to coincide with her personal needs', as the *Guinness Book of Records* so discreetly puts it!

What may well at that time have seemed a level of strain intolerable to the feminine structure is unremarkable today, as witnessed by the dramatic and strenuous sports achievements of many women. Nevertheless in 1927 Frenchwoman Violette Morris, in her little 1100 cc BNC at the Bol d'Or 24 hour race, achieved a performance that even today would have us take off our hats in admiration. Not only did she drive against the clock, but raced 309 laps against numerous male competitors, all of whom were beaten by the lady driver, a charming woman ungallantly described by the sports press as 'masculine'. And at the 1927 Coppa Florio, held in France that year, Violette Morris achieved a high placing.

The 'car of cars' appears

In the 'golden twenties', as described by D. B. Tubbs in his book *Art and the Automobile*, a sports car first saw the light of day whose type designation alone sends shivers of envy down the spine of connoisseurs – the Mercedes-Benz S class, with later model variants SS, SSK and SSKL. Developed by Dr Ferdinand Porsche, these super-sports cars became the apogee of the performance car, princes of fast travel. The famous American architect Frank Lloyd Wright referred to them as the realization of his dictum that 'form must respond to function' – in other words they *looked* like sports cars. Compared with the filigree thoroughbred Bugattis, in particular the 35 B, the S-types were like giant battle-chargers.

It is difficult to imagine that it was at the wheel of just such a lusty car that Ernes Merck, a young woman motor racing enthusiast from Darmstadt, achieved her greatest successes. On 4 September 1926, the *Darmstadter Tageblatt* named her 'Germany's most outstanding driver', and continued: 'A woman at the wheel of a car is a particularly attractive sight – with certain exceptions, of course. Being women, they also have to concern themselves with matters of external appearance simply of no concern to males in sport.... The lady has to take considerable account of the field of her sport. She will never quite set the objective of her sports activity exclusively as sporting success: even in the keenest sporting battle, she will still remain a lady with all the strengths and weaknesses associated with her sex....' This and much other fulsome nonsense somehow found its way into print in the so-called emancipated twenties.

Ernes Merck did not make it easy for them, as she was in fact an excellent sportswoman. Her husband, pharmaceuticals manufacturer Wilhelm Merck, consistently supported her sporting ambitions. Her first driving experience was in a 30 bhp NSU, and she subsequently used models produced by Wanderer, Opel, Adler, Minerva and Steiger. In 1922 she began to satisfy her desire for sporting honours; she first piloted a Benz, came second in her first race, and in 1923, in addition to many other successes, took third place in the famous Solitude race. That same year, at the wheel of a Mercedes, she took part in the Krahberg race, and in 1924 she took the ladies' first prize at the Hesse AC hill climb and flat races, and fourth place in the Konigstuhl hill climb. In 1927, she took over her first Mercedes-Benz S, and drove this colossus to second spot in the International Klausenpass race. The one-ton S type was hard work even for fully trained racing drivers; Rudolf Caracciola and Otto Merz had many a tale to tell about their own difficulties. Contemporaries spoke highly of Ernes Merck's considerable technical understanding, her unfailing sense of the possibilities and limits of the engine, and the sure instinct with which she handled her sports car. Sadly, she died in December 1927 at the age of 29.

A woman round the world

There can be little doubt that Ernes Merck devoted herself to motor racing as an enjoyable diversion, a hobby, but to Clarenore Stinnes, who was almost the same age, motor sport was anything but a matter of diversion. This girl, daughter of a prominent industrialist, wanted to drive her car around the world! It seemed sheer madness, but she did the impossible. Clarenore Stinnes, with her team of three, covered 29,037 miles between 1927 and 1929.

There was no money available from family funds. Her mother and brothers refused to finance the young girl's crazy plans. True, Clarenore Stinnes had already made a name for herself as a rally driver, and in 1925 in the Leningrad-Tiflis-Moscow Rally she had beaten 52 male competitors – but to drive around the world was something very different. So she raised 100,000 Marks in cash, mainly by badgering motor accessory companies, and motor manufacturers Adler provided her with two trucks. The plucky team of travellers comprised the 26 year old expedition leader Clarenore, cameraman Carl-Azel Soderstrom, the man who was later to become her husband, and two mechanics. The book *Soderstrom's Photographic Diary* by Michael Kuball and Clarenore Stinnes about the two-year tour is a chronicle of barely believable adventures, punctuated by some masochistic episodes.

The round-the-world safari began on 25 May 1927. For thousands of miles there were no motor roads, and long stretches had to be covered with no detailed maps. In Siberia, the temperature dropped to 52 degrees below

zero. When the engine failed to start at such cold temperatures, a fire was lit under the oil sump, hot water was poured into the radiator, and the sparking plugs were heated in the oven. At considerable risk to their lives, they crossed the frozen Lake Baikal. Clarenore Stinnes and her team were also the first drivers to cross the South American Andes in a motor car. They frequently had to clear their way with pick-axe and dynamite in a life-and-death rally that ended in Berlin on 29 June 1929.

Signora Elisabetta, Bravissimo!

At almost the same time as the manufacturer's daughter was travelling through Russia, another young woman was taking up a similar challenge 2000 kilometres further south. In April 1927, the Sicilian shepherds on the dusty roads east of Palermo gazed in wonder at an elegant sporting couple who, armed with a writing pad, measuring tape and binoculars, were meticulously recording road widths, bends, uphill and downhill gradients and checking road surfaces.

The couple were Czech banker Vinzenz Junek and his wife Elisabeth. For five days, morning till night, they walked on the road, noting the Targa Florio route metre by metre. Each day they covered around 20 kilometres, returning after dusk to Polizzi, town of the notorious Mafia headquarters. By 1927, the petite and charming Liz was already a personality in international racing circles, and not without reason – she had made sports and racing cars her passion. She had learned to drive in 1921. Three years later she began to take part in races, almost exclusively in Bugattis. In the European racing circus, she started her career the hard way, beginning with local 'farmers' races', through the numerous hill climbs, including that of the daunting Klausenpass in Switzerland.

The first circuit race that Elisabeth Junek entered was the 1927 Targa Florio. It was to prove the breakthrough. This tough adventure in Sicily was already among the classic public road circuit races, one that Vincenzo Florio (1883-1958) had conceived in 1906 to make his native island of Sicily attractive to a wider public.

The first race on the road circuit known as the 'Great Madonie', after the mountain range dominating the region, took place in 1906. The course was 92.48 miles (148.82 kilometres) and had to be lapped three times. The winner was Alessandro Cagno in an Itala (time 9:23:23 hours, average speed 29 mph). When Elisabeth Junek rolled up to the start of the Targa Florio on 24 April 1927 in her Bugatti 35 B, she knew precisely what to expect: five laps, each 67 miles in length (once again, Florio had changed the course), 335 winding miles of dusty tracks, narrow passes, steep precipices – with hundreds of goats, mules, dogs and widlfowl on the roads. It was, however, neither a chicken nor a goat, but a wretched breakdown, that put an end to Elisabeth Junek's Targa Florio ambitions. As a result of damage to the steering, she crashed in lap two *when she was leading the race.*

Shortly afterwards, she managed the dangerous Nürburgring without injury, winning the Group II (sports cars up to 3000 cc) category of the German Grand Prix in her Bugatti 35 B.

In 1928, Elisabeth Junek arrived at the Targa Florio with two Bugattis; one of the cars, a 1.5 litre Bugatti Type 37, serving as a training vehicle and spares carrier. Florio had arranged for the course to be improved, and some of the bends had been made sharper. The road surface, too, was less blindingly dusty. In harsh training, Elisabeth drove no less than 47 laps, wearing out more than 50 tyres.

In the race itself, she was among the leaders in the first four laps, but in the fifth she was forced to slow down by damage to the water pump. Nevertheless, she still took fifth place, leaving drivers of such renown as Minoia, Dreyfus, Lepori, Foresti and Maserati behind her. Madame Junek became winner in the private drivers' class, and took the ladies' prize. The Italians acclaimed her vigorously, cheering 'Elisabetta, Signora Elisabetta, bravissimo!' She ended her brilliant career as a racing driver after her banker husband suffered a fatal accident in his Bugatti 35 B at the Nürburgring that same year.

THE OWNER-DRIVERS – OFTEN IMITATED, NEVER SURPASSED

When racing driver Otto Merz pulled in at the pits at the Nürburgring and raised his 3000 lb Mercedes Benz S with his hands to allow a faster tyre change . . . it saved him several crucial seconds! Merz then went on to win the German Grand Prix with his 6.8 litre supercharged car.

English journalists at the 1929 Tourist Trophy in Ulster reported in amazement that Merz tore off a damaged mudguard with his bare hands, as others might tear a sheet from a calendar. The strength of the man was legendary. It was said in racing circles that Otto Merz could drive a four-inch nail into a board with his bare hands, that when he greeted the wife of a racing driver colleague her wedding ring had to be removed from her finger with a pair of pincers . . . some man! Otto Merz witnessed the assassination of Archduke Franz Ferdinand in Sarajevo on 28 June 1914; he was driving the car of Count Boos-Waldeck, the Archduke's Honorary Adjutant. Merz carried the fatally wounded successor to the Austro-Hungarian throne up the steps to the state president's palace, where the Archduke died in his arms.

In the first three decades of this century, strong men such as Merz were predestined for motor racing, which involved hard, grinding physical work. Racing cars often seemed to develop an elementary life of their own – as in the case of the Peugeot driven by France's racing ace Georges Boillot in the 1914 Lyon Grand Prix. The steering wheel vibrated so much that Boillot had his left forearm tied to the wheel with cord. Drivers like Merz and Boillot entered into a symbiosis with their vehicles, a kind of shared fate where the upward development of the racing car's power and engineering was matched by increased driving ability of the drivers.

The relationship between owner-drivers and their sports and racing cars was quite different. They were devil-may-care madcaps too, audacious to a fault, but always 'on the sunny side of the street'. An owner-driver was a man who loved his sports or racing car so deeply that he cossetted it and spoiled it as he might his wife or mistress – sometimes more so. In the salad days of the twenties he was a man who would be seen gambling in Monte Carlo, on a yacht in Madeira, with a gun at a shooting lodge in Scotland, the champagne bottle always beside the oil can. Owner-drivers were rich, otherwise they wouldn't have been able to afford the expensive sport with its chic ambiance. Money was never discussed – they just had it. Owner-drivers preferred the finest and fastest; if the vehicle they were searching for was nowhere to be found on the market, they built it themselves, as in the case of Count Louis Zborowski, whose Chitty-Chitty-Bang-Bang (I, II and III) is described elsewhere.

Gold cufflinks sealed his fate

English-born Zborowski was the prototype owner-driver. Even in his giant car, he liked to be clad in a made-to-measure flannel suit from Savile Row. At his country house at Higham, near Canterbury, he engaged a chief engineer, Clive Gallop, who 'tailored' racing cars for the slender count. In 1923, in the hope of winning at Indianapolis, Zborowski shipped a complete squadron of Bugatti 30s to the brick track. But success eluded him and he consoled himself by buying a 2 litre 8-cylinder Miller, which he later drove at Brooklands. When Zborowski acquired a taste for road racing, he gave Aston Martin a hefty injection of capital to build him some suitable sports cars. His engineer designed a 1.5 litre engine with a twin camshaft and 16-valve cylinder head to give the Aston Martin a further boost.

The Spaniards called the Count *el eterno segundo* (the eternal second) as time and again he took the flag just behind the victor in numerous races in the Iberian peninsula, but Zborowski, an amateur of the first order, was regarded as such a good driver that Mercedes took him into their team in 1924, a position that was anything but amateur.

In Monza a racing driver's fate befell him. For inexplicable reasons, his 2 litre 8-cylinder Mercedes left the track at the notorious Lesbo bend, and crashed into a tree. The Count died immediately of his injuries. Zborowski's mechanic, who was in the car with him, escaped with injuries. There are many opinions as to the cause of the accident; historians now generally agree that Zborowski's gold cufflinks caught on the throttle lever on the steering wheel. They pulled it to the full-throttle position, and the Mercedes bounded away out of control – a tragic case of history repeating itself, for Count Zborowski's father had died in 1903 at the La Turbie hill climb when *his* sleeve caught the throttle and dragged it to the fully open position . . . some say he was wearing the same cufflinks.

Own-brand spark plugs and a crazy wager

Owner-drivers would constantly expose themselves to terrifying risks with an abandon that often defied reason. The two brothers, Sir Algernon and Kenelm Lee Guinness, financially well-heeled, connected with the well-known Irish brewing clan, were cast in the mould. Algernon attracted attention back in the first decade of this century with his exploits in his various Darracq models. With a fearsome 200 bhp V8 Darracq he stormed over the long flat beach in Ostend, at Brooklands and at Saltburn Sands in Yorkshire in speed record attempts. The car, looking like an early dragster – a bare chassis and two basic bucket seats with a 22,518 cc machine between them – clocked up several obscure records while driving well beyond any rational hope of survival. . . .

Sir Algernon took part in many races and speed record attempts before and after the First World War. He was placed in the 1906 and 1908 Tourist Trophy at the Isle of Man and in 1922 won the event in a 1.5 litre 16-valve Talbot-Darracq (distance raced 226 miles; average speed 53.3 mph), and brother 'Bill' (Kenelm Lee Guinness), who had been his riding mechanic before the war, drove a 3.3 litre Sunbeam to victory in the 1914 TT.

But what made 'Bill' famous among his contemporaries were his 'KLG' spark plugs. He had been dissatisfied with the miserable quality of the spark plugs available on the market – a weak point in automotive engineering

mainly because of their poor insulation. 'Bill' decided to manufacture his own spark plugs in a rented workshop in London. His 'own brand' quickly gained such a high reputation in the racing fraternity that the brewery heir moved into industrial manufacture.

One day before the First World War the Guinness brothers attempted to set up private speed records on the landing strip of a disused aerodrome west of London, marking out the distances to be covered with sprinkled flour. Meanwhile, friends blocked access roads with their cars to allow the massive Darracq enough room to run-up to the start. When the 8-cylinder engine began its shattering roar, local residents went into shock. The police in nearby Camberley swung onto their motorbikes in search for the scene of the crime. By the time they reached the aerodrome the Darracq, silent once more, was being towed behind another car. They had had their fun, and ultimately that was what counted. . . . Another story often told with relish is the occasion when Kenelm Lee Guinness, who never rolled to the start line without his woollen hat, avenged himself for some brusque words and harsh gestures from the barrier marshalls at a French Grand Prix. When the Marseillaise was played and everyone stood to attention, he started up his engine, and the music was drowned by the infernal noise. His eccentricity extended to shipping his racing cars and mechanics on his yacht, *Ocean River*, whenever he needed to travel to faraway courses.

Kenelm Lee Guinness became a World Land Speed Record holder in 1922, when he drove a V12 350 bhp Sunbeam at a speed of 133.75 mph, a record he held for two years until he was beaten by Parry Thomas in a Delage. He suffered an accident in the Sunbeam at the 1924 San Sebastian Grand Prix when he was badly injured, and never really recovered. He died in 1937; his brother Sir Algernon lived until 1954.

The Bentley Boys

While the Guinness brothers tended to go it alone, the famous 'Bentley Boys' were a sworn association of friends – smart, well-to-do amateur racing drivers for whom team spirit and fairplay were all-important. It is largely thanks to them that the great sports car make became world-famous, keeping the threat of the company's collapse at bay for several years.

The Bentley Boys included a number of winners of the 24 hour Le Mans race: Frank Clement with his co-driver John Duff (1924); Dr J. D. Benjafield and S. C. H. 'Sammy' Davis (1927); and Woolf Barnato, who, with co-drivers B. Rubin, Henry 'Tim' Birkin and Glen Kidstone, was the first to cross the finishing line for three consecutive years, from 1928 to 1930. Three times Le Mans winner Woolf Barnato was a multi-millionaire; his father had made his money in diamond prospecting in South Africa. No wonder, then, that the son used his money freely, calmly spending astronomical sums on his hobby. He it was who lent W. O. Bentley a helping hand in 1926 when his works were on the brink of closing down, becoming chairman of the Bentley works, but remaining a stalwart of the works team. At that time he was rated the best English racing driver, a man who 'never made a mistake on the road', as W. O. Bentley said time and again.

Woolf Barnato was in fact an outstanding example of that rare breed of gentleman, a sportsman, financier and playboy. He was also a stylish high-liver and enjoyed the odd wager. At Cannes, in the south of France on 13 March 1930, he bade farewell to a friend who was travelling back to London on the Blue Train, pride of the French railroads: 'I'll bet you £100 that I can get back to London in my Bentley before you'. The friend laughingly took up the bet, and Barnato began his chase through the length of France. There were no motorways or 6-lane highways in those days, of course, but the numerous towns and villages on the 700-mile drive from Cannes to Boulogne were negotiated without incident — at the remarkable average of 44 mph. Woolf Barnato was lucky. The ferry connection went smoothly, and he was already in London when the Blue Train arrived at Calais Maritime. Barnato ate a hearty breakfast in the Reform Club, took a nap and met his friend four hours later at Victoria Station. When the details and outcome of the wager became known in France, furious protests were made. The French authorities simply could not understand such a joke (and perhaps they cannot be blamed) and the Association of French Car Manufacturers wanted to fine Bentley £150 for Barnato's jaunt. They argued that the fine should be imposed because Barnato, chairman of the company, had held a race on French roads without first obtaining the necessary permission. It riled the French that Woolf Barnato's successful chase through France had provided such tremendous publicity for the Bentley marque, and it irked the French state railways to be forced to admit that an English sports car had beaten their famous *Train Bleu*! The £150 fine, incidentally, remains unpaid. . . .

Pile-up at White House

The animosity of the French towards Bentley and Barnato was also partly due to the Le Mans trauma. Since the first Twenty-four Hours of Le Mans race in 1923, French cars had managed to win only three times; in 1923, when a Chenard Walcker won, and in 1925 and 1926 when a Lorraine-Dietrich took the laurels. In 1924, 1927, 1928 and 1929, it was the turn of the Bentley Boys. And worse was to come when Woolf Barnato won in 1930, too. . . .

The Le Mans event of 1927 is remembered in the history of this annual French motor racing spectacle for the multiple pile-up at White House, a fast bend before the pits. The French *pilote* Tabourin in his Theophile Schneider went into a skid and partially blocked the road. The same thing happened to the 4.5 litre Bentley driven by L. G. Callingham. Four more cars crashed into the mess, an Aries, a second Theophile Schneider and two more Bentleys — one of which was driven by Sammy Davis. None of the drivers was injured, but all the cars were badly damaged. Davis's 3-litre sustained a bent front axle and broken headlamps; the right hand side running board holding the battery had come adrift, and the front right wing was torn away. However, the damaged car managed to limp to the pits where basic essential repairs were carried out. Drivers Benjafield and Davis examined the cracked chassis and bent front axle. They decided to take a chance, continued the race — and won! At the victory celebrations in London's prestigious Savoy Hotel, Lord Iliffe proposed the toast to the victors. He made a humorous speech, and at the end announced that there was a lady outside who wished to be allowed in. The double doors of the banqueting hall were thrown open — and in rolled the victorious 3 litre Bentley, which the mechanics had manhandled into the hotel as a surprise.

Given the strictly regulated, highly commercial world of motor racing today, well might we join nostalgically in the song: 'Where have all the good times gone?'

Previous page: 189. 1901 Oldsmobile. 190. 1902 Holsman.

191

191. 1903 Cadillac.

192

192. 1911 Stanley Steamer.

193. 1911 Overland.

194. 1914 Ford T.

95. 1914 Franklin. Following pages: 196. 1934 Packard.

197

197. 1930 Chrysler.

198

198. 1929 Ford Model A.

DID YOU KNOW?

Motoring history is even richer in facts, fables and curious phenomena than fisherman's lore. It would have proved a fertile source of inquiry for psychologist Sigmund Freud – finding out, for example, why car drivers seek a cure for their neuroses by working off their frustrations at the steering wheel, giving expression to their libido by chasing up the outside lane of the motorway, headlights flashing impatiently. It is a broad subject – and one that Theodor Fontane might enjoy discussing. His novel *Effi Briest* was first published in 1895, in the same year as the first accident in the history of motor racing took place – in the Paris-Bordeaux-Paris race when Panhard driver Prevost ran into a dog and was forced to retire with a broken wheel. If former reporter Fontane had heard of this accident, he would have been fascinated by its drama, and by the way in which the history of the motor car is always uncovering something new – such as the odd fact that Pope Pius X was made a gift of an Itala in 1909, and refused to use it. . . .

AEG AND SIEMENS – CARS AS A SIDE-DISH

'Old Rathenau isn't what he used to be. He's beginning to lose his senses. He dreams of cars, he sees every street covered with automobiles, no horses in the shafts anywhere – even to pull ploughs. In short, his mind is becoming befuddled.' This was the kind of comment that Emile Rathenau, founder of Allgemeine Elektricitäts-Gesellschaft had to put up with when he announced his decision to become actively involved in the up-and-coming automobile industry.

He wanted to go into the infant automobile business with a ready-made design that he had found in the Allgemeine Automobil-Gesellschaft (AAG) in Berlin – its similar-sounding name in itself seeming to invite a partnership. The company had begun business by selling electric vehicles, then took over the production of a small gasolene car of its own, a rear-drive 5 hp runabout. The purchase of AAG came about at the end of 1901, and its name was subsequently amended to Neue Automobil-Gesellschaft (N.A.G.). The production plant was installed in AEG's Oberspree cable works.

A year later, the new organisation was joined by the autombile department of Messrs. Kuhlstein Wagenbau whose origins lay in the days of the horse-drawn carriage. With this company, they also took over a talented designer, Joseph Vollmer, who was responsible for developments over the next few years and contributed to the high reputation acquired by N.A.G. products. As taxis, they were a common sight in Berlin, and N.A.G.'s double-decker buses also became a significant feature of the Berlin city scene. N.A.G. also manufactured commercial vehicles, and in terms of quality and popularity they were second to none. A 40 bhp car was installed in the Kaiser's imperial stables, and became his wife's favourite transportation. Aero engines were produced too, the first being installed in August von Parseval's airships. AEG believed that they owed it to their reputation as a company in the electrical industry to become active in the electric vehicles industry too, where they saw good prospects in taxis and delivery vehicles for urban transport. The first N.A.G. electric vehicles were exhibited at the Berlin Motor show in 1907, and the company founded its own taxi-operating firm.

N.A.G. – A marque is born

During the First World War, the company's name was changed. The initials N.A.G. were retained, but now stood for 'Nationale Automobil-Gesellschaft'. By 1919 the breakaway from the earlier multitude of car types had been completed. At the first post-war show in Berlin in

1921, the company launched the C4, a 10/30 bhp 4-cylinder car of 2536 cc, with which the N.A.G. became seriously active in motor sports for the first time. The show coincided with the first Avus race (then known as the Grünewald race) which saw the C4 winning its class in the hands of its designer Christian Riecken.

At the international 24 hour Touring Car Race in Monza in 1924, N.A.G. was again victorious, with a modified type C4b which covered 1604 miles at an average 67 mph – a high speed for the day. On return to Berlin, the N.A.G. team was given a triumphant reception, and by way of a special distinction was permitted to drive through the central arch of the Brandenburg Gate. But N.A.G. achieved its greatest sports success with Riecken as driver in the first German Grand Prix on the Avus circuit in 1926. The 2½ litre side-valve N.A.G. took second place after Caracciola in a Mercedes – at an astonishing 84.3 mph average.

N.A.G. are certainly able to lay claim to the distinction of having built the first German car with a V8 engine (launched in 1931) but sadly there were no buyers. Another product from N.A.G. was the unusual *Ei des Kolumbus* (Columbus's egg) as a magazine dubbed the automatic clutches developed by N.A.G. and based on the principle of the centrifugal coupling. As a publicity stunt, a car was driven from Berlin to Frankfurt without the clutch being operated, or gear being changed.

In 1933 the company came back down to earth and introduced a smaller car, the 'Voran' with front wheel drive, a fan-cooled 1.5 litre 'boxer' engine with independent suspension and integral (monocoque) body construction. But even this model failed to turn the tide of destiny and in 1934 N.A.G. discontinued car manufacture.

The name of N.A.G. lived on until 1948 at the Bussing Company, to whom commercial vehicle production had been transferred back in 1931. It is interesting to note that MAN, successor to Bussing, is still supplying double-decker buses for Berlin even today, representing a continuity of supply of approximately 75 years.

Siemens and the Protos

The starting point in car manufacturing for another major company in the electrical industry – Siemens – was Nuremberg. The electrical engineering company, formerly Schuckert AG Electromobil, had been building passenger coaches and three-wheeler delivery vehicles for the Bavarian postal authority since 1899. Siemens took over the company in 1903, and as Siemens-Schuckert built the Nonnendamm car works in Berlin which produced the first electric vehicles in 1906. Just one year later it was producing gasolene engines, and a further year on, the Berlin company Protos was acquired.

Protos had begun by building engines, but from 1900 onwards also marketed complete cars, these soon enjoying an excellent reputation. Protos were active in motor sports, too, largely as the proprietor's wife was an eager participant in the touring car competitions popular at the time. Indeed, the only German car to take part in the New York-Paris long-distance contest in 1908 was a Protos.

The company's early range extended from 4.6 litre models through to large 6.8 litre 50 hp cars. The German Crown Prince Wilhelm drove Protos cars exclusively – publicity that in those days was not to be underestimated. Protos were involved in the commercial vehicles sector, too, making both electric and gas-engined vehicles. They also offered the 'combination' drive, in which a petrol engine was used to feed a generator that supplied energy for electric automotive power. Surplus energy was released to a battery which supplied additional energy at times of high power consumption on hills.

After the First World War, Protos concentrated on a single model, the Type C, with a 2613 cc 10/30 bhp engine. This was welcome as a high quality product, and was adopted by many bodywork companies for special vehicles. Local and postal authorities bought large batches fitted out with appropriate modifications for their specialist uses. In the twenties, production at Protos was

around 130 to 150 vehicles per day – a considerable output for the time.

Siemens recognized, however, that a car factory within an electrical group was bound to remain an outsider in the long term, and when funds were needed to counter the imports flooding into the German market it was decided that the car factory should be sold. It was bought in 1926 by N.A.G., but on 1 July 1927, the last Protos car left the conveyor belt. It bore a plate with the words:

> In the prime of your life,
> At the peak of your strength,
> You, the much prized,
> Were snatched away.
> In the pages of glory
> At the time recorded
> In large gold letters
> Is Protos's reliability!
> Protos passed through many hands
> With their excellent design,
> But to what avail if now and finally,
> You are scrapped,
> Kaputt.
> As the last – and unforgotten –
> We shall watch you as you leave,
> Who would oft and gladly own you
> Believing you will rise again.
>   HANS OTTO NEUBAUER

FIRST, FASTER, BIGGER AND BETTER

● Compressed-air 'self-starters' had a certain popularity before electrical ones came into use. The once-famous pioneer American firm of Winton fitted them, as did Delaunay-Belleville in France, Minerva in Belgium, and Wolseley in England.

● The controls of early cars varied greatly. The reliable and popular belt-driven Benz cars of the 1890s had seven or eight (according to type) hand controls but only one pedal, while a number of later cars, such as some Mercedes, Delaunay-Bellevilles and Gobron-Brillies had four pedals to confuse the driver. The gear change on Model T Fords was pedal-operated with no hand lever to bother about.

● Aluminium was used for crankcases and other mechanical parts in the 1890s

and it soon found its way into the coach-builder's art. The Paris coachbuilders, Rothschild et Cie, introduced aluminium panelling in 1902, and the first production-model Lanchesters (1900-05) had Lanchester-made bodywork, with aluminium mudguards and other parts, the entire structure being made integral with a composite steel and aluminium chassis.

● All-steel bodywork (with no wood framing) was introduced on a small B.S.A. car in 1912, and the 1913 model Hupmobile, made by the Hupp Motor Car Corp. of Detroit, was also steel-bodied. But the real pioneers of the modern system of making pressed-steel bodywork were the Dodge brothers, who broke away from their association with Ford and began making Dodge cars in Detroit in 1914.

● Modern-type brake-linings of woven or bonded asbestos were developed by Herbert Frood of Chapel-en-le-Frith (hence the trade-name 'Ferodo'), but they were not in evidence until after 1905. Before that, leather, wood, compressed fibre, or woven camel-hair were used for brake-lining; these gave fair results but were short-lived and easily burnt out. Metal-on-metal brakes were used on many cars; these were long-lived and could not burn out, but were often noisy and apt to snatch badly when hot.

● The most usual arrangement of brakes before 1914 was for the pedal brake to act on a drum on the transmission shafting, and the hand brake (then often called the 'side brake') to act directly on the rear-wheel brake-drums. Most motorists normally 'drove on the side brake' and kept the foot brake in reserve for emergencies: it was more powerful but imposed a great strain on the final-drive gears, half-shafts, etc.

● Brakes on all four wheels did not come into general use until the mid-1920s, but many firms experimented with them. They were optionally available on some Mercedes models in 1903 but it is doubtful if anybody actually opted for them. The Scottish firm of Arrol-Johnston fitted them as standard equipment to their 15.9 hp model in 1909. Most 'experts' were against the idea, however, and Arrol-Johnston dropped their four-wheel brakes after eighteen months.

● Opposed-piston engines, with two pistons in each cylinder working outwards from a central combustion chamber, were used by Arrol-Johnston (Scotland) from 1898 to 1906, and Gobron-Brillie (France) from 1898 to 1914. A 4-cylinder, eight-piston, 100 hp Gobron-Brillie was officially timed at 103.56 mph in 1904, and a 2-cylinder, four-piston, 18 hp Arrol-Johnston won the Tourist Trophy Race in 1905.

● Tyre troubles caused many breakdowns and much expense. In 1902 it was reckoned that a light car, carefully driven at not more than 25 mph, might do 2000 miles on a set of tyres. Heavy, fast cars could do less than a thousand. George Lanchester, delivering a car to Rudyard Kipling, suffered twenty-one punctures or bursts on the 200 miles from Birmingham to Rottingdean.

● Detachable and interchangeable wheels or rims were not available before 1905. The troublesome tyres had to be repaired or replaced by the roadside with the wheels in situ. The first device was the Stepney spare rim which clamped beside the rim of the deflated tyre and allowed the car to be driven slowly home. Then followed the Captain, the Warland and other types of detachable wheel rims, and the famous Rudge centre-lock detachable wheel was marketed in 1908. The modern-type bolt-on wheel was originated by the Sankey Co. soon afterward, in 1910.

● The first European Grand Prix cars to use hydraulic brakes were the 1922 Bugatti and the 1922-23 Rolland Pilain, both to the front wheels. The first to use them on all four wheels was a Maserati in 1933 – twelve years after they had appeared on the 1921 French Grand Prix-winning Duesenberg from America.

● The first monocoque racing cars were built by Gabriel Voisin, and first raced in the 1923 French Grand Prix. In latter-day terminology these might be described as 'semi-monocoque', but at least in principle they anticipated the true monocoque in Grand Prix racing by 39 years.

● The first Grand Prix car to have its engine behind the driver and its gearbox and differential attached to the chassis – and thus part of the sprung mass – was the Benz Tropfenwagen.

● Left-hand drive is almost as old as the industry, having been seen on Benz cars at the beginning of the twentieth century. By 1914 the majority of American makes had left-hand drive, and by 1918 only Pierce-Arrow and the American-built Fiat (the latter in its last year of production) retained the right-hand layout. Pierce-Arrow, however, defended their conservatism on the ground that it was more convenient for chauffeurs, and did not fall into line with the rest of the industry until 1920. Early Springfield-built Rolls-Royces were also right-hand drive. Packards of the 1913-17 era had the curious combination of left-hand steering and a left-hand gear change. Though left-hand steering was general practice on popular continental cars by 1929, the more expensive models retained right-hand drive well into the 1950s. No Bugatti ever had left-hand drive and Lancia's switch in 1956 was dictated only by a growing interest in American exports.

● Horstman light cars of the 1913-26 period had mechanical kick-starters in their cockpits, operating on the Archimedes screw principle. These were retained even after the firm went over to electric starting.

● The first recorded use of an oil-pressure warning light was on the 14-15 hp Talbot of 1926.

● Mechanical windscreen-wipers were first seen on closed cars in America in 1916. One of the earliest was the Willys-Knight. The first firm to fit windscreen-washers as factory equipment was Triumph in 1935. The first American use of these was by Studebaker in 1937.

● The foot-operated parking brake is generally believed to be a by-product of automatic transmission, but the Chevrolet 490 of 1916 had no handbrake; instead a ratchet incorporated in the pedal mechanism could lock it for parking. The modern foot-operated type was standardised by Buick in 1942, six years before the company offered an automatic.

● Quickly detachable wheels were almost universal on British and continental cars by 1920, but the fixed wood wheel with demountable rim survived in America on many makes until 1932. It was claimed that these were easier for a woman to handle in the event of a 'flat'.

● Tubeless tyres were used (without much success) on motorcycles and American light cars in the 1890s, but reinvented by Dunlop in 1953. Balloon tyres were pioneered by Firestone in America in 1923, and first offered later in the year by Cole. The first car to be designed for balloons was the Chrysler 70 of 1924.

● Illuminated radiator emblems were pioneered by Wolseley in 1933, though the American Fageol luxury car of 1917 (which did not go into production) had a similar device made of ivory.

● The first car to be offered with a reversing light was the American Wills-Sainte Claire, in 1921.

● Doors opening into the roof were pioneered on a custom sedan body built for a Duesenberg Model J chassis in 1930 by Murphy of Pasadena. Their first use on a series production body was on the Riley Falcon saloon introduced for 1933.

● Detachable hardtops, transforming open cars into formal carriages, were common in the early days of the century, e.g. Lanchester (1901), Cadillac (1903). Similar styles of all-year bodyworks were also listed by a number of American manufacturers during the First World War and immediately after, but the first series-production, European style, in the modern idiom was the Lancia Lambda (1922). No suggestion was offered as to the best means of storage for this ponderous component when out of use!

● The first standard body to conceal its spare wheel in the tail was the Austin Twenty tourer of 1919.

● Seats convertible into a bed were found on the 1921 Pan, an American car.

● Curved windscreens were first used on factory-bodied cars in 1914 by Kissel. The first British use was on 1922 Arrol-Johnston models.

● Tartan loose covers for upholstery are common practice, but at least two manufacturers used tartan for the exterior finish of their bodies: Voisin on a *conduite intérieure écossaise* in 1922 and Willys-Knight on a 'Plaidside' roadster in 1930.

● Electric fuel-pumps were first used on the 1923 Wills-Sainte Clare. The first British car so equipped was the 2 litre Arab of 1927.

● Safety-glass was first fitted as factory equipment on Stutz and Rickenbacker cars in 1926.

● Headlamp flashers were first used on the Fiat 1500 of 1935.

● Smith's Jackall permanent four-wheel jacks were introduced in 1929, and first fitted as factory equipment to Star cars in 1931.

● An ingenious solution to the parking problem was the Parkmobile of 1928, a species of four-wheel retractable undercarriage which could be lowered to give

lateral movement. It was standard on an obscure American car of the period, the New York Six.

● Heaters are almost as old as the industry, hot-water bottles (upholstered to match the interior trim) being recognised as accessories in the first decade of the twentieth century. The hot-water type fed off the car's cooling system made its appearance in America in 1926, though a foot-warmer so operated was found on Cannstatt Daimlers of the 1897-1900 period. Defrosters were recognised accessories by the middle 1930s. One of the oddest arrangements of all was found on the 1954 air-cooled Dyna 54 Panhard. This had a catalytic-type petrol heater mounted on the engine bulkhead and fed from the main tank. It was asserted that this device worked at a temperature low enough to eliminate any fire risk, but it was soon discarded in favour of a more conventional installation drawing hot air off the cylinders of the engine. Air-conditioning was first offered on private cars in 1938 by Nash.

● The world's first old-car club was the Veteran Car Club of Great Britain. It was founded in November 1930, at the end of that year's London-Brighton Run, at a meeting at the Ship Hotel, Brighton. The three 'founding fathers' were S. C. H. Davis, J. A. Masters and J. A. Wylie.

● The Vintage Sports Club was founded in 1934 to promote the use of sports cars made up to the end of 1930. It is currently Britain's biggest old-car club, with a paid-up membership of approximately 5700.

● The largest-capacity 6-cylinder private car made since 1918 was the 11,160 cc Stower D7 of 1919. It used what was basically a First World War aero-engine. The largest-capacity engine fitted to a rear-engined car in series production since 1918 was the 3.4 litre air-cooled V-8 Tatra of 1937. Only one of the British Burneys (1930-33) had the bigger Lycoming straight-eight and the American Stout Scarab and Tucker Torpedo were never made on a commercial scale. The largest air-cooled

engine fitted to a production car after 1918 was the 6.4 litre 12-cylinder Franklin of 1932. The largest 4-cylinder private car listed after 1918 was the Belgian Pipe of 1921. It had a bore and stroke of 120×200 mm, giving a capacity of just over 9 litres. There was no series production, but at least one was exported.

● The greatest number of forward-gear ratios offered on a private car for normal road use was eight, on Maybachs with their own *doppelschnellgang* (dual overdrive box) as fitted in 1931-39. Four reverses went with this package, which was available as an option in Britain on 1932 models of the 3 litre Lagonda.

● The world's first series-production 12-cylinder car was the Packard Twin-Six, introduced for 1916 and made until 1932. In 1932 American buyers had the choice of six different makes using 12-cylinder motors: Ashburn, Cadillac, Franklin, Lincoln, Packard and Pierce-Arrow. In the same year France offered two twelves (Hispano-Suiza, Voisin) as did Germany (Horch, Maybach) and Czechoslovakia (Tatra, Walter). Britain, however, offered only one (Daimler) and Italy none at all.

● The first touring car to be made in series with a twin overhead-camshaft engine was the D Type Salmson of 1922. The Ballot 2LS, introduced during 1921, was a super-sports car made in very small numbers.

● The world's first series-production straight-eight was the Type 8 Isotta Fraschini of 1919, which was reaching customers by the end of 1920. A contemporary in America was the Kenworthy Line-O-Eight of 1920 but it is doubtful if any of these cars were sold commercially.

● The world's first production 6-cylinder engine with a capacity of less than 1.5 litres was the PS Type Mathis, marketed in 1922. Capacity was 1140 cc.

● The first car to be offered with a synchromesh gearbox was the 1929

Cadillac. The first British makers to adopt synchromesh were Vauxhall and Rolls-Royce in 1932. The first all synchromesh gearbox was announced by the German ZF component firm in 1931, but the first car to fit such a gearbox as standard was the British Alvis Speed Twenty in October 1933. The first German production car so equipped was the 3 litre Adler Diplomat of 1935.

● Two-speed rear axles supplementary to the main gearbox were first seen on the British Cooper two-stroke car of 1909. They were rediscovered by Voisin in 1928, and reintroduced to America by Auburn in 1932. The first hypoid bevel rear axles were found on 1927 Packards. Their first European application was by Mathis in 1928. The first production car with swing-axle rear suspension was the rear-engined Rumpler of 1921.

● The last private car to be offered with solid tyres was the Type XL Trojan of 1929.

● The last private car to be marketed with a double-sleeve-valve engine was the 6-cylinder Panhard of 1939. The last models to be marketed with single sleeve-valve engines were the Scottish Argyll and Arroll-Aster, discontinued in 1931. Slide-valve engines were used by Imperia of Belgium until 1934.

● All-wooden unitary construction was used in prototype cars by Frederick and George Lanchester in 1922-23, and by Marks-Moir in Australia in 1923. The first production application of this system was on the original Marcos GT coupe of 1960. Wooden chassis were standard on all Franklin cars up to the end of the 1927 season, and on certain 1928 models.

● Pre-selective gears are not an invention of the 1920s, much less of the 1930s, though they were one of the fads of that decade. Lanchester had them in 1900, and three-speed De Dion-Boutons of 1902 also had a primitive system of pre-selection. The Wilson box (best known of the pre-selective systems) was tried experimentally by Vauxhall in 1927 and first catalogued as an option in the 1929 Armstrong Siddeley range. It was, however, anticipated by the German ZF-Soden box, fitted to several makes of car (Fadag, Lindcar, Szawe) in 1923.

● Hydraulic four-wheel brakes were pioneered by Duesenberg on their Model A straight-eight in 1921. The first mass-produced car to fit them was the Chrysler 70 of 1924. First British use was on the 1925 models of Horstmann and Triumph.

● Cruciform-braced frames were first seen on the 1921 6.6 litre 6-cylinder Hotchkiss, a prototype which did not go into production.

● More than one make of car changed nationality after the Armistice of 1918. When Alsace and Lorraine were returned to France Bugatti and Mathis (both formerly German) became French. The new state of Czechoslovakia acquired three ready-made makes from the defunct Austro-Hungarian Empire – Nesselsdorf (Tatra), Praga, and Laurin-Klement (later Skoda).

● In over forty years of manufacture, Ettore Bugatti never made a 6-cylinder car. Other long-standing firms with similar records include Bianchi, Cadillac and Isotta Fraschini.

● Perhaps the most unusual warranties ever issued by the motor industry were bore guarantees given by two British makers in the 1930s. British Salmson cars of the 1934-39 period had their cylinder bores guaranteed for 40,000 miles, and a 25,000 mile guarantee on similar lines was offered for 1939 Singers.

● The Bucciali Double-Huit exhibited at the 1931 Paris Salon, but never marketed, had a 16-cylinder power unit made up of two straight-eights mounted side by side and driving the front wheels. Twin radiators were used.

● Six-wheeled private cars are usually adaptations of commercial or military vehicles, but at the 1930 London Motor Show Crossley exhibited a six-wheel limousine with a 3.8 litre 6-cylinder engine. It did not go into production.

● Airscrew-propelled motor cars were offered in the 1920s by two small French firms: Leyat in 1920-21 and La Traction Aérienne in 1921-26.

● Mail-order cars are traditionally associated with the motor buggies offered by the American firm of Sears Roebuck from 1908 to 1912, but other concerns tried their hand at this game. Between 1916 and 1924 two Chicago makes (Birch and Bush) were sold exclusively through mail, and Sears Roebuck themselves had a second try in 1952 with their Allstate, a special version of the small Kaiser model. It lasted no more than two seasons.

● Contrary to general belief, the first foreign car owned by a reigning British Monarch was not the 'famous black Buick' (CUL 421) which King Edward VIII bought in 1936. His grandfather Edward VII purchased a 14/20 hp Renault landaulette in 1906, and this was retained by his widow, Queen Alexandra, until her death in 1925. In 1908 the King bought a 45 hp Mercedes. In 1901, incidentally, Queen Alexandra took delivery of a 'City and Suburban Electric Phaeton' which she used to drive about the grounds of Sandringham House. For all its English-sounding name, this was a Columbia, made in Hartford, Connecticut.

● William Crapo Durant, founder of General Motors, died a relatively poor man in 1947. After the collapse of his last automobile empire (comprising Durant, Star, Locomobile, Flint) in 1932 he went into the supermarket business, but without outstanding success.

From the Guinness Book of Car Facts & Feats.

PERSONALITIES

GENERAL & TECHNICAL

Bold figures indicate illustrations

BIBLIOGRAPHY

J. Bentley, F. Porsche: Porsche–Ein Traum wird Wirklichkeit. Ein Auto macht Geschichte, Düsseldorf 1978

Anthony Bird, Ian Hallows: The Rolls-Royce Motor Car, London 1972

Griffith Borgeson: Bugatti – The Dynamics of Mythology, London 1981

L'Ebé Bugatti: The Bugatti Story, London 1967

Donald Clarke (Ed.): The Encyclopedia of Transport, London 1976

H. G. Conway: Bugatti – Le pursang des automobiles, Sparkford 1979

Richard Crabb: Birth of a Giant, Philadelphia 1969

John Day: The Bosch Book of the Motor Car, London/Glasgow 1975

Eugen Diesel, Gustav Goldbeck, Friedrich Schildberger: Vom Motor zum Auto – Fünf Männer und ihr Werk, Stuttgart 1968

Erik Eckermann: Vom Dampfwagen zum Auto – Motorisierung des Verkehrs, Reinbek bei Hamburg 1981

Raymond Flower, Michael Wynn Jones: One Hundred Years of Motoring, Maidenhead 1981

Richard v. Frankenberg, Marco Matteucci: Geschichte des Automobils, Künzelsau 1973

Luigi Fusi: Alfa Romeo – Tutte le vetture dal 1910, Milano 1978

G. N. Georgano: A History of Sports Cars, London, New York, Sydney, Toronto 1970

– (Ed.) The Encyclopaedia of Motor Sport, London 1971

– (Ed.) The Complete Encyclopaedia of Motor Cars – 1885 to the present, London 1971

Anthony Harding: The Batsford Colour Book of Historic Racing Cars, London and Sydney 1975

Anthony Harding (Ed.): The Guinness Book of Car Facts & Feats, Enfield 1980

August Horch: Ich baute Autos, Berlin 1937

Thora Hornung: 50 Jahre Nürburgring – Kurvenlabyrinth für Könner, Koblenz n.d.

Monika und Uwe Hucke: Die Geschichte der Bugatti-Automobile, Nettelstedt n.d.

Peter Hull: Alfa Romeo, Sparkford 1975

Judith Jackson: Eine Jahrhundertliebe – Menschen und Automobile, München 1979

Dennis Jenkinson, Peter Verstappen: The Schlumpf Obsession, London 1977

Brad King: All Colour Book of Racing Cars, London 1973

Richard Kitschigen: Rennen, Reifen und Rekorde – die AVUS-Story, Stuttgart 1972

Michael Kuball, Clärenore Stinnes (Ed.): Söderströms Photo-Tagebuch 1927-1929, Die erste Autofahrt einer Frau um die Welt, Frankfurt am Main 1981

Lord Montagu of Beaulieu, F. Wilson McComb: Behind the Wheel – The Magic and Manners of Early Motoring, New York and London 1977

Giovanni Lurani: A History of Motor Racing, London, Sydney, New York, Toronto 1972

Peter Müller: Ferdinand Porsche – Ein Genie unserer Zeit, Graz und Stuttgart 1965

L. C. Munro: Motor Cars – A Picture History, London 1970

Alfred Neubauer, Harvey T. Row: Männer, Frauen und Motoren, Stuttgart 1970

T. R. Nicholson: Sports Cars 1928-1939, London 1969

T. R. Nicholson: Racing Cars and Record Breakers – 1898-1921, London 1971

– Sports Cars Book Two 1907-1927, London 1970

Werner Oswald: Alle Audi-Automobile, Stuttgart 1979

– Alle Horch-Automobile, Stuttgart 1979

Juraj Porázik: Oldtimer-Autos aus den Jahren 1885-1940, Hanau 1981

Cyril Posthumus: The Story of Veteran & Vintage Cars, London, New York, Sydney, Toronto 1977

Peter Roberts: Racing Cars and the History of Motor Sport, London 1973

Graham Robson: The Encyclopedia of the World's Classic Cars, London 1982

L. T. C. Rolt: Motoring – A Pictorial History of the First 150 Years, New York 1974

L. J. K. Setright: The Designers, London 1976

Ernest Schmid: Schweizer Autos, Lausanne 1978

Halwart Schrader: Die Automobile der Gebrüder Schlumpf, München 1977

– Oldtimer-Lexikon, München, Bern, Wien 1976

Louis William Steinwedel: The Mercedes-Benz-Story, Radnor 1975

Hans Stuck: Sekunden erobern die Welt, Berlin 1939

Erwin Tragatsch: Die großen Rennjahre 1919-1939, Bern 1973

D. B. Tubbs: Art and the Automobile, Guildford and London 1978

David Burgess Wise: Classics of the Road, London 1981

PICTURE CREDITS

BUGATTI